SAN FRANCISCO
IN MAPS & VIEWS

SAN FRANCISCO
IN MAPS & VIEWS

SALLY B. WOODBRIGE
INTRODUCTION BY
DAVID RUMSEY

RIZZOLI
NEW YORK

First published in the United States of America in 2006 by
RIZZOLI INTERNATIONAL PUBLICATIONS, INC.
300 Park Avenue South, New York, NY 10010
www.rizzoliusa.com

ISBN-10: 0-8478-2871-9
ISBN-13: 978-08478-2871-5
Library of Congress Control Number: 2006928781

Page 2: *San Francisco, Looking South From North Point* (p. 86)
Page 4: Detail, *Map of the State of California* (p. 62)
Pages 6-7, 8-9, 10-11: *San Francisco, 1862, from Russian Hill* (p. 68)

Designed by Aldo Sampieri

Printed and bound in China

2006 2007 2008 2009 2010/ 10 9 8 7 6 5 4 3 2 1

CONTENTS

THE GOLD RUSH DECADE, 1848–1859

THE PROGRESSIVE MOVEMENT

Plan of the Civic Center, from the Report of D. H. Burnham on the Improvement and
Adornment of San Francisco

THE RISE OF THE PHOENIX: POST-1906-EARTHQUAKE SAN FRANCISCO

POST-WAR SAN FRANCISCO

THE CONTEMPORARY CITY

ACKNOWLEDGMENTS

I am indebted to the following people for their generous contributions of time and information to the enrichment of this book. Heading my list is Philip Hoehn, librarian of the David Rumsey map collection and former librarian of the University of California, Berkeley map collection, who patiently answered my numerous queries about historic maps of San Francisco and reviewed my text. David Rumsey, author and map collector extraordinaire, not only wrote the introduction to this book, but also provided information and advice along with reproductions of many of his maps for this book. Another Bay Area map collector, Warren Heckrotte, also shared his knowledge of historic maps and allowed me to reproduce one of the many important maps in his collection.

The staff members of the San Francisco Public Library's San Francisco History Center and the University of California, Berkeley Earth Sciences and Map Library were unfailingly helpful in guiding my search through their collections for notable historic maps and views of San Francisco.

Finally, I am grateful to the contemporary map makers who gave me permission to reproduce their work. Reineck and Reineck have designed many of the locally well-known maps of the city; four of their maps are reproduced here. Rick Waterman is starting a career in map design; the map of his reproduced here was created in his student days at San Francisco State University's Department of Cartography. Peter Brastow belongs to a group involved in mapping natural open spaces in San Francisco. The map included in this book shows the current state of their project.

Although they are not professional mapmakers, the architects working on the map project in Skidmore, Owings & Merrill's San Francisco office have demonstrated that, given the motivation, current technology can enable mapmaking that competes with the best commercially available products.

INTRODUCTION
by David Rumsey

SAN FRANCISCO: THE INSTANT CITY

San Francisco is a city that sprang to life in a relatively short time. From its burst of growth during the California gold rush in the mid-nineteenth century, the city took only a few decades to extend its reach from San Francisco Bay to the Pacific Ocean. In many ways the change in landscape has continued with remarkable dynamism right to the present day. The initial frenzied pace of development was caused by the immense wealth that poured into San Francisco from the gold mines. But the dynamic of boom, followed by bust, continued as the city moved into the twentieth century, punctuated dramatically by the immense destruction of the 1906 earthquake and fire. The rapid changes in the city are graphically recorded through historical maps of San Francisco. Mapmakers struggled to keep pace with the landscape morphing around them as they worked, with the result that maps were often out of date before they hit the press. Economic booms and busts were not all that made their mark on the ground. Even after the city was fully built out, earthquakes and fires continued to alter the physical environment. After each such event the city would rebuild and give birth to a new version of itself. All of these changes can be seen today through the prism of San Francisco's cartographic past.

This book presents a new way of seeing that past. More conventional urban histories may use an occasional map or view, by way of illustration at best. But here the maps are the narrative, with words acting as glosses on what the maps make vivid to us. This approach has certain unique advantages: telling the story through maps and views brings into focus the spatial aspects of the history. Events are always grounded, so to speak, firmly in physical space. Viewing a city such as San Francisco by examining its representation in maps and views allows the reader to move through space as well as through time. Thus we see the city evolve before our eyes. And we see not only the physical evolution of its urban space, but also—and again uniquely—the ways that cartography itself evolves as it develops and deploys new visualization techniques and tools.

It is especially appropriate to have Sally Woodbridge, an architectural historian intimately familiar with San Francisco's built environment, write this book. Situated on a peninsula, San Francisco has been destined by nature to be a compact city. Architecture and the built environment play outsized roles in determining its physical form. Consequently, the history of its architecture closely parallels and influences its cartographic history. Woodbridge is able to bring a fresh perspective to maps, seeing them in ways that a purely cartographic historian might miss and highlighting features that buildings and maps have in common. For me, a map collector with a special focus on my adopted home of San Francisco, it is especially exciting to see the ways that she tells the stories of the maps and buildings together, foregrounding the many issues affecting city planning in the past, the present, and into the future.

The progression of maps in this book reveals many of the basic features of mapping that inform cartography. Maps are never completely neutral, and in many ways their points of view are somewhat arbitrary, even if fixed in conventions we take for granted. The sheer conventionality of the orientation of north-at-the-top, south-on-the-bottom can be seen in the Vincent 1860 *Map of The State of California* (see page 62), a stunning image that places the state on its side in order to emphasize the centrality of San Francisco Bay. Maps also frequently distort space in order to respond to the needs of their users or sponsors: a case in point is the 1893 *View of the Midwinter Fair in Golden Gate Park* (see page 98), which prominently features the property for sale by the map's sponsor, Baldwin and Hammond, just beyond the park. Maps commonly respond to events: war, gold discoveries, land rushes—all produced prodigious numbers of maps. The 1848 *Map of the Valley of the Sacramento including the Gold Region* (see page 36) is an excellent example of the many California gold rush maps that proliferated during that tumultuous time. More endearingly, maps always strive to be useful, especially at the local level; guides and directories try to help the user navigate and find information, a task particularly important in a city whose topography is constantly shifting. *The Illustrated Directory of San Francisco* of 1895 (see page 101) is not only a superb example of this, but is also one of the best surviving visual records of the built city largely destroyed in the 1906 earthquake and fire. And maps have their own genealogies: they usually grow out of each other, with one influencing many succeeding maps as cartographers learn from each other and codify that learning in new maps. The U.S. Coast Survey maps of San Francisco of 1853, 1859, and 1869, grow out of each other and form the basis of many other maps because of their highly accurate cartography, one example being the state sponsored *Map Exhibiting the Salt Marshes, Tide and Submerged Lands in and adjacent to the Bays of San Francisco and San Pablo* (see page 80).

The narrative of maps in this book also reveals the growth of cartographic science and art from rather simple manuscript beginnings to our current day, three-dimensional Geographic Information Systems (GIS) maps. The Cañizares manuscript map of 1776 showing San Francisco Bay (see page 18) is more a work of art than science, yet it does give us a fairly accurate view of the landscape and it is certainly beautiful in its graphic art. This map for the first time establishes the magnificent San Francisco Bay as a body of water that is separate from Drake's Bay, and one that has its own entrance from the ocean, the Golden Gate. The Cañizares map begins the process of increasing accuracy in mapping San Francisco Bay for the next seventy-five years until the Gold Rush of 1849. At that time, maps shift in focus from the bay to the emerging city. In the maps of the city over the next one hundred and fifty years we see a steady progress of cartographic science that culminates in the present with the fortuitous marriage of efforts by both cartographers and architects to render three dimensions in two, stunningly demonstrated in the combination Computer Aided Design (CAD) and GIS maps of the built city in 2006 by the architectural firm of Skidmore, Owings & Merrill (see page 154). To have traveled from the Cañizares map to these last two in the short space of just over two hundred years is remarkable, and this book documents the journey.

The technology of mapping and the technology of rendering buildings come together through the computer programs of GIS and CAD. Both use software to render space. And both are part of a growing trend of harnessing the power of computers to render spaces—both geographical and architectural —with astonishing degrees of accuracy. Now we can move through these spaces in real time on our computers. These computer programs engender maps, in a sense, but not like our static maps of the past. Rather, they allow for the creation of dynamic documents that tell us where we are going, how to get there, and what the world will look like when we arrive. Combining this with instant delivery of maps over the Internet means that maps are returning to a more central role in our world, a role they clearly had in the past, as evidenced by the numerous entries in this book.

Maps of San Francisco have proven to be very important in shaping the destiny of the peninsula and its people, both in the practical sense of sorting out conflicting land titles, and in the larger sense of showing the potential redesign of the entire city (as we see [beginning on page 108], for example, in the Burnham maps of 1905). And today, with the San Francisco Bay area playing a central role in the Internet and software revolutions, it is especially appropriate that it should be providing us with the very latest in Internet mapping from many search engines. The new three-dimensional, GIS-enabled globe programs that are proliferating on the Web let us see exactly how San Francisco fits in with the rest of the world, at many different scales. As more people experience maps in their everyday lives, they will begin to think in time and space as dynamically as must have the cartographers from the Gold Rush era, and see how we are all tied together on our small, finite planet. This is bound to help us better navigate the immense environmental challenges of our time.

The map of San Francisco Peninsula on the opposite page is a composite of two maps: the 1869 U.S. Coast Survey Map on the east side of the Peninsula and a 2000 Air Photo USA Satellite Image on the west. I have composed two maps into one to show in one view how the technology of mapping has changed over the last one hundred and thirty years, as well as how the city these technologies visualize has evolved. Visualization of landscape and space was once the purview of the cartographic draughtsman using lines for streets, shading for wetlands, and hachures for hill shapes. All this is now captured by camera from above and enhanced through various manipulations of digital imagery and colors. Yet each method, the old and the new, has aspects that the other lacks. One hopes that in the future, the art of the old cartography can be combined successfully with the precision and comprehensiveness of the new. Looking at the two maps together, contrasting their styles and methods, shows part of the journey traveled by the maps and views in this book as San Francisco evolved into the city it is today.

SAN FRANCISCO

San Francisco Peninsula

DISCOVERING THE SAN FRANCISCO BAY

From today's vantage point, the discovery of the San Francisco Bay, the Pacific coast's largest natural harbor, should have been an easy matter, particularly for the experienced navigators whose ships then sailed the Pacific Ocean. That it took over 200 years to find a body of water with a shoreline of about 100 miles that encloses 450 miles of water, is a mystery that may be explained only by chronicling the confusion caused by the instances of mistaken identity and misguided exploration that defeated its dedicated seekers.

Although Spain had claimed the land along the North American continent's Pacific coast, the decline of the Spanish empire during the eighteenth century delayed the colonization of the northern reaches of what became the United States. What interested Spain was maintaining profitable trade with her possessions across the Pacific Ocean. From 1566 to the end of Spain's control of Mexico in 1821, the Manila Galleons (very large ships that not only traded Mexican silver and gold for far eastern luxuries such as tea, spices, and porcelain, but also carried as many as 600 passengers) carried on this trade. The limit of one round-trip per year set by the king in 1593 increased the need to find a good North American harbor where the ships could stop for repairs, supplies, and a respite from the pirates that preyed on them during their six- to seven-month voyages across the ocean.

The desire to find a way to the Pacific Ocean that would shorten the long voyage around South America's Cape Horn kept alive the hope of finding the fabled Strait of Anián, reputed to cut through the North American continent. In 1542, the Spanish Viceroy Mendoza sent Juan Rodríguez Cabrillo north along the California coast to search for the strait. Cabrillo, who had served under Hernando Cortés, the conqueror of Mexico, sailed as far north as the Punta Arena. He not only failed to find the strait the English called the Northwest Passage, but also missed the entrance to the bay later named San Francisco.

Cabrillo was not incompetent. The lack of accurate maps and the limits of navigational science deterred ships from sailing close to the uncharted and frequently fog-bound coast, which was likely to be dangerous. Ships set their course out beyond the Farallone Islands, some 30 miles offshore. Taking into account the earth's curvature, this distance put the narrow entrance to the bay below the horizon seen by those on shipboard. Consequently, the high landmasses on either side of the Golden Gate appeared to be continuous.

The second known European to explore the Pacific coast in search of the Northwest Passage was the English navigator and privateer, Sir Francis Drake, who was also attracted to the treasures of the Manila Galleons. In 1579, Drake sailed down the Pacific coast and claimed for Queen Elizabeth the land around the coastal inlet east of Point Reyes, calling it New Albion. Although the Spanish were aware of Drake's incursion into their territory, nothing further came of it. When Sebastián Rodríguez Cermeño, commander of the 1595 Manila Galleon, took his vessel, the *San Augustin*, into Drake's Bay he found no trace of the English on the shore. He then named this estuary the Bahía de San Francisco and thereby initiated a confusion of identity that plagued later coastal explorers.

In 1602–03, the Conde de Monterey, then viceroy of New Spain, sent Sebastián Vizcaíno with two small ships up the California coast from Mexico to find a harbor for the Manila Galleons. Although Vizcaíno sailed as far north as Cape Mendecino, he too missed the entrance to the big bay. However, he found another bay, named it Monterey for the viceroy, and highly recommended it as a suitable harbor in his report, which the Spanish officials unfortunately took seriously.

Through Vizcaíno's descriptions and maps, the Monterey Bay became important to Spain's colonization plans for Alta California. In 1765, Charles III appointed José de Gálvez *visitador-general* of New Spain. Gálvez chose Don Gaspar de Portolá, the first Spanish governor of Baja California, to be head of the so-called Sacred Expedition. Its purpose was to establish a chain of missions and forts along the coast to defend the lands against colonization by the Russians and incursions by the British and French. Four contingents of settlers and supplies set out, two by sea on the vessels San Carlos and San Antonio in January and February of 1769, and two by land under the separate commands of Captain Rivera y Moncada and Portolá, who departed San Blas, Mexico, in March and May.

After a rendezvous with Moncada in San Diego in June, Portolá set out on land with the Franciscan monk, Junipero Serra, some Christian Indians and servants, and about 60 soldiers to search for Monterey Bay. Although the party reached the bay near the mouth of the Salinas River without difficulty, the vagueness of Vizcaíno's description of landmarks in the area prevented them from recognizing it. Continuing their search north along the San Francisco peninsula they were confronted by the Montara Mountain in presentday San Mateo County and decided to camp over night by a creek at its base. The next day, October 31, they climbed the western side of the mountain to the top, and were able to see the coast ahead. By consulting the maps and descriptions they carried with them of Vizcaíno and José Gonzalez Cabrera Bueno, a pilot of the Manila Galleons, they learned that they had passed Monterey and that the headland they saw jutting into the sea in the distance was Point Reyes. The ocean islands to the west were the Farallones, and the watery expanse they faced was the Gulf of the Farallones. Had they looked east from the top of Montara Mountain they would have seen the bay, but there is no evidence that they shifted their gaze from the west coast, and perhaps some part of the mountain blocked their view to the east.

Instead of immediately retracing their course Portolá directed Sergeant José Francisco de Ortega to lead a scouting party to search for Cermeño's Bahía de San Francisco and explore Point Reyes for three days. While they were gone, another group of soldiers explored the nearby Santa Cruz Mountains and while hunting for deer reported that they had seen "an immense arm of the sea" that extended landward as far as the eye could see. When Ortega's scouting party returned, they reported that their route along the coast was obstructed by an immense estuary that penetrated inland and branched to the north and south. Both parties had seen the harbor of their dreams, but since the descriptions did not fit that of Monterey Bay, Portolá discounted them. Ailing and exhausted, his party returned to San Diego, once again passing Monterey without recognizing it, in January 1770. Although a second trek up the coast succeeded in locating the Monterey Bay, Portolá did not pursue exploration of the reported inland sea to the north.

In 1772, Pedro Fages, Portolá's successor as governor, attempted to find Cermeño's Bahía de San Francisco by exploring the east side of the huge unnamed estuary. But despite having followed the north arm of the bay as far as the Carquinez Strait and Suison Bay they returned to Monterey without a real understanding of what they had seen.[1]

1. *The bay extends from the Golden Gate, so named in 1846 by the American explorer John C. Fremont, about 10 miles northeast to the entry of San Pablo Bay and about 40 miles southeast along the east shore of the San Francisco Peninsula. The bay's maximum width is about 13 miles.*

THE CAÑIZARES MAP

The final installment in the history of the San Francisco Bay's discovery began with the plans made by Viceroy Antonio María Buchareli y Ursúa, now residing in Monterey. Again, the plans called for expeditions on land and sea. In September 1775, under the command of Juan Bautista de Anza and José Joaquín Moraga, a party of 240 people that included women, children, cattle, and supplies began the 1500-mile route from Sonora to the peninsula; they arrived on its fog-bound east side in July 1776.

> Title: Untitled Map of San Francisco Bay
> Date: 1776
> Cartographer: José de Cañizares
> *Hand-colored manuscript, 19 ⁷⁄₁₀ x 13 ⁴⁄₁₀ inches*
> *The Bancroft Library, University of California, Berkeley*

To prepare for their arrival Buchareli ordered the Spanish navigator Juan Manuel de Ayala to precede the land party and establish a settlement near the bay. Ayala's ship, the *San Carlos*, left San Blas in March 1775 and entered San Francisco Bay on August 5. This time an exploration of the bay that included mapping was ordered, but Captain Ayala was not able to participate in it because of an accidental foot wound from a pistol shot. Instead, his pilot, José de Cañizares, and ten other members of the crew, were sent to explore the bay in a launch. For the next 44 days while the *San Carlos* anchored off Angel Island, Cañizares and another crew member, Juan Bautista Aguirre, explored the bay with a sounding line and compass. Cañizares compiled the results and created a report and a detailed chart, which showed that the great body of water was not connected to Drake's Bay. In 1776, Cañizares returned to the bay as captain of the *San Carlos* and made further explorations from which he refined his chart. He named the new bay the Bahia de San Francisco, describing it as "not one body of water, but many." The Presidio and the Mission Dolores are represented on the map with symbols, and 28 additional sites such as the Farallon Islands are lettered. Although many of the names are no longer associated with these sites, their identification reveals an intention to identify the geographical features considered important at the time. The explorers' interest in the groves of great trees meticulously dotted over the landscape is revealed in note 1a (on the map), which identifies them as redwoods. At long last a visual record of the San Francisco Bay had been made.

Anza and José Joaquín Moraga, his second-in-command, proceeded north to select a site for a mission in the bay area. The march took four days and led them to a lake later called Mountain Lake near the site selected for the Presidio. Returning south they found a stream, which Father Pedro Font considered sufficient to operate a mill. Since it was Good Friday, the Friday of Sorrows, they named it the Arroyo de los Dolores. Although the mission sited near

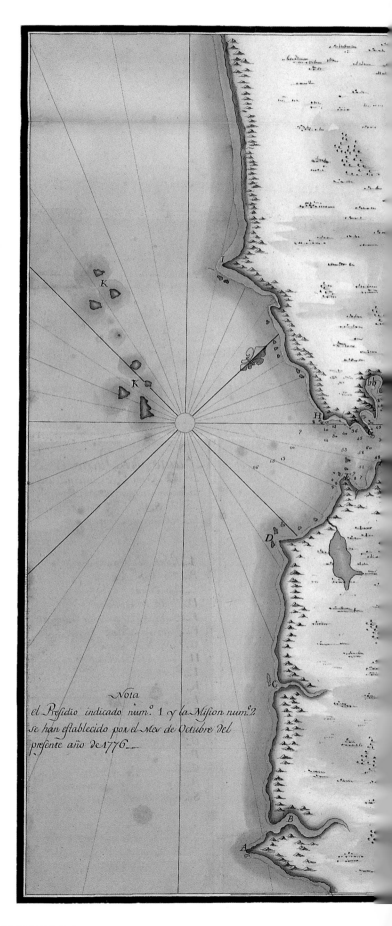

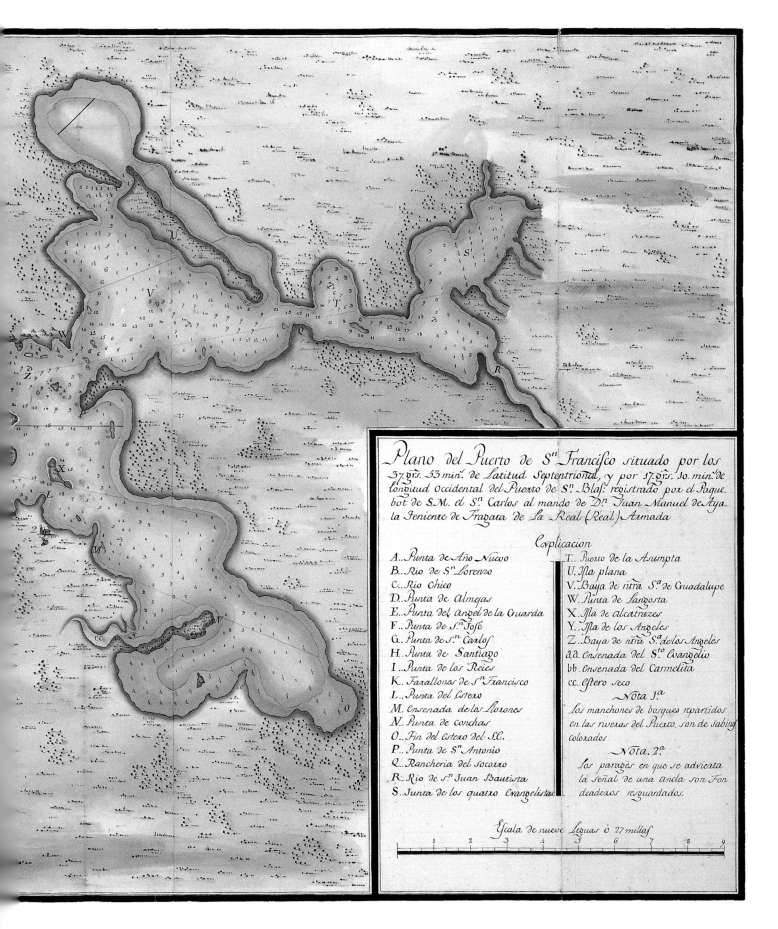

Plano del Puerto de Sn Francisco situado por los 37 grs. 53 min. de Latitud Septentrional, y por 17 grs. 30 min. de Longitud Occidental del Puerto de Sn. Blas: registrado por el Paquebot de S.M. el Sn. Carlos al mando de Dn. Juan Manuel de Ayala Teniente de Fragata de la Real (Real) Armada

PLAN

DU PORT DE

St. FRANÇOIS,

Situé sur la côte de la *CALIFORNIE* Septentrionale :
La Pointe des Rois par 37.° 59.′ de Latitude Nord et 124.° 54.′
de Longitude Occidentale.

Les sondes sont exprimées en Brasses d'Espagne, de deux vares ou six pieds de Castille.

A. Pointe des Almeras.
B. Laguna de la Merced.
C. Laguna del Presidio.
D. P.ta del Angel de la Guarda.
E. P.ta del Cantil Blanco.
F. Presidio de San Francisco.
G. Pequena Laguna.
H. Mission de San Francisco.
I. Laguna de los Dolores.
J. Ile de Alcatraces.

K. Ile de los Angeles.
L. P.ta de San Antonio.
M. Ile del Carmel.
N. Anse des Carmelites.
O. Anse de Consolation.
P. P.ta de S.t Carlos.
Q. P.ta de S.t Iago.
R. P.ta de Reyes.
S. Farallones.
T. Arena y lodo.

V. Arena y Franyo.

Lieues Marines de 20. au dégré.

Prix Deux Francs.

the arroyo was formally named San Francisco de Asís, it became know as the Mission Dolores. The mission was formally dedicated on October 9. The settlement at the Presidio, although located near the bay's entrance, grew slowly in part because the main trade routes were on the Pacific Ocean, while the settlements were tied to the bay.

MAPPING THE BAY

In September 1786, the French navigator Jean François Galaup, Comte de la Pérouse, undertook an exploration of the Pacific coast sponsored by the French government and devoted to scientific, geographic, and commercial purposes. His two vessels carried botanists and geologists and sailed from Alaska to Monterey. They were the first European ships to tour the coast since Sir Francis Drake in 1579.

La Pérouse arrived in San Francisco on September 10, 1786, and in Monterey on September 13 where he stayed until September 24. While there La Pérouse arranged for a ten-day exploration of the San Francisco Bay, which produced an hydrographic chart of the bay that he sent to the Ministry of Marine in France. The chart was published along with an account of his explorations in *A voyage round the world, in the years 1785, 1786, 1787, and 1788*, published in Paris in 1797. Although the expedition continued across the Pacific Ocean, the last communication from it was dated February 7, 1788. Later the wreckage of what was judged to be La Pérouse's ship, *La Boussole*, was found on the reefs of an island near New Hebrides; all aboard were presumed lost.

Title: Plan du Port de St. François
Date: 1797
Cartographer: Jean François Galaup, Comte de la Pérouse
Published: 1828, Depot-General de la Marine (Paris)
Atlas Map; Chart Map
Engraved map. Relief shown by hachures; soundings in brasses d'Espagne,
19 ⁷⁄₁₀ x 13 ⁴⁄₁₀ inches
David Rumsey Collection

The 1797 chart of the San Francisco Bay in La Pérouse's report was based on earlier maps made by José de Cañizares, pilot of the 1775 exploratory expedition led by Captain Juan Manuel de Ayala. While Cañizares's maps were not accurate, the errors occurred mainly in the San Pablo Bay adjoining the San Francisco Bay. Although the map from La Pérouse's report shown here differs from those of Cañizares in respect to San Pablo Bay and may indicate his own findings, inaccuracies persisted.

For today's viewers the absence of graphic information about the land around the two bays is striking. A simple square denotes the Presidio, and several smaller squares aligned along a brief street at an undefined distance from the Presidio mark the mission complex. Because nothing connects these two outposts of New Spain, they appear to float in empty space.

The point of view from which the cartographer presents the two-bay system is high above the ocean. Rhumb lines, which enabled seamen to steer a direct course from point to point, radiate from the compass centered near the bay entrance. Stretches of the Pacific coast north and south of the entrance are drawn, and the Farallone Islands are clearly marked. Although the importance of the bay as an extension of the ocean is clear, the lands to either side of its entrance appear to be of almost equal significance. In fact, more of the territory to the north of the entrance is rendered than that of the future home of San Francisco to the south. Another indication of a lack of interest in the region's landscape is the oval frame within which the 18 or so points of navigational importance around the bay and west of its entrance are marked with letters. The inaccurately drawn San Pablo Bay has no letters.

For a better understanding of what was happening on the ground, we turn to the account of the explorations of it by the Englishman George Vancouver. England's Royal Commission sent Vancouver to make hydrographic surveys along the coast of what he called New Albion, echoing Drake's name for the area. He completed several tours between 1790 and 1795. In *A Voyage of Discovery to the North Pacific Ocean and Round the World,* published in London in 1798, Vancouver gave a detailed account of his experiences of the bay and its shores along with maps.

After entering the bay on November 15, Vancouver anchored his ship "in a most excellent small bay within three-fourths of a mile to the nearest shore." Cattle and sheep grazed on the surrounding hills. In response to a flag raising and a salute fired to signal the Presidio of their arrival, a group of men on horses, including a priest and a sergeant, came out in a small boat to meet Vancouver's party.

"We soon arrived at the Presidio, which was not more than a mile from our landing place. Its wall, which fronted the harbor, was visible from the ships, but instead of the city or town, whose lights we had so anxiously looked for on the night of our arrival, we were conducted into a spacious verdant plain, surrounded by hills on every side, excepting that which fronted the port. The only object of human industry which presented itself was a square area … enclosed by a mud wall resembling a pound for cattle … low small houses were along the wall. Facing the gated entrance to the square was the church which, though small, was neat in comparison to the rest of the buildings."

The commandant's house to the left of the church consisted of two rooms and a closet. Vancouver thought that during the winter rainy season the houses "must at best be very uncomfortable dwellings" since the windows cut in the front wall had no glass or any other covering. He judged the large room of the commandant's house where he and his men were received to be about 30 feet long, 14 feet wide, and 12 feet high. "The floor was of the native soil raised about three feet from its original level, without being boarded, paved or even reduced to an even surface; the roof was covered with rushes, the walls on the inside had once been whitewashed; the furniture consisted of a very sparing assortment of the most indispensable articles, of the rudest fashion, and of the meanest kind; and ill accorded with the ideas we had conceived of the sumptuous manner in which the Spaniards live on this side of the globe."

The hills surrounding the Presidio appeared barren, their summits composed of "naked uneven rocks." On the next day, Sunday, the party visited the mission accompanied by men from the Presidio. There they found soil "infinitely richer than that of the Presidio" and pastures with a "more luxuriant herbage", and consequently a greater number of sheep and cattle. The mission church, "for its magnitude, architecture, and internal decorations, did great credit to its constructors." Vancouver noted that the building and decorating of the church had been the main object of the *padres'* efforts. Everything else, including their own quarters and gardens, which occupied about four acres, had barely been developed.

Although they ate well and enjoyed the hospitality of their hosts, Vancouver noted, "the distressing inconvenience these valuable people labor under, in want of almost all the common and most necessary utensils of life." He had been led to expect that the colony was in a very different stage of improvement. "Why such an extent of territory should have been subjugated, and, after all the expense and labor bestowed upon its colonization, turned to no account whatever is a mystery in the science of state policy not easily explained." He questioned the ability of the Californians to resist invasions, mentioned the difficulty of landing in shallow waters, and noted the remoteness of any sources of water from the only anchorage he could recommend. [1]

In brief, Vancouver's description of the two rudimentary settlements suggested that they were not likely to promote development of the peninsula, a prediction reinforced by Spain's preoccupation with sea trade to the detriment of settlement.

Still, some planning had occurred. In 1773, distribution of land to Indians and *popladores* who were committed to farming and cattle-raising was approved. In 1779, Governor Filipe de Neve had codified rules for the administration of California. His *Reglamento* provided for the establishment of civilian towns, or pueblos, associated with missions and Presidios and entitled to town councils called *ayuntamientos.* The recruitment of settlers and the granting of land that would enable them to build residences, raise crops, carry on trade, maintain herds of cattle, cultivate the public lands, and serve military needs when necessary, were also covered in the *Reglamento.* The pueblos were to be the bulwarks of civilization.

But Neve's laws were never fully implemented, and Alta California's isolation prevented news of the revolutions against Spanish rule in the south from reaching the northern region. Spanish Governor Diego de Borica even wrote at the closing of the century that Alta California was "the most peaceful and quiet country in the world" with a healthy climate and plenty to eat.

Even though Mexico won independence from Spain and gained control of California in 1821, the unprofitability of the settlements in Alta California did not attract the settlers needed to ensure the government's firm control. As Neal Harlow observed in his book, *California Conquered* (p. 22), "Mexico sent a series of governors—four of whom were shortly expelled—and dispensed laws, many of which proved to be irrelevant, inappropriate, or simply inconvenient and were consequently ignored, tempered, or supplanted by local initiative."

Still, news about California reached well beyond its borders. In November 1826, Frederick William Beechey, commander of the British exploring vessel *Blossom,* came down the coast to San Francisco, proceeded south to Monterey in December, and returned to carry out a new survey of the San Francisco Bay in October 1827. [2] In 1831, Beechey described the bay as, "sufficiently extensive to contain all the British navy, well sheltered, and with good anchorage everywhere, surrounded with a country varied with hills and valleys, partly wooded and with fine pasturage, and abounding with cattle of every kind." Beechey also observed the lack of an industrious population and predicted that if nothing changed, the province would fall into other hands because its natural importance would prevent it from remaining in a neglected state.

Two weeks after Beechey departed, the French trader, Auguste Duhaut-Cilly, arrived on a California tour that took him as far south as Los Angeles. He found the Californians hospitable, but vain and easily offended. He judged the men handsome and well-formed, but awkward when not on horseback, lazy, ruined by gambling, and degraded by drunkenness. It appeared that California was wasted on its inhabitants.

In 1824, Mexico's Sovereign General Congress enacted a colonization law intended to encourage settlement and trade. California's ports were opened to ships from all nations, an action that tied the ranchos and missions to a system of trade linking the Pacific and Atlantic coasts. The Yerba Buena settlement on the bay cove south of the Presidio became the economic center of the region because it was used as an embarkation and debarkation point for trading vessels that entered the bay. More foreign traders arrived. Although fur traders were numerous, the most established trade besides whaling was in the hides of cattle slaughtered and tanned for shipment around Cape Horn to New England; there the leather supplied the money-making manufacture of shoes and clothing. Likewise, the tallow from the cattle was used to make candles. Shortages of coins and valid paper money turned hides and tallow into California's currency.

By 1834, the increase in trade from ships anchoring in the bay prompted Governor José Figueroa and the Territorial Deputation, the local legislature, to secularize the missions in stages and to move the soldiers at the Presidio to a new garrison in the Sonoma valley. With the Presidio garrison departed and the mission largely deserted, the presidial population had decreased to about 200 inhabitants. The inhabitants had begun moving south from the unpromising location near the bay's entrance to the muddy and shallow Yerba Buena cove. While it was initially seen as a possible landing place, ocean-going vessels could not dock there because of the shallowness of the cove.

At this point Governor Figueroa and the Deputation turned to the *Leyes Vigentes*, the Laws of the Indies, to authorize the election of an *ayuntamiento* based at the Presidio of San Francisco that would establish the legal basis for a larger area. [3] The town council was elected in December 1834 and installed in January 1835. The pueblo's boundaries were set as a line running from the south side of Rincon Point on the bay around 4th and Berry streets, to the Divisadero at Lone Mountain, and from there to the south side of Point Lobos on the ocean. The council was renewed each year until 1838 when the population declined to less than was required for this designation—the Mexican Constitution of 1836 had increased the population requirement for a pueblo to 4,000. The *ayuntamiento* was then suspended until the population increased to the required number. Instead of an *alcalde*, the pueblo was governed by justices of the peace who formed a municipal *junta* for the purpose. The names Yerba Buena, San Francisco, and the Puerto de San Francisco were all used for the pueblo.

THE GROWTH OF YERBA BUENA

Whereas only one land grant had been made in Alta California prior to 1833, in the next decade more than 300 grants were made from lands formerly part of the missions. In October 1835, William A. Richardson, one of the entrepreneurial foreigners who had come to Yerba Buena, submitted a petition for land on its beach. Richardson, an English seaman, had come to the bay area as first mate on a whaler. He abandoned ship, became a resident, formed alliances with the *Californios*, and married the daughter of the Presidio *comandante*, Ignacio Martinez. The location of his claim was based on its convenience to trade around the bay. Richardson was known as a surgeon, bricklayer, and carpenter. Having taught the Indians at the Missions Dolores and Santa Clara to build boats, he used two of them in his trading enterprises around the bay. Attached to his petition for land was the *disegno*, or drawing required by law. In effect, it was a plan for the pueblo of Yerba Buena. The town he drew had one short street, the Calle de la Fundación, set back from the shore of the cove about 900 feet. The road meandered along the base of the steep sandy hills to the west and intersected with the trail to the mission at the south end and the Presidio trail on the north end.

Richardson's account of laying out the town that followed his *disegno* was recorded as follows in the transcript of records from the 1854 proceedings of the US Board of Land Commissioners and the U.S. vs. José Y. Limantour:

1. *Servin, Manual P.* CHS Quarterly *49: 221-32, Sept. 1970. Miguel Costanso, diarist, military engineer, and navigator under Portolá, also advised Governor Borica in 1794 of the area's continued backwardness, and lack of settlers, shipping, and trade.*
2. *Beechey produced the first accurate chart of the bay; it was published by the British Hydrographic Office in 1833.*
3. *Las Leyes Vigentes—the laws still in force—refer to orders and decrees of the Cortes of Spain, which, being municipal laws, were considered still in force in Mexico after the revolution of 1821 because, although a change in the sovereignty of a country changed the political laws, the laws respecting private property remained in force. Dwinelle, op. cit, pp. 338-39.*

They measured off two hundred *varas* from the beach in a southwest direction, and then told me that I could select some place out of that limit.… I told them I wished to go a little higher up.… They then measured off another one hundred *varas* in the same direction … the magistrate, Don Francisco de Haro … appointed me the first sand hill to the southeast from where we were standing as the southeast boundary. He then went to the first sand hill with the *Ayuntamiento*, and I accompanied them, and he pointed to the direction in which the street must lay. He commenced measuring, and measured off the first three 100-*vara* lots.… I selected the fifth l00-*vara* lot from the starting point. He measured off no more in that direction but declared all the land in that direction, on the line to the waters of the bay [north beach] as the northwest boundary for the small settlement of Yerba Buena, and at that same time laid off the street in that same direction, which he called the Calle de la Fundación.… The first 200 *varas* measured off on the beach were reserved for government purposes. [1]

In 1837, Richardson replaced his first structure, a tent of pine posts covered with canvas, with a large adobe he called the Casa Grande. The following year he moved with his family to his 20,000-acre Rancho Saucelito (Willow Grove) from which he conducted a profitable trade in a variety of commodities including fresh water, which was in short supply in Yerba Buena.

Another important early Yerba Buena resident was Jacob Leese, an Ohio-born merchant, who arrived in 1836 and formed a partnership with William Hinckley and Nathan Spear to exchange hides and tallow for Yankee goods. Leese built a house sheathed with clapboards, a rarity at the time; it was the first residence worthy to be so called and stood next to Richardson's first house. Leese became a naturalized citizen, and after marrying a sister of General Mariano Vallejo dissolved his partnership, sold his business to the Hudson's Bay Company, and moved to Sonoma in 1841.

Leese's house was built on one of the lots drawn by Jean Vioget, a Swiss engineer, who came to Yerba Buena in charge of his own ship to trade with the *Californios*. Vioget also owned surveying equipment, which apparently got him the job of laying out an official town plan for Yerba Buena's first *alcalde*, Francisco de Haro. De Haro's concern about the growing number of land acquisitions that were not associated with a system of streets prompted the survey.

Title: Plan of Yerba Buena, California
Date depicted: 1839, redrawn 1855?
Cartographer: after Jean-Jacques Vioget
Pen-and-ink, pencil, and watercolor on paper,
17 ³⁄₁₀ x 21 ¼ inches (sheet)
The Bancroft Library, University of California, Berkeley

1. *Transcript of record of the case: The United States vs. José Limautour, 1857. v. 1, p. 26.*

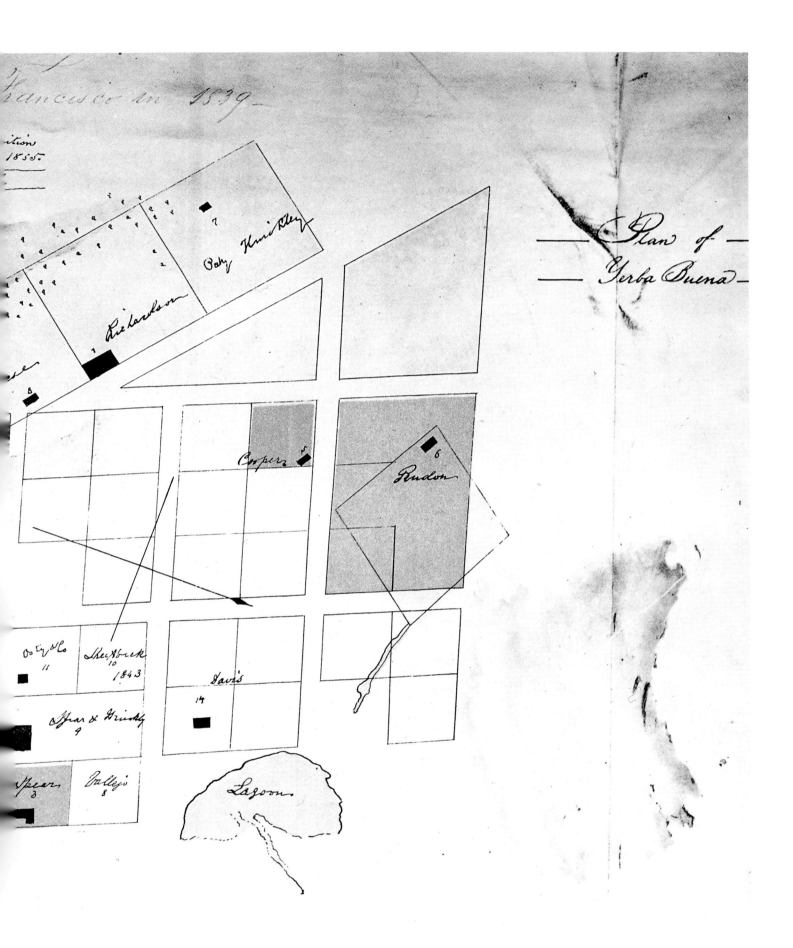

Francisco in 1839

Plan of —
Yerba Buena —

Richardson

Poly Knickley
7

Cooper
5

Rudon
6

Ochs&Co
11

Sherbeck
10
1843

Davis
14

Spear & Grissly
9

Spear
3

Vallejo
8

Lagoon

Vioget's survey included the existing houses standing in fenced lots in the area bounded by California, Dupont, Montgomery, and Pacific Streets (now part of Chinatown and the financial district). The survey began on Montgomery and encompassed three blocks to the west and four from north to south between Sacramento and Pacific Streets. One oversized lot was set between Sacramento and California Streets. Richardson's Calle de la Fundación was incorporated but did not conform to the direction of the other streets. Vioget laid out 12 rectangular parcels of fifty *varas*, approximately 137 feet square, and parts of others in a northwest to southeast grid that was not aligned with Richardson's and Leese's lots on the Calle de la Fundación. In fact, the Calle was abandoned as a base line and later disappeared along with the Mission Plank Road to the Presidio. Although no street names appear on Vioget's map, Dupont, Kearny, and Montgomery, which more or less followed the bay shore, are easily identified. A plaza that recalled the Law of the Indies' town center replaced Richardson's government preserve on the bay shore.

Given the need to incorporate the existing dwellings and properties within the town, Vioget's plan seemed logical. As a guide for extending the network of streets, it made little sense because many steep hills barred their path. Still, in 1839, the massive immigration caused by the Gold Rush was nearly ten years away, and Yerba Buena's prospects for settlement were not bright.

FURTHER EXPLORATIONS OF THE BAY AND THE CONQUEST OF CALIFORNIA

Westward migration over the Oregon Trail from 1843 to 1845 brought more Americans to Yerba Buena. Russians pursuing the fur trade also came down the coast regularly and in 1812 had established a fort on the northern coast near Bodega. But having hunted the sea otters to near extinction, the Russians left the fort and sold it to John Sutter in 1841. That same year Lieutenant Charles Wilkes of the United States Navy arrived as commander of yet another a

scientific mission to chart the bay. Wilkes wrote a five-volume narrative that gave California a rather negative review and predicted that it would separate from Mexico and possibly be joined with Oregon. Still, Wilkes was confident that when populated by the "Anglo-Norman race" California would "fill a large space in the world's future history."

Title: Port de San Francisco Dans La Haute Californie
Date: 1844
Cartographer: Duflot de Mofras, Eugene
Publisher: Arthus Bertrand, Editeur, Libraire de la
Societe de Geographie (Paris)
Atlas map, 17 ³/₁₀ x 9 ⁴/₅ inches
David Rumsey Collection

Other nations were interested in California's future. Eugène Duflot de Mofras, an attaché of the French legation in Mexico City, also came to California after touring the northern Pacific coast. After arriving in Monterey in May 1841 with appropriate letters of introduction, he spent the next two years exploring the bay and visiting California's missions, villages, and ranchos, to assemble information on the military resources, geography, agriculture, natural history, and other aspects of the culture. The chart of the Port de San Francisco, to which a chart of the *Entrée du Port de San Francisco* is appended, was included in his book, *Exploration du territoire de l'Oregon, des Californies et de la Mer Vermeille, executée pendant les années 1840, 1841 et 1842*. The widely read book was published in Paris in 1844. Although the chart of the San Francisco Bay was based on Beechey's chart of 1833, it was redrawn, translated into French, and improved by de Mofras's own explorations, particularly in the north bay where he entered the names of the San Joaquin and Sacramento Rivers at its east end and also that of Carquinez Bay.

De Mofras's book was considered to be the best one on California prior to the American occupation; it made these western regions

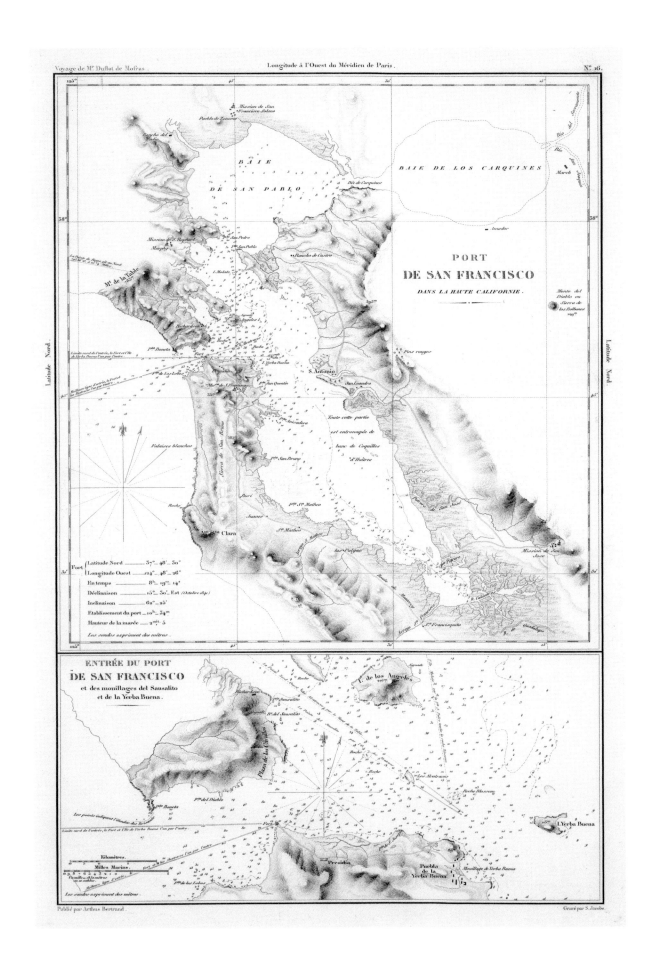

PORT
DE SAN FRANCISCO
DANS LA HAUTE CALIFORNIE .

ENTRÉE DU PORT
DE SAN FRANCISCO
et des mouillages del Sausalito
et de la Yerba Buena .

Publié par Arthus Bertrand . Gravé par S. Jacobs .

known in official European circles. A comparison of de Mofras's chart of the early 1840s with that of La Pérouse in 1786 shows the progress of the bay's development in some fifty years. The west shoreline of the bay is rendered in detail along with important geographic features such as Point Lobos, Point San Quentin, Points San Bruno, and San Mateo. The islands of Alcatraz, Los Angeles, Yerba Buena, and Molate are rendered. The land around the bay is no longer featureless as it was in La Pérouse's map; a road marked from Fort Point to the Presidio divides there with one branch leading to the settlement on Yerba Buena Cove and the other to the mission. This road, which became El Camino Real, is labeled the Route de Monterey. It linked various way stations and after crossing the Arroyo San Francisco reached the south part of the bay.

North of the watery delta in the south bay, a road beginning at the Porte de Potrero leads east to the Mission de San Jose. The road northward along the east bay passes a stretch of the bay labeled as a *banc de Coquilles de Huitres*, or a bank of oyster shells. A few structures dot the shores of two rivers indicating rudimentary settlements at San Leandro and San Antonio where Oakland later developed. Proceeding northward, this road terminates at the Rancho de Castro east of the Porte de San Pablo. North of the Bay's entrance, present day Marin County is marked by Richardson's rancho on what was named

Richardson's Bay. De Mofras noted Richardson's residence in his book and stated that Richardson was "an excellent pilot." On San Pablo Bay the Rancho del Indio, the Pueblo de Sonoma, and the Mission de San Francisco de Solano are marked. The bay region had become a geographic entity known to travelers on land and water.

De Mofras was a keen observer of California's culture. He noted that the parish priests, who were supposed to replace the Franciscan monks formerly in charge of the missions, never came. The Indians were left without teachers or protectors, and non-Indians associated with the missions were appointed managers of them. Rural and illiterate, they persecuted the remaining missionaries and deprived them of all means of support. De Mofras concluded that the country had lost its civilizing institutions and drifted into anarchy. The missions' property, deserted and looted, was released to private individuals, mainly rancheros of Spanish or Mexican heritage, called *Californios*, who were born or had long resided in California.

Charles Wilkes, a U. S. naval officer and commander of six ships, which carried out a major exploratory and scientific expedition from 1838–1842 that covered the northwest coast of North America, echoed de Mofras's statements, saying that the remaining inhabitants did not profit wisely from the spoils of the mission. "Most of them," he stated, "instead of preserving the cattle, kill them in order to sell their hides and tallow to trading ships; the soil rests untilled, for hardly anyone but the Indians cultivated it."[1] These accounts reinforced Richard Henry Dana's much quoted description of the Californians in his popular book of 1835, *Two Years Before the Mast*, as an "idle and thriftless people who can make nothing for themselves."

De Mofras also testified that the Californians were very friendly to France. "They hate the Americans," he stated, "because they are rapacious, Protestant, and Republican. They incline toward France because she is monarchical, powerful, Catholic, and of the same Latin race to which they themselves belong."[2]

During his stay, de Mofras visited Wilkes's ships in the San Francisco Bay as well as English men-of-war ships, which anchored in the same harbor and cruised along the coast, as did the American ships. According to de Mofras, the commanders of these ships had instructions to seize the capital at Monterey upon news of a probable conflict between Mexico and the United States. As for military installations, de Mofras stated, "There is no military force in California. There are no garrisons at the Presidios. The gun carriages at the forts have rotted away, and the guns, which were mostly cast in Manila more than 100 years ago, lie rusting on the ground. It is perfectly clear that California will belong to whatsoever nation will take the trouble to send there a ship of war and 200 soldiers."

Wilkes had also described the Presidio in bleak terms: "After passing through the entrance of the Bay we were scarcely able to distinguish the Presidio, and had it not been for its solitary flag staff, we could not have ascertained its situation. From this flag staff no flag floated; the buildings were deserted, the walls had fallen into decay, the guns were dismounted, and everything around it lay quiet ... the remnant of troops there consisted of no more than an officer and one soldier."[3]

In 1845, President Andrew Jackson offered Mexico $3,500,000 for the part of California north of the thirty-eighth parallel. Had the offer been accepted, it would have given the United States control of the San Francisco Bay a year earlier than the actual event.

With the annexation of Texas in 1846, the country lacked only Oregon, New Mexico, and California to complete its coast-to-coast expansion. On May 13, 1846, President Polk proclaimed a state of war with Mexico. This news took weeks to reach California and brought confusion to both the Mexicans and the Americans in the area. On July 9, Captain John B. Montgomery, whose ship the *Portsmouth* was anchored in the bay, rowed ashore at Clark's Point in a launch with 70 men in their dress uniforms. To the sound of a fife and drum, the flag was hoisted in the public square in front of the customhouse. The only shots fired in this definitive attack on the town came from the 21 guns on the *Portsmouth* that were fired in salute and then followed by three cheers by those on shore and on board.

---

1. *Wilkes, Charles.* Narrative of the United States Exploring Expedition. *Vol V, 1841: 106, 176.*

2. *Dwinelle, John W.* The Colonial History, City of San Francisco. *San Francisco: Ross Valley Book Co., 1978: 12.*

3. *Wilkes,* Narrative of the United States Exploring Expedition. *Vol V, 1841: 152.*

YERBA BUENA BECOMES SAN FRANCISCO

CIVIL GOVERNMENT AND LAND

1846 was a momentous year in the bay area. In January the *alcalde*, Washington A. Bartlett, changed the town's name, Yerba Buena (whichhad been derived from its location on Yerba Buena cove), to San Francisco. The "good herb," which inspired the name, was a minty plant with medicinal uses that grew wild in most parts of the bay—most notably Yerba Buena Island. The change was motivated by the desire to more clearly identify the town with the bay and thus ward off the rise of the competing east bay cities of Vallejo and Benecia. General Stephen Watts Kearny, commander of the Army of the West, arrived in 1846 to bring order to a chaotic situation and establish a legal government. Although his term in office lasted for only 100 days, he managed to appoint and instruct the *alcaldes*, whose office had survived the overthrow of the Mexican government. On March 1, Kearny proclaimed that Mexican laws would remain in force until superceded by a more competent legal framework.

Also in 1846, John Charles Fremont named the entrance to the bay the Golden Gate or the Chrysopylae, to recall the harbor of Constantinople, which was called Chrysoceras (the Golden Horn). The shape of the two harbors suggested to Fremont golden advantages for commerce. His inclusion of the explanation of the name in the Geographical Memoir he published in 1848—the first year of the Gold Rush—made him seem prophetic.

Title: View of San Francisco, formerly Yerba Buena,
in 1846–7 before the Discovery of Gold
Delineator: Captain W. F. Swasey
Publisher: Bosqui Eng. & Print Co.
Copyright date: 1884
Colored lithograph, 16 ⁹/₁₀ x 20 ½ inches
San Francisco Public Library

The date of 1846–1847 places this scene in the era of popularity of the bird's-eye view, which began to be produced around 1840 and continued to be in vogue until the 1910s. As was typical of the genre, the scene is tilted up as if set on an easel. The use of color enhances its picturesqueness.

Although the copyright date indicates that the view was made many years after the scene it records, the publishers have attempted to make it authentic by adding facsimiles of the signatures of General Mariano G. Vallejo, J. D. Stevenson, George Hyde, and Captain Swasey. These important early residents—Swasey stated that he had been a "continuous resident since 1845"—bolstered the credibility of the scene by adding a note to the lithograph stating, "We the undersigned hereby certify that this picture is a faithful and accurate representation of San Francisco as it really appeared in March, 1847."

As for the scene itself, the streets are eerily empty and little indication is given of what life in Yerba Buena was like. The important features are indicated by letters and numbers. The *U.S. Portsmouth* is prominently located in the bay

DESIGNED & COPIED FROM VIEWS TAKEN AT THE TIME & PUBLISHED BY.

VIEW OF SAN FRANCISCO, FORMERLY YERBA BUENA, IN 1846-7

BEFORE THE DISCOVERY OF GOLD

WE THE UNDERSIGNED HEREBY CERTIFY THAT THIS PICTURE IS A FAITHFUL AND ACCURATE REPRESENTATION OF SAN FRANCISCO AS IT REALLY APPEARED IN MARCH 1847

J. D. Stevenson

COMMANDING 1ST REGT. OF N.Y. VOLS. IN THE WAR WITH MEXICO.

Gen. M. G. Vallejo

George Hyde

FIRST ALCALDE DIST. OF SAN FRANCISCO 1846-7

Capt. W. F. Swasey
A CONTINUOUS RESIDENT SINCE 1845.

ase.
ffice.
owned by Wm. A.

Hotel.
vis' Store.

re. The
building.
sidence.
Ware-

Cottage.
he Russ

13—John Sullivan's Residence.
14—Peter T. Sherback's do.
15—Juan C. Davis'   do.
16—G. Reynolds   do.
17—A. J. Ellis Boarding House.
18—Fitch & McKurley's building.
19—Capt. Vioget's Residence.
20—John Fuller's Residence.
21—Jesus Noe's   do.
22—Juan N. Pidilla's   do.
23—A. A. Andrew's   do.
24—Capt. Antonio Ortega's Residence.
25—Francisco Cacerez's Residence.
26—Capt. Wm. Hinckley's do.

27—Gen. M. G. Vallejo's building.
28—C. L. Ross' building.
29—Mill.
30—Capt. John Paty's Adobe building.
31—Doctor E. P. Jones' Residence.
32—Robert Ridley's Residence.
33—Los Pechos de la Choco.
34—Lone Mountain.
35—Sill's Blacksmith Shop.
➝—Trail to Presido.
⬅—Trail to Mission Dolores.

31

along with other ships of varying sizes. The important buildings are numbered and include: 1. Customhouse; 2. Calaboose (jail); 3. School; 4. Alcalde Office; 5. City Hotel, owned by William A. Leidesdorff; 6. Portsmouth Hotel; 7. William H. Davis Store; 8. Howard & Mellus Store (former Hudson's Bay Company); 9. Leidesdorff's Warehouse; 10. Sam Brannan's residence; 11. Leidesdorff's Cottage; 12. The first Russ residence; 19. Vioget's residence; 21. Jesus Noe's residence; 24. Captain Antonio Ortego's residence; 27. General M. G. Vallejo's building; and others. Important natural features were Lone Mountain, Twin Peaks, the Trail to the Presidio, and the Trail to the Mission.

T. A. Barry and B. A. Patten, bar owners in the vicinity of Portsmouth Square, wrote *Men and Memories of San Francisco in 1850*, to recall the Gold Rush era that they watched transform the rudimentary settlement of Yerba Buena into the teeming city of San Francisco. While their memories may not always be accurate, they enliven views like those that follow here. Montgomery Street, they noted, was not graded in 1850. "It was like any hillside, with a gradual slope. Not that it was so gradual either," they stated, "for the western side was several feet higher than the eastern." They noted that the Hudson's Bay Company building, a large wooden structure of two-and-a-half stories with a high, sloping roof, faced Montgomery Street; that William H. Davis (who imported some 25 knocked-down houses for Happy Valley and other locations) erected the building at California and Montgomery Streets; and that the brick customhouse had verandas on each of its four stories connected by exterior stairs.

In 1849, Barry and Patten recalled that the tents pitched in the middle of California Street above Montgomery Street were interspersed with boxes, bales of goods, and piles of lumber. A large corrugated iron warehouse stood on Sansome between Jackson and Pacific Streets.

In 1849 or 1850, they recalled "The old road, or path, to the Mission Dolores was the same as had been used for eighty years prior to the gold discovery—a winding way among the sand hills and chaparral…. A vehicle was rather a curiosity until the plank-road was constructed…. Nearly all the residents of San Francisco in those days rode horseback, used the Mexican saddle, and had all the jingling

accoutrements. They wore the vicuna hat or the broad-brimmed glazed sombrero, and the comfortable, convenient, protecting serapa…. The horse's hooves made no sound on the trail because they sank deep in the unresisting sand at each step." On present day Eddy Street between Powell and Mason Streets, they described the Mission Road winding "in and out amongst mounds and ridges of sand piled up like dirty snow-drifts, with here and there a charcoal-burner's hut and clumps of scrub oaks."[1]

Barry's and Patten's description of Kearny Street is particularly evocative: "Kearny Street's narrow sidewalks were wonderfully made and composed of a great variety of queer materials… In front of one man's property, the walk was made of barrel staves nailed upon stretchers; the one adjoining had thin, springing boards, threatening at every step to let you through; then a mosaic made of sides and ends of packing-cases, some portions covered with tin or zinc—the jagged, saw-like edge making business for the dealers in boots and shoes; now you trod upon the rusty tops of old stoves or heavy iron window-shutters, or an old ship's hatchway covering; then a dozen or two heads of kegs, set close together, imbedded in the mulch of last year's rainy season; and so on, in great and curious variety."

In 1850, the road to the Presidio was probably unchanged from the time recaptured in Swasey's view. According to Barry and Patten, it had "no level way for vehicles along the hard steep sloping hill corrugated with rain-washed ruts and ugly gulleys… In summer the adobe soil was hard as stone; in the winter rainy season, gummy, sticky, and disagreeable. A carriage always seemed to be toppling over or sliding down the hill. It went past cattle pens and corrals, brick-yards, and butchers' shambles looking baked and hard as slag with no sign of vegetation but everywhere a surface blown bare by the continuous winds of summer, after the rains came wild flowers and grass. Past Sutter, a road led to the Laguna or Washerwoman's Bay and then cow sheds, and barns, and milk ranches, and a little wayside inn for soldiers, and then a few cottages until the Government reserve and the Presidio, which was then a few dilapidated old adobes, some long shedlike barracks and a cottage or two for officers."[2]

1. Barry, Theodore Augustus, and Benjamin Adam Patten. Men and Memories of San Francisco. *San Francisco: Burger and Evans, 1972: 13-16.*
2. Ibid: 133.

THE FIRST SURVEYS

Following his renaming of the town in 1847, Alcalde Bartlett hired Jasper O'Farrell to revise Vioget's plat of San Francisco. O'Farrell was the former Surveyor General of Alta California and had carried on his surveying work after the American conquest. He conducted two surveys of the city. The first eliminated the Calle de la Fundacion, but extended Vioget's grid without altering it significantly south to Post Street, west to Taylor Street, and north to Francisco Street. O'Farrell then found this first plat untenable because of the oblique angles Vioget had drawn for his blocks. He then reset his survey as an orthogonal grid.

While O'Farrell was occupied with the survey work from mid June to mid July, Edwin Bryant was elected *alcalde*. He implemented General Stephen Watts Kearny's decision to enable the development of land to help pay down the municipal debt by releasing from federal control the so-called water lots in the cove's tidal lands from Rincon Point to Clark's Point. The lots were sold at auction from July 20–23 to "speculative citizens and wharf-builders." Over 250 lots were sold. Some of the 45 x 137 ½-foot beach lots went for $600. Lots of the same size that were under water sold from $50 to $400.

In addition to extending Vioget's 50-*vara* grid further west and south, O'Farrell also established a second grid south of Market Street, which he made an artery 110-feet wide. He set this grid parallel to the Mission Road at about 45 degrees from true north to connect on a diagonal line to the Mission Dolores. He then shifted the line of the streets parallel to the waterfront by two and one half degrees in a northeast and southwest direction. This shift was called the O'Farrell swing because it shifted the line of the streets from a pivot at the corner of Washington and Kearny and altered most of the lot lines in the previous surveyed section. Instead of the 50-*vara* lots traced in Vioget's plat, the blocks south of Market Street were given 100 *varas*, effectively preventing the streets defining these blocks from intersecting directly with those north of Market.

Neither the passage of time nor other plans for correcting the dysfunctional traffic pattern caused by O'Farrell's survey have succeeded in marrying the areas north and south of the 120-foot wide avenue once called "the slot" for the cable car slot that ran up the street. O'Farrell's grid, extended by William Eddy in 1849–50, was lamented by Frank Soulé, John H. Gihon, and James Nisbet, authors of the *1855 Annals of San Francisco*: "If the great thoroughfares had been adapted to the natural configuration of the tract of country upon which the city stands," they said, "there might have been some apparent irregularity in the plan, and some, perhaps some little ground available for building purposes lost, yet many millions of dollars would have been saved to the community at large, which, as matters stand, have already been unprofitably expended, while millions more must be spent in overcoming the obstacles willfully placed in the way by the originally defective plans."[1]

Title: Official map of San Francisco. Compiled from the field notes of the official re-survey made by Wm. M. Eddy, surveyor of the town of San Francisco
Date: 1849
Cartographer: William M. Eddy
Delineator: Alex Zakrzewski
Lithographer: Francis Michelin
Colored cadastral map, 20 x 20 inches
Library of Congress
[see following page]

Eddy was hired in 1849 to enlarge O'Farrell's 1847 survey. Following the official chartering of the city in 1851, Eddy submitted his map. A cadastral map, it was intended to provide a standardized basis for buying and selling city land.

The water lots platted on the tidal lands east of the high tide line had been released from federal ownership by General Stephen Watts Kearny in 1847 and authorized for sale to raise money for the municipal treasury. These lots, which were 45 feet wide, are darkened for emphasis in Eddy's map. Private developers have created a number of secondary streets through the 100-*vara* blocks south of Market. Since a *vara* was 33 inches or 84 centimeters long; the 100-*vara* lots were about 274 feet or 168 meters on each side—too large for efficient residential development, which required more street frontage. The skewed northeast/southwest plat of the south-of-Market blocks was a better orientation for this area of the city than the north/south plat of the north-of-Market area; it connected the bay and the settled area around the Mission Dolores, which in turn, veered toward the south bay. An odd 24-block plat in the northeast part of the city between Larkin and Fillmore streets was the result of the unused 1847 "Laguna Survey" located near the fresh water lake called "washerwoman's lagoon."

Eddy's map defined the city for the years prior to the 1855–56 Van Ness Ordinances that extended the survey area west of Larkin Street to include the Western Addition.

1. *pp. 489-490.*

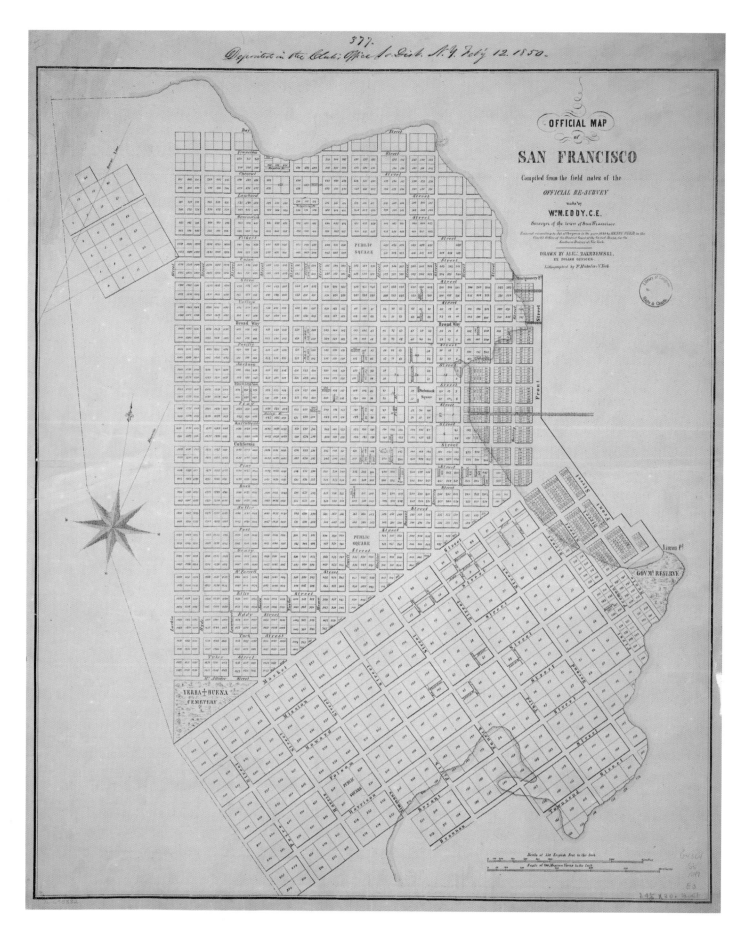

PRE-GOLD RUSH LAND RUSH

On July 31, 1846, 238 Mormons led by Samuel Brannan, a convert to the Mormon faith in 1842 and publisher of a religious newspaper in New York, arrived in Yerba Buena. They had come to establish a colony outside the United States, which did not sanction such articles of the Mormon faith as multiple marriages. Finding that U.S. forces had preceded them and conquered California, many of the party left for Utah. But for a while their numbers doubled the local population, and Brannan later became one of San Francisco's prominent citizens.

On January 24, 1847, a gold nugget found in the tailrace of a sawmill on the south fork of the American River led to the great migration to California known as the Gold Rush. James W. Marshall, supervisor of the sawmill's construction, reported the discovery to the owner, John Augustus Sutter, but the news was not released. Then, on May 12, the Mormon leader Samuel Brannan rode into San Francisco, announced the discovery, and brought some gold dust to prove it. The rush was on. Not only people already in California, but many others from Oregon, Utah, Hawaii, Mexico, Chile, and other coastal areas of South America came as fast as they could. Their numbers increased exponentially after President Polk's official confirmation of the discovery and the display of 230 ounces of California gold in the capitol on December 8, 1848.

In that year San Francisco's population was between 850 and 1,000. Gold fever soon depopulated all the settled communities in northern California, and by the beginning of June, San Francisco was almost empty with most of its houses boarded up and no work in progress.

In February 1849 military Governor Persifor Smith arrived determined to fine and imprison non-citizens prospecting for gold on public lands. He found that the high rate of desertion in the military made enforcing all laws nearly impossible. Smith had even heard that the most trusted marines in the British Navy had deserted along with their non-commissioned officers. He wrote President Polk that all vessels going to San Francisco lost their crews and from all he had learned about California he did not see how it would be possible to live there. San Francisco was not suitable for military or commercial purposes, he stated. It had no harbor, no landing place, bad water, an inclement climate, and in times of war it could be isolated by a short blockade across the peninsula.

Although the popular account of the Gold Rush migration's composition favored the adventuresome individuals—mainly young white males—who came to the state by land and sea, in fact, most immigrants, particularly after the placer mining phase of the rush ended, came as members of companies. Their final destination was the so-called Mother Lode region, which extended roughly from Mariposa north to Georgetown in El Dorado County. This mining country in the Sierra foothills was mainly reached from San Francisco. None of the ways of getting to the foothills was fast or comfortable; all had life-threatening aspects. The city itself was chaotic and lacking in most of the things necessary to sustain life and the pursuit of the promised gold. There were no buildings to speak of and no people or materials with which to construct any.

In November 1849, Colonel James Collier, custom collector for California, arrived in San Francisco to arrange for strict enforcement of the revenue laws. Astonished by the business of the port, he noted that with 312 vessels in the harbor and 697 arrivals since April, the port's business equaled that of Philadelphia. The city's cost of living was also unheard of: a two-story, four-room house might rent for between $400 and $2000 a month, depending on location.

Despite the chaotic conditions, plans to establish a state government proceeded. On June 4, 1849 Thomas Butler King, an emissary of President Zachary Taylor, arrived for a meeting with Governor Bennett Riley and told him that it would not matter whether the first step toward a provisional government was taken by the people or at the invitation of Congress. Riley then called for an election to fill vacant offices and select delegates to frame a constitution to submit to the people and to Congress. The constitutional convention met from September to November, and the state government was activated prior to admission to the Union in 1850.

THE GOLD RUSH DECADE, 1848–1859

THE DISCOVERY OF GOLD

Title: Map of the Valley of the Sacramento
including the Gold Region
Date: 1848
Cartographer: Thomas O. Larkin
Lithograph, 21 ⅜ x 17 inches
Warren Heckrotte Collection

The dramatic shift in geographic interest from the San Francisco Bay to the mining country in the early Gold Rush period is apparent in this 1848 map. It was created as a manuscript map in 1844 by John Bidwell, who in 1841 came to California as a leader of the first overland immigration train. He stayed to work for Captain John A. Sutter, explored the Sacramento Valley, and acquired a knowledge of surveying that he put to good use finding land for such clients as Thomas O. Larkin in 1844. Relying on information from his surveys and explorations, Bidwell made the first detailed map of the valley's waterways and ranchos, many of which were granted by the last governor sent from Mexico, Manuel Micheltorena, in 1844.

Thomas O. Larkin, a New Englander, arrived in California in 1832, became a successful merchant, speculated in real estate, and went on to be the first and only United States consul to Mexican California from 1844–48. In the mounting excitement that preceded President James K. Polk's message to Congress—delivered on December 5, 1848—concerning the discovery of gold in California, Larkin traced the "Mapa del Valle del Sacramento" his friend Bidwell had given him and had it copyrighted and published in Boston. Larkin gave proper credit for the "correct tracing of the map of Bidwell/Land Surveyor" and stated that it was the best one for

California. He also added the words, "Gold Region in bold letters in the upper right corner and, on the left side, a Table of Distances, of which the most awesome was surely the 17,000 miles from New York to San Francisco via Cape Horn.

The circumscribed map area resembles the spinal column of some prehistoric vertebrate. It stretched from the Barranca Colorado (now Red Bluff) of Josiah Belden to the Campo de los Franceses Rancho of Charles M. Weber near present-day Stockton in the south. In addition to the central valley, the map recorded the important settlements of Yerba Buena Pueblo or San Francisco, the Saucelito "watering places", the Missions of San Rafael and Sonoma, and Sutter's Fort as well as the topographic features of Mount Diablo and the Sutter Buttes. The Bahia de San Francisco, the primary focus of early maps, was relegated to the lower lefthand corner of the map, its entrance minimized. Directions for entering the bay from the valley are given below Mount Diablo near the map's lower edge. The Angel, Yerba Buena, and White Islands are shown much larger relative to the size of the bay than they actually were. The White Islands were later called Isla de las Alcatrices for the pelicans that nested there.

Although the Larkin/Bidwell map scooped other mapmakers, theirs was not the most accurate map in respect to the size of the mining region and its activities . As Larkin himself realized too late, the map opened his land and that of others to hordes of squatters and scavengers with no respect for boundaries or landowner's rights whose main legacy was lengthy legal disputes over land titles. Today the map is most important for the picture it provides of the pastoral pre-Gold Rush era of the Sacramento Valley ranchos and for the portent given in the two words, Gold Region, of the momentous times that followed.

36

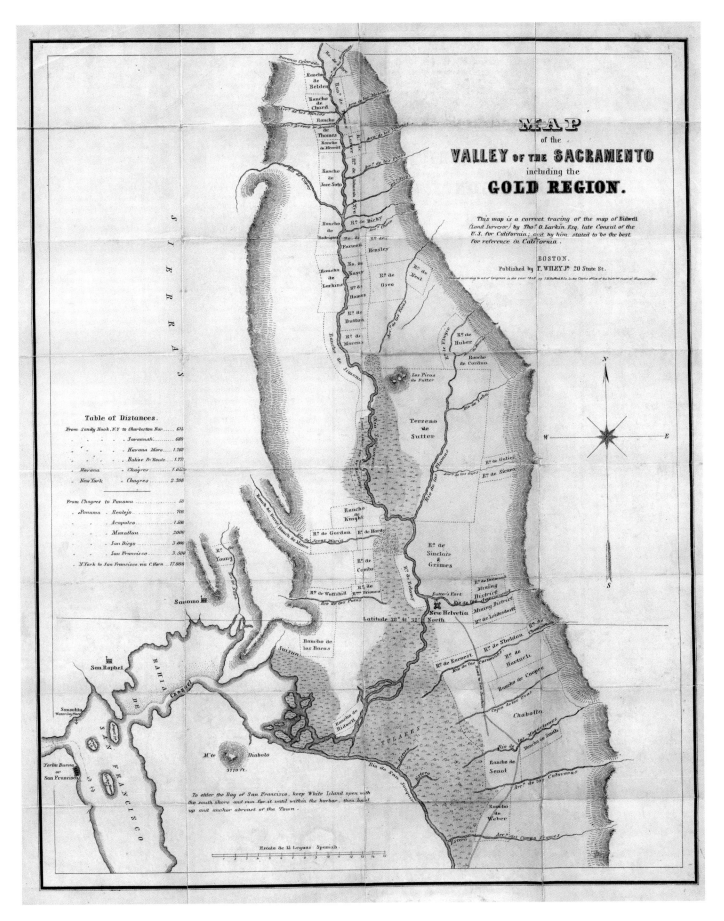

MAP
of the
VALLEY OF THE SACRAMENTO
including the
GOLD REGION.

This map is a correct tracing of the map of Bidwell
(Land Surveyor) by Thos. O. Larkin, Esq. late Consul of the
U.S. for California; and by him stated to be the best
for reference in California.

BOSTON.
Published by T. Wiley Jr. 20 State St.

Table of Distances.

From Sandy Hook, N.Y to Charleston Bar 614
" " " Savannah 680
" " " Havana Moro 1.260
" " " Balize Pt. Route 1.770
Havana " Chagres 1.030
New York " Chagres 2.308

From Chagres to Panama 50
" Panama " Realejo 700
" " " Acapulco 1.500
" " " Mazatlan 2000
" " " San Diego 3.000
" " " San Francisco 3.500
" N.York to San Francisco via C.Horn 17.000

Latitude 38° 41' 32"

To enter the Bay of San Francisco, keep White Island open with
the south shore and run for it until within the harbor, then haul
up and anchor abreast of the Town.

Escala de 15 Leguas Spanish.

S I E R R A S
BAHIA DE SAN FRANCISCO
TULARES

THE APPEARANCE OF TRANQUILITY

Title: The Port of San Francisco, 1849, from
Rincon Hill, drawn on the spot by Henry Firks
for W. H. Jones,
Esq. of San Francisco U. C.
Date depicted: 1849
Delineator: Henry Firks
Publisher: G. T. Brown & Co (San Francisco)
Uncolored lithograph, 12 ¹⁵/₁₆ x 31 ¾ inches
Formerly Burger and Evans Collection
San Francisco Public Library

Because accounts of the city's disorder were commonplace, this map's view appears far from truthful. The three hundred and some vessels reported to be adrift without any human hand to guide them have been replaced by an orderly set of vessels of various sizes. A few people stroll the nearly empty streets, but no activity enlivens buildings such as Leidesdorff's pyramidal roofed warehouse in the foreground on the left. Portsmouth Square, seen in the distance with the nation's flag above it, is located on the hillside above the cove. Also notable is the unlikely fringe of vegetation that defines the hillside where Firks set up his easel. This cosmetic touch contributes to the peaceful quality of the scene.[1]

1 Am. Ship Huntress. 2. Br. B. Azenath. 3. Dan. B. Neptunas 4. Fr. B. Stacesul. 5. Fr. Schr. Chateaubriand. 6. Mex. Sch. Victoria. 7. Am
9. Am. B. Superior. 10. Am. Sh. Philadelphia (Burned June 24ᵗʰ) 11. Ch. B. Carmen. 12. Haw. B. Mary Frances. 13. Am. Sh. Ed
15. Dan. Sh. Addia. 16. Am. Sh. Grey Eagle 17. Br. B. John Ritson. 18. Am. B. Col Fremont. 19. Ch. Sh. Virginia. 20. Am.
21. Ch. B. Maria Louisa. 22. Ch. B. Romano. 23. Am Scr. Thomas. 24. Am. B. Quito. 25. Am. B. Louisian

---

1. *The time of the Gold Rush coincided with the rise of the clipper ships that were a boon to west coast trade because of their greater speed. Too large to navigate the inland waterways, they anchored in deep water just inside the San Francisco Bay and their shipments were transferred to steamers. The development of the north waterfront with wharves, warehouses, and fireproof buildings made it the logical place for this operation.*

beron.

SAN-FRANCISCO
1849.

DRAWN ON THE SPOT BY HENRY FIRKS, FOR

und.

W.H. JONES ESQ.
OF SAN-FRANCISCO U.C.

27_Ch.Sh California Dorado. 28. Am. Steamer Panama. 29._Am B.Col Benton 30._Am Sh Massachusetts 31. Am B Lucy Penmunan. 32_ Fr B Limanienne. 33_Ch Sh. Gen Ferrias. 34. Am Sh Honolulu 35 Fr B Olympa 36. Am Sh Hebur 37. Am Steamer Oregon 38.U S S Warren 39._U S S Southampton. 40_Quartm P Invincible. 41. H B M Inconstant 42. Launch for Stockton. (Emily & Jane) 43 _ Customhouse 44 Golden Gate 45_ Parkers Hotel. Isld Yerba Buena 46 PM S S Cos Office. 47 S H Williams & Cos Store 48 G B Post & Cos Store 49. Leidsdorff's Residence 50. Gross Hobson & Cos Store 51 Starkey, Janion & Cos Warehouse.

VIEW OF SAN FRANCIS

TAKEN FROM THE WESTERN HILL AT THE FOOT OF TELEGRAPH HILL, LOOKING TOWARD RINCON POINT AND MISSION V

The City is located about 7 miles from the entrance of the Harbor. The Harbor with its imposing Grandeur and beauty, were solely by
in the World. At Present there are between 4 and 500 square rigged vessels at anchor in the Bay, many of which are hidden from t
In the extreme left will be seen the Island of Yerba Buena, and also in the same direction about 50 Miles distant, Mount Diablo peering

Published by Geo H Casilear New York City, and by Atwell, San Francisco California

Title: View of San Francisco, Taken from the Western hill at the foot of Telegraph Hill, looking toward Ringon(sic) Point and Mission Valley
Date: 1851
Delineators: Henry Bainbridge and George W. Casilear
Lithographers: Sarony & Major (New York City)
Publisher: George W. Casilear (San Francisco)
Tinted map, 26 x 38 ¾ inches
Library of Congress

This lightly tinted bird's-eye view looks southeast across the bay with Yerba Buena Island on the far left. Conventionally picturesque groups of travelers occupy the scene's foreground. They probably represent newly arrived prospectors for gold encamped here en route to the mines. Tents have been pitched and various activities are taking place in an orderly way that contrasts with the firsthand accounts given by many who joined the rough-and-tumble existence in the boomtown that was San Francisco. The distant city also appears orderly. Various points of interest are indicated, and the whole scene is inviting. The "Western Hill at the foot of Telegraph Hill" would be the lower slope of what was later named Russian Hill.

THE "WHOLE EXPANSE OF NAVIGABLE WATERS AT ONE VIEW"

Title: Chart of the Farallones and entrance to the
Bay of San Francisco, California
Date: 1850. Entered 1851 in the District of Columbia.
Cartographer: Cadwalader Ringgold, Commander,
U. S. Navy. Assisted by Simon F. Blunt, Lieut. U.S. Navy
Delineator: Constructed, projected and drawn by
Fred. D. Stuart, hydrographer.
*Lithographed chart map. Relief shown by hachures and spot heights,
soundings in fathoms. Place names in English or Spanish,*
20 x 30 ³⁄₁₀ inches
David Rumsey Collection

During a stay in San Francisco in 1849–50, U. S. Navy commander Cadwalader Ringgold was asked by some unidentified private citizens to survey the bay, described as "a vast and unknown sea," and remove the many obstacles to "intercourse with the mines." Ringgold began his survey by triangulation and azimuths from a base on the plain of New York of the Pacific, present day Pittsburgh, California, at the head of Suison Bay, and ended at Spear and Semple Points. In his 1851 account, *Memoir and Maps of California*, Ringgold stated that he was not aware of any other surveys connecting the bay with its tributaries.

To fulfill his goal of presenting the "whole expanse of navigable waters at one view" necessitated using other surveys, notably Frederick Beechey's 1833 chart. Ringgold quotes Beechey's description of the entrance to the harbor: "The port of San Francisco does not show itself to advantage until after the port is passed, when it breaks upon the view and forcibly impresses the spectator with the magnificence of the harbor. He then beholds a broad sheet of water, sufficiently extensive to contain all the British Navy…. The only objects wanting to complete the interest of the scene are some useful establishments and comfortable residences on the grassy borders of the harbor…. A sickly column of smoke rising from within the dilapidated walls, misnamed the Presidio, was the only indication we had of a country being inhabited."

Ringgold's chart presents more information than de Mofras's chart of 1844. The Golden Gate is lettered along with the Bays of Richardson, Aspinwall, Lejuanjelua, and San Rafael, which scallop the shoreline before the entrance to San Pablo Bay. Petaluma, Sonoma, and Napa Creeks are indicated, and Mare Island, which would become a U. S. Navy Base in 1854, is shown across from the city of Vallejo, established by General Mariano Vallejo in 1850. The plat of Vallejo extends along

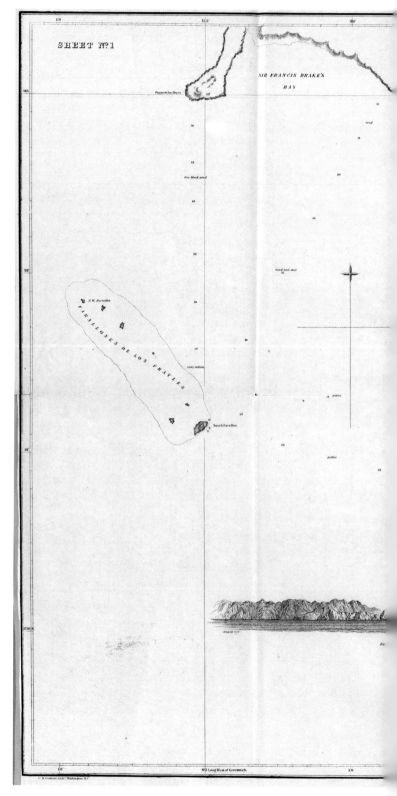

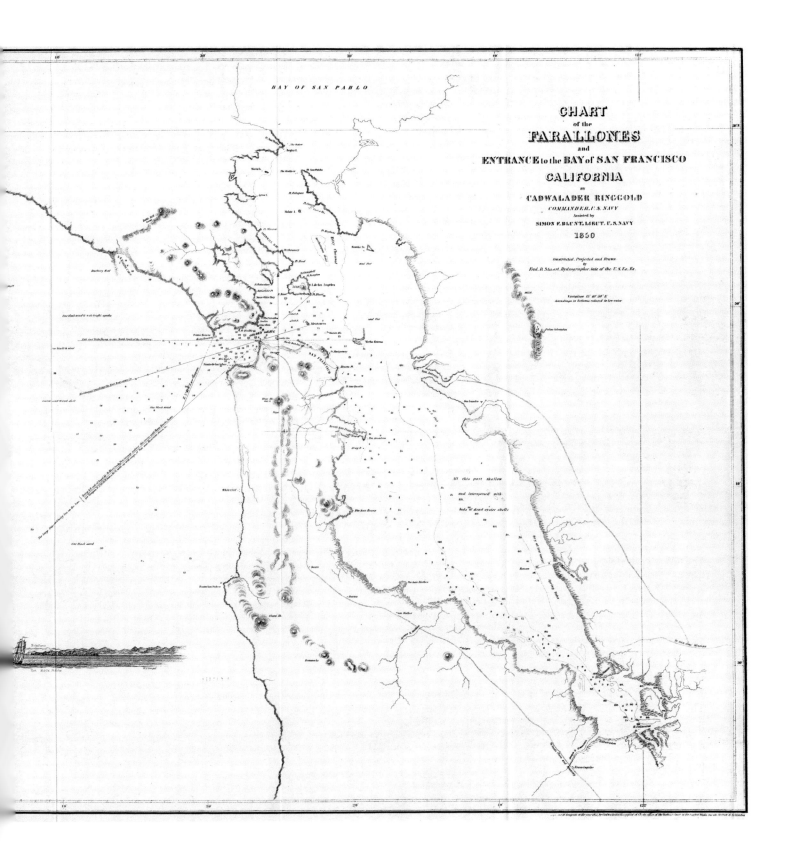

CHART
of the
FARALLONES
and
ENTRANCE to the BAY of SAN FRANCISCO
CALIFORNIA
BY
CADWALADER RINGGOLD
COMMANDER, U.S. NAVY
Assisted by
SIMON F. BLUNT, LIEUT. U.S. NAVY
1850

Constructed, Projected and Drawn
by
Fred. D. Stuart, Hydrographer late of the U.S. Ex. Ex.

Variation 15° 40' 30" E
Soundings in fathoms reduced to low water

BAY OF SAN PABLO

View of San Francisco from Yerba Buena Island.

Fort   Pta. Boneta.

Pt. Finley.

W. H. Dougal.

the shore of the Napa River and appears to be about the size of San Francisco. To the south the Carquinez Straits are shown in detail as well as the city of Benecia. The Contra Costa's shoreline is delineated with hachuring and other graphic conventions. The owners of ranchos are lettered. A trail running south connects the ranchos of Don Castro, Salvio and Fernando Pacheco, the Peralta familes, and Joaquin Estudillo on the San Leandro Creek.

The promontory jutting into the bay that terminates in the Punta San Pablo is detailed; the mud flats between it and the Punta Penole are indicated. Two slivers of sketches show the location of Invincible Bueys, one off Marin Island north of San Rafael and the other on the east end of Angel Island in line with Signal (Telegraph) Hill. The San Francisco peninsula is shown in some detail with the city's grid of streets extending into the bay and further west than was the case. The roads linking the city with the now defunct Presidio and mission are tied into the Camino Real, and South San Francisco is lettered on the hilly terrain south of Point San Quentin.

Title: View of San Francisco from Yerba Buena Island
Date: 1852
Delineator: William H. Dougal
Publisher: Jno. T. Towers, Washington
Lithograph, 5 ½ x 9 ½ inches
David Rumsey Collection

Appended to the chart is a small engraving depicting the view of San Francisco from Yerba Buena Island. Introduced by vegetation, the foreground has two figures, one standing, the other reclining, who represent the viewers. They contemplate the distant harbor dotted with tiny ships and the rolling land of sand and scrub with buildings scattered like pebbles over the lower slopes. The distant hills include Twin Peaks rising above Rincon Point and Signal Hill (Telegraph Hill). Fort Point and Punta Boneta bracket the Golden Gate. The scene is orderly. If anything, the two observers suggest a *dolce far niente* ambience beside the placid waters of the bay. The vignette is signed by W. H. Dougal, a Gold Rush artist, who wrote about his California experiences in *Off for California: The Letters, Log, and Sketches of William H. Dougal, Gold Rush Artist.*

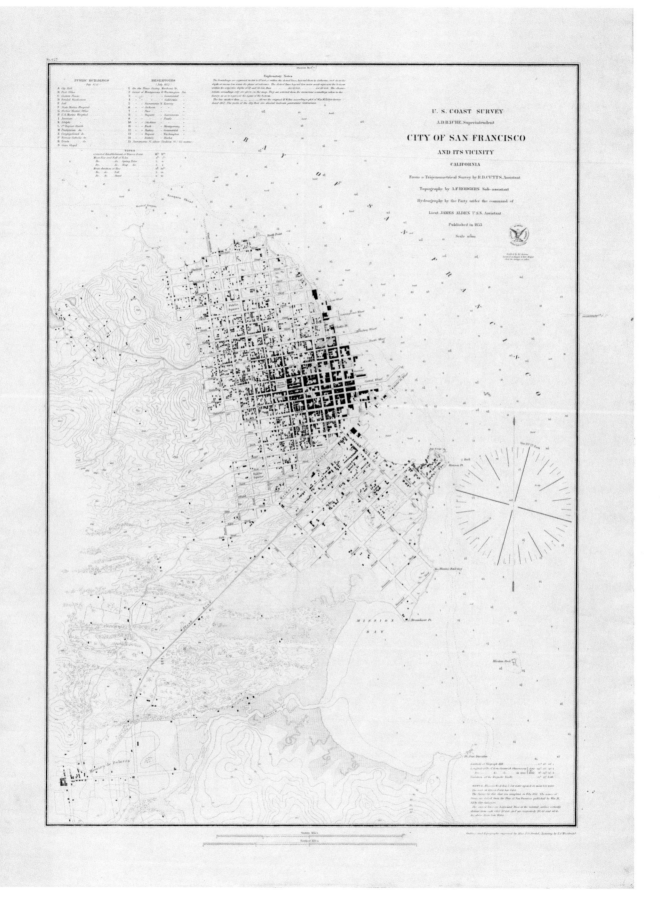

ON THE WATERFRONT

Title: City of San Francisco and its vicinity, California
Date: 1852, published in 1853
Cartographer: U. S. Coast Survey
Publisher: Washington: U. S. Coast Survey
Chart map taken from a trigonometrical survey by R. D. Cutts, assistant to Superintendent A. D. Bache, with topography by A. F. Rogers and hydrography by the survey party under the command of Lieut. James Alden of the U. S. Navy.
Uncolored map, 26 x 17 ¾ inches
David Rumsey Collection

The city map and related topography were taken from William Eddy's 1851 survey, but the grid has been softened, and the dense numbered lots have yielded to the footprints of real buildings that decrease in number away from the central downtown area and the bay shore. Of the many wharves built into the bay, the Central Wharf, which became Commercial Street, and the Market Street Wharf are still the longest. But the wharves are becoming streets made of wood planks laid on top of piles that are connected to hulks of ships converted to lodgings, warehouses, and commercial enterprises.

Barry and Patten described this scene when recalling the transformation of the Niantic Hotel: "Today rows of warehouses stand where the old dismasted hulks floated with their stored merchandise." The Niantic Hotel had been an English ship that lost her crew within a week of docking in San Francisco in April 1849. The ship was hauled in near the foot of Clay Street and used as a storeship. Its cargo was gradually sold until the May 4, 1851 fire, which reduced it to a charred hulk. A building called the Niantic Hotel was erected on the hulk and later known as one of the city's best.

Between December 24, 1849, and May 4, 1851, six fires devastated the city. The 1853 map reveals the after-effects of the fires in the greater density of buildings south and east of Portsmouth Square. The May 4 fire destroyed the early city center around the square including the very important customhouse at the corner of California and Montgomery Streets. The Sydney Ducks, Australian convicts who came to San Francisco during the Gold Rush, were said to be responsible for the fires. These inhabitants of a collection of shanties and hovels at the base of Telegraph Hill called Sydneytown had easy access to the commercial enterprises around Portsmouth Square. The fires they set spread rapidly through the flimsy buildings around the square, enabling the arsonists to loot the businesses and gambling houses there. In 1852, the on-going threat of fire caused the city to prohibit tents and wooden buildings within the limits of Union, Powell, Post, Second and Folsom Streets, a territory that included most of the built area of the city.

Even before 1850, financial institutions had begun to move south, erecting the brick buildings that subsequently lined Montgomery and Kearny Streets. The heaviest concentration of buildings occurs in the north-south blocks from California to Washington Streets and the east-west blocks from Kearny to Front Street.

An area marked "hard sand" on the coast survey map defines a tidal inlet extending from the Market Street Wharf to Rincon Point. The so-called water lots auctioned off in 1847 were located in this marshy zone. The aggregation of structures around Rincon (the Spanish word for corner) Point probably included both residential and industrial building as well as the Marine Hospital, located on government owned land at the tip of the point. Near the intersection of First and Market Streets, Peter and James Donohue opened the Union Iron Works in 1849 and began making mining equipment, which led to the development of the city's first manufacturing district.

In the vicinity of First and Second and Market and Mission Streets, sand hills as high as 60 feet on either side of Market Street protected an area supplied by spring water, which was called Happy Valley. Perhaps 1,000 tents had been pitched there. Wooden buildings, some of them pre-built on the east coast in states such as Vermont were "knocked down," and the sections were then numbered and shipped in pallets stacked on the decks of ships. William D. Howard, one of the city's early successful merchants, imported 25 of these prefabricated dwellings, which reportedly had high-pitched gable roofs with Gothic trim attached to the eaves and porches with turned posts and balustrades.[1] A number of them were located in Happy Valley, which became the city's working class district. Many Happy Valley residents worked in the nearby Union Iron Works.

Rincon Hill rose above Happy Valley; its proximity to the business district and freedom from low-lying fog attracted prominent citizens who built their mansions there beginning in 1849. The entrepreneurial financier William Ralston, the industrialist Peter Donahue, the engineer and inventor of the cable car, Andrew Hallidie, and many other city magnates populated Rincon Hill.

Near the old road to the Presidio around Washerwoman's Lagoon (the Laguna Pequena noted by Anza in 1776 as a source of fresh water) is a smattering of buildings that may have been on small farms fed by the fresh water of the lake. Its site is now bounded by Lombard, Filbert, Octavia, and Franklin Streets.

1. *Kirker, Harold.* California's Architectural Frontier: Style and Tradition in the Nineteenth Century. *San Marino, California: Huntington Library, 1960: 39-40.*

SAND

Title: San Francisco in the 1850s
Date: 2005
Graphic designer: Chuck Byrne
Unpublished colored map, variable measurements
Chuck Byrne

This map was created to show what the north end of the peninsula that became the city of San Francisco was like on the ground before the city was built up as it is today with residential neighborhoods, parks, and other open spaces. In brief, most of the city was a sandy desert that in its early decades of settlement resisted the kind of verdant vegetation so dear to the settlers from the eastern part of the country.

The geology the map depicts was taken from geologist Clyde Wahrhaftig's book *Streetcar to Subduction*, published in 1983 by the American Geophysical Union. In it he describes the effects of the subduction of tectonic plates on the formation of San Francisco's landscape. A linear map of the city on page nine was used as the basis for the colored map shown here.

This map is a conceptual rendition of the landscape of the northern tip of the San Francisco peninsula around 1850; the author makes no claim for total accuracy. The colors include two shades of blue: a lighter one for the waters of the bay and ocean and a darker gray-blue for the tidal lands that were later filled. The parts of the bay that were filled in the 1850s are indicated in a light brown tone. A medium brown tone was used to depict areas composed of "mélange," a mixture in which rocks have been crushed beyond recognition to form dune sand and lagoonal and alluvial deposits, sometimes bearing Franciscan rocks. The dark brown areas indicate surface deposits of Franciscan rocks that occurred on Nob, Russian, Telegraph and other hills in the city as well as San Bruno Mountain. The light tan color indicates areas covered for the most part by Holocene dune sand.

Some early accounts of San Francisco mentioned gardens cultivated in areas where dune sand and lagoonal and alluvial deposits existed. The light sandy soil moistened by frequent fog cover enabled the cultivation of plants, and native grasses made pasturing cattle possible in some areas. But the kind of gardens conjured up by these accounts should not be taken as the equivalent of those made in the rich soil found in other parts of the bay area and the state, not to mention other parts of the country and the world where some of the writers came from. The history of Golden Gate Park testifies to the difficulties of stabilizing the sand dunes and creating the topsoil that turned the 1,017 acres of desert into the present lush oasis.

The following comments made by visitors and residents during the early days of American settlement in San Francisco reveal their reaction to a physical environment that, today, is almost impossible to imagine.

Richard Henry Dana wrote perhaps the most famous early account during his 16-month visit to the California coast as a seaman from January 1835 to May 1836. The 19-year old Bostonian made many observations about the settlement that became San Francisco in his best-selling book, *Two Years Before the Mast*, published in 1840. Although Dana found the bay spectacular, he was not so impressed with the barren landscape around it, which he described as composed of sand dunes of varying heights that often shifted their positions overnight.

Steve Richardson, son of Yerba Buena's early settler, William Richardson, said that the persistent winds bore "an almost incredible burden of both fine and coarse sand that got into clothes eyes, nose, mouth … penetrating the innermost recesses of the household."

In 1845, a visitor named Henry Wise observed, "The site seems badly chosen, for although it reposed in partial shelter beneath the high bluffs of the coast, yet a great portion of the year it is entirely enveloped in chilling fogs, and invariably, during the afternoon, strong sea breezes are drawn through the straits like a funnel, and playing with fitful violence around the hills, the sand is swept in blinding clouds over the town and adjacent shores of the bay … in the vicinity of Yerba Buena all looks bare and sterile from a distance, and on closer inspection, the deep sandy soil is covered with impervious thickets of low thorny undergrowth, with none of the rich green herbage, forest, or timber as in Monterey.[1]

In 1853 City Engineer Milo Hoadley, William Eddy's successor, confronted the problems caused by the many sand dunes blocking the westward extension of the street grid beyond the relatively flat land around Yerba Buena Cove. Although large sand dunes had been removed between California and Mission Streets, they continued to impede growth southwest along Market and Mission streets.

Steam shovels scraped away many of these hills, depositing the sand in railroad cars that dumped their loads into the cove. The rocky eastern slope of Telegraph Hill was blasted away with dynamite, and the rock carried away by ships for use in often-faraway road-building projects. Although buildings filled the valley between Nob and Russian Hills, development bypassed the steep sandy slopes of Nob Hill to follow Market and Mission Streets when they were graded. In 1853 Rincon, Nob, Russian, and Telegraph Hills were nearly free of structures. The western edge of development was around Mason Street. The 1853 U. S. Coast Survey map shows only a few structures along the Plank Road leading to the settlement around the Mission Dolores.

1. *Vance, James E., Jr.* Geography and Urban Evolution in the San Francisco Bay Area. *Berkeley: Institute of Governmental Studies, University of California, Berkeley, 1964: 12.*

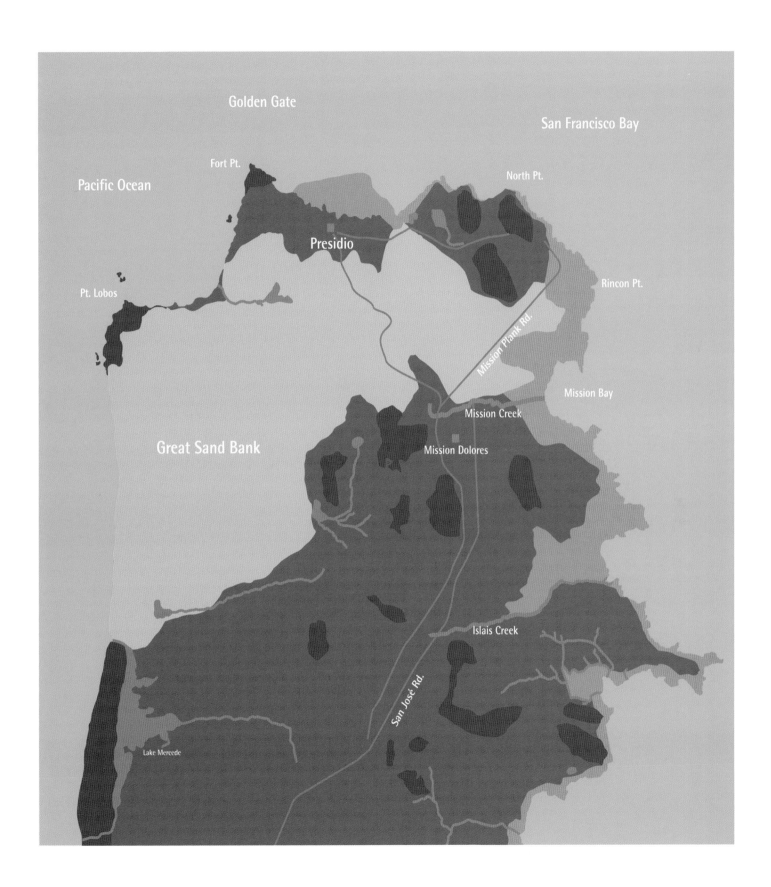

Golden Gate

San Francisco Bay

Pacific Ocean

Fort Pt.

North Pt.

Presidio

Rincon Pt.

Pt. Lobos

Mission Plank Rd.

Mission Bay

Mission Creek

Great Sand Bank

Mission Dolores

Islais Creek

San José Rd.

Lake Mercede

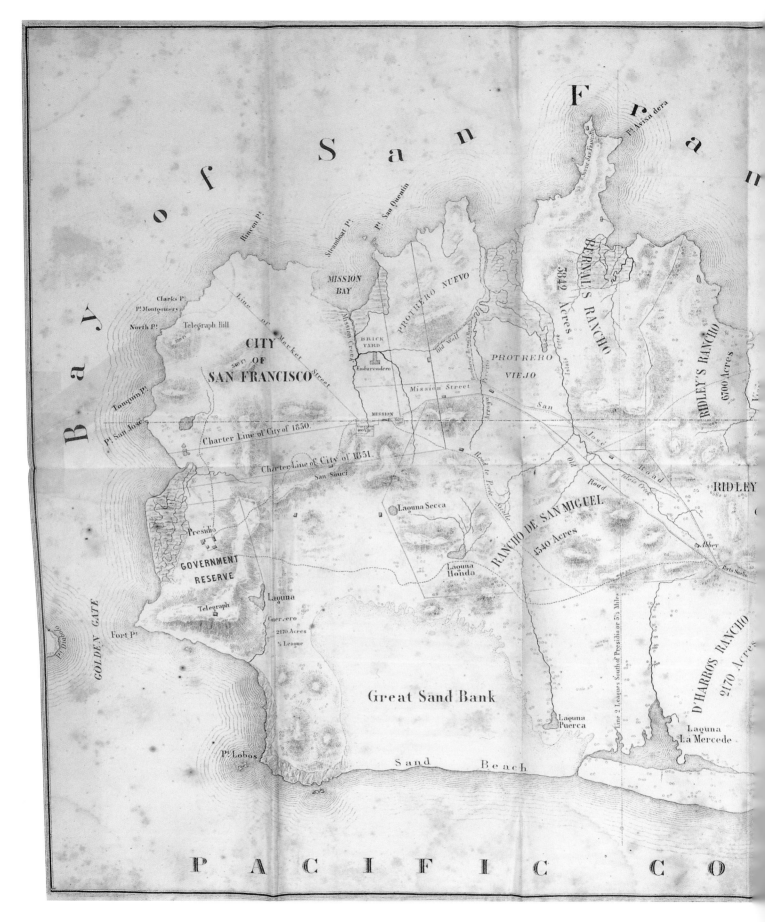

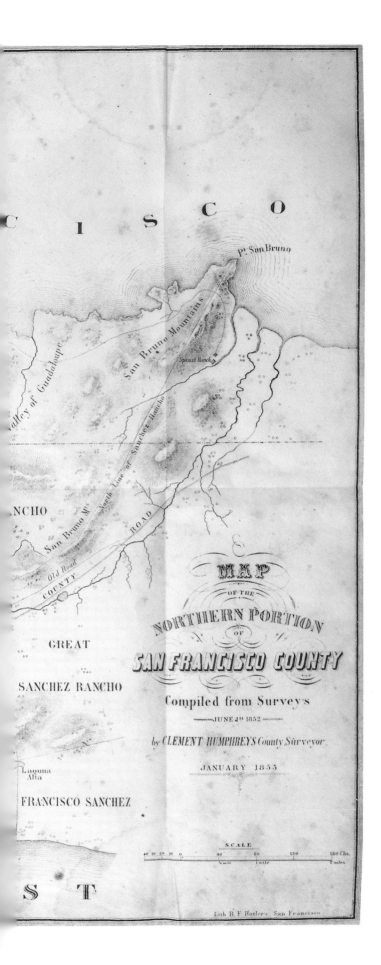

Title: Map of the Northern Portion of San Francisco County
Date depicted: Compiled from Surveys, June 1852
Cartographer: Clement Humphreys, County Surveyor
Published: January 1853
Publisher: G. K. Fitch &Y Co.
Engraved map, 15 ½ x 19 ¾ inches
San Francisco Public Library

County Surveyor Clement Humphreys compiled the information on this map of the northern portion of San Francisco County from various surveys he conducted in 1852. The map was folded into the Manual of the Corporation of the City. Its intent seems to have been to record the ranchos of the *Californios*, the first families of San Francisco— some of the ranchos were larger than the city itself. Important natural features such as the Great Sand Bank that covered much of the Pacific coast south of Point Lobos and the lakes west of the city charter lines were noted. Mission Bay, Mission Creek, and the mission's Potreros Nuevo and Viejo (New and Old Pastures) are shown along with the brickyard on Mission Creek which developed there because of the area's fine clay. The old roads from the Presidio and mission are shown connecting to the New County Road to the south-bay area. The map presents the image of a landscape embedded in the past during the time of transition in the post-Gold Rush decade.

Benjamin F. Butler, the engraver of the map, relocated his lithography business from New York City to San Francisco about 1850. He may have started the first lithography plant in the city. If so, Humphrey's map was one of his early cartography ventures; it followed the firm's 1851 issue of *The Official Map of the City of San Francisco Full and Complete* to the present date by William Eddy, the city surveyor.

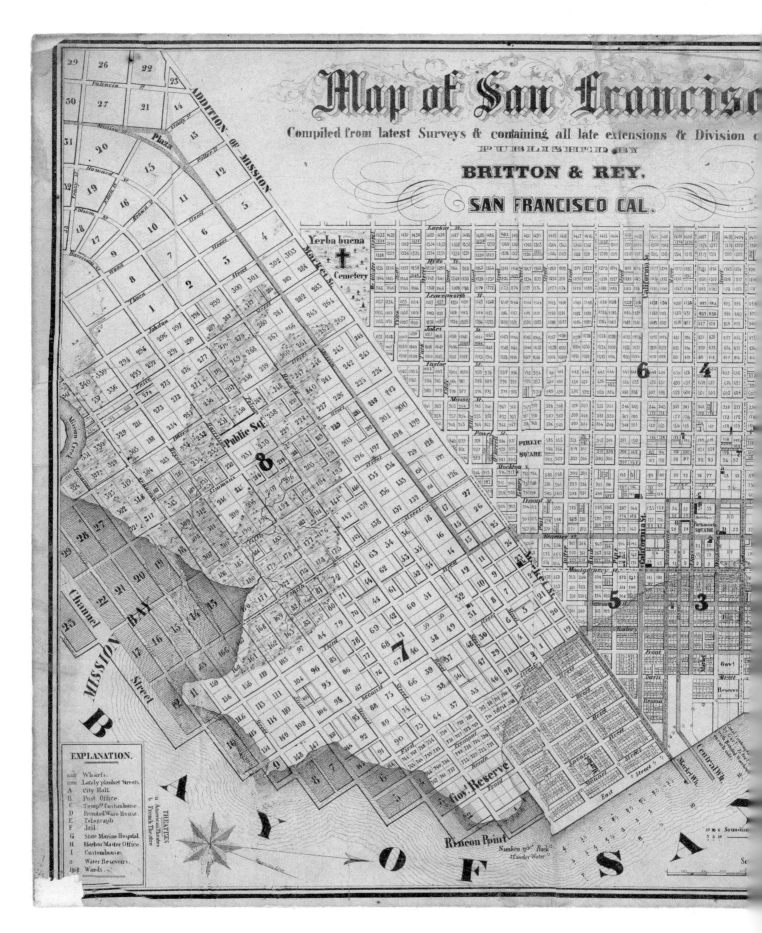

WALKING CITY AND "THE WALL STREET OF THE WEST"

Title: Map of San Francisco, Compiled from latest Surveys & containing all late extensions & Division of Wards
Date published: 1852
Cartographer: Britton & Rey
Publisher: Britton & Rey (San Francisco)
Letter sheet map, 8 ⅔ x 10 ⅔ inches
David Rumsey Collection

The 1852 letter sheet map of San Francisco shows the city's original shoreline and the filled areas darkened and laced with wavy lines. The water lots in the central business district are numbered; many had been sold at auction by the city in 1847 to pay down the municipal debt. The Market Street Wharf on the bay is the focus of the map, which extends southwest along Market to the triangular site of Yerba Buena Cemetery. Larkin Street traces the western edge of city development north to the bay where the grid extends westward to Webster Street. The small, untitled 24-block plat drawn diagonally across the grid represents the 1847 Laguna Survey, which was never approved or developed; its upper corner touches Washerwoman's Lagoon. With a population of about 40,000 and an area of about two square miles, San Francisco was a "walking city" not yet expanded by streetcar lines into its future suburbs.

The planked streets are marked in darker tones and the extra width of Market Street is indicated. California Street, sometimes called the "Wall Street of the West," is also extra wide. City wards one through eight are marked with large numerals. The city hall, post office, customhouse, harbor master office, jail, and state marine hospital are lettered, and the water reservoirs are marked with a symbol.

The Mission Plank Road, a toll road, was built in 1851 by the Mission Dolores Plank Road Company, which had a contract in 1850 for the city's first wooden highway. The company was responsible for maintenance of the road and could collect tolls for seven years following its completion. After that the property reverted to the city. The Mission toll road ran from the Plaza (Portsmouth Square) down Kearny and proceeded to Market Street. From there the road proceeded southwest to the Mission Dolores. A parallel route was initiated on Folsom Street in 1852, and more planked roads followed in other parts of the city. Barry and Patten noted that in 1850 the tollgate for the Mission Plank Road was on Third Street. "When you turned the corner on Third Street to Mission, going west," they said, "you were pretty well out of town."

Because the city fills the sheet, the viewer may not realize that only a small part of the lands within the city's boundaries are depicted. The orderly numbered parcels convey real estate opportunities, not the city as it was built up at that time.

In the lower right corner of the map sheet is a cameo view of a business block designed in the popular Renaissance Revival style and labeled above as Page, Bacon & Adams & Co. Fashionably dressed people are shown passing by on the street. These firms, which apparently commissioned the map, contributed importantly to the evolution of banking in the Gold Rush city after 1849. The St. Louis bank, Page & Bacon, opened its San Francisco branch in 1850. James King of William, one of the city's bankers, wrote that "the same banker who in '50 and '51 considered himself tolerably well patronized with $200,000, found himself in '52 with nearly $600,000, far behind Page, Bacon & Company who had three times that amount." In 1852, the year of this map, its sponsors were clearly leaders in the city's financial sector. Like Wells Fargo, the firms were both bankers and express companies.

The financial panic of 1855 changed this situation. The run on the banks occurred when word reached San Francisco that the main office of Page & Bacon in St. Louis had experienced heavy losses on a Midwestern railroad loan. Although the company had raised enough gold in California to cover the losses, news spread that the bank had folded while the gold was en route to St. Louis. This news triggered the fateful run. The panic began in February with lines of people outside the Montgomery Street banks demanding their deposits. When it ended, both Page, Bacon and Adams & Company were ruined along with other prominent firms such as Wright's Miners' Exchange. Wells Fargo and Company was temporarily suspended. By the year's end there had been 197 bankruptcies. Considering the misfortune that came to its sponsors, this map may serve as a memorial to their time of prosperity.

The intense competition that marked San Francisco's business climate in its early post-Gold Rush years may be surmised from the recollections of William Tecumseh Sherman, who was a banker in the city from 1853 through 1856. The rebellious actions of the 1856 Vigilance Committee caused him to leave California. In 1864, after the capture and burning of Atlanta, Sherman wrote that although he could handle a hundred thousand men in battle and take the City of the Sun, he had been afraid to manage a lot in the swamp of San Francisco.

LAND

Although acquiring land titles had been a somewhat informal matter during the Mexican period, under American rule, the hunger for property produced a multiplicity of claims and claimants, all demanding settlement. For advice on this matter Governor Riley relied on the judgment of his Secretary of State, Captain Henry Halleck, who had served in that capacity under Governor Mason. As a civilian lawyer, Halleck had established a law firm, which mainly dealt in land claims, in partnership with Frederick Billings and Archibald Peachy.

The adjudication of such claims required knowledge of Mexican law as well as deferring judgments until competent courts were established to deal with the differences in California and Mexican legal traditions. In July 1849 William Carey Jones, an expert in Spanish land laws, was sent by the U.S. Department of the Interior to review the California and Mexican archives for a report on land titles. After some time in San Francisco and Monterey, where he found confusion and no records before 1839, and some time in Los Angeles and Mexico City, he returned to Washington to prepare his report. The reports on land titles that Carey and Halleck produced in 1850 had different conclusions. Whereas Carey found that most of the claims were legitimate, Halleck determined that they were precarious. This division of opinion continued the uncertainty that clouded land titles.

The state legislature approved a charter incorporating the City of San Francisco in 1851. That same year Congress created a Board of Land Commissioners, which held that Mexican property rights would be respected and that all titles were valid until proven otherwise.

WASHINGTON ST.   622   MERCHANT ST.   600   CLAY ST.

MONTGOMERY ST.—EAST SIDE—FROM CLAY TO WASHINGTON ST.

622. **THE EVENING BULLETIN**   600. **C. SCHAEFER.** Dealer in   543. Clay Street.
Daily and weekly   Havana and Key West Cigars   **PACIFIC PRINTING CO.**
Editorial Rooms 517 Clay Street   and Smokers' Articles   Pernau Bros. & Pitts Co., Props,
Printing and Bookbinding.

17

Title: Montgomery St.—East Side—from Clay to Washington St.
Date published: 1895
Publisher: Glover's Illustrated Directory, Vol. 1 #5, p. 17
Engraved from line drawings
Measurements: 9 ⁵/₇ x 13 ¾ inches
David Rumsey Collection

The phenomenal number of court cases dealing with disputes over land titles enriched many of the city's lawyers. This page from *Glover's Illustrated Directory* depicts the physical result of this situation. The 1853, Montgomery Block is shown occupying the street frontage between Merchant Street, a narrow secondary street, and Washington Street. The adjacent block between Merchant and Clay Streets is also shown with two buildings that appear slightly higher than the Montgomery Block. The drawing is deceptive. By showing the windows and other details of the neighboring buildings at a slightly larger scale and compressing the Montgomery Block to provide an angled view down Merchant Street, the delineator has made the much larger building seem smaller. The drawing also omits the Montgomery Block's sculpted portrait blocks described above.

Henry W. Halleck, the building's developer, had studied civil engineering at the United States Military Academy at West Point. He designed the building's foundation as a raft of redwood logs that could withstand movement in the marshy land beneath Montgomery Street without sinking into it. Another structural innovation was tying the walls together with iron rods to resist seismic torquing. Estimates of the costs of the building ranged from $600,000 to several millions of dollars. Halleck financed the land purchase and the building with fees won from the settlement of land grant cases by his firm, Halleck, Peachy & Billings. The Montgomery Block was the largest business building erected in the West at that time.

Designed by an English architect, Gordon P. Cummings, in a simplified Classical Revival style, the facade of the four-story building occupied 122 feet of Montgomery Street and was 138 feet deep. It had over 150 rooms including 28 commercial spaces on the arcaded ground floor.

The arcade was made of granite, the upper three stories of the building were plastered brick, and a cement-asbestos compound fireproofed the roof. The Montgomery Street facade featured a sculpted stone bust of Washington above the bronze entrance doors and heads of Franklin, Clay, and Jackson, along with those of the architect, the contractor, the sculptor, and the collector of the port of San Francisco, all of which were set on the keystones of the arches.

One of the most famous tenants was the Bank Exchange Saloon. Contrary to state law, the saloon engaged in trading mining stocks and banking. California had no chartered banks until the 1860s because, as stated in the state constitution, "The Legislature of this State shall prohibit by law any person or persons, association, company, or corporation from exercising the privilege of banking or creating paper to circulate as money." The prohibition stemmed from the memory of previous financial disasters associated with the circulation of paper money that bred a determination to deal only in "hard money." However, such currency was scarce in the Gold Rush economy, and gold dust or nuggets often took its place. Because one needed a secure storage place for gold, those enterprises that had burglar-proof safes became informal banks. The Bank Exchange was one of these. Prior to the Mexican-American War of 1848, a chronic shortage of paper money and coinage existed that even led to hides— California banknotes—being used in trade.

CITY OF SAN FRANCISCO.

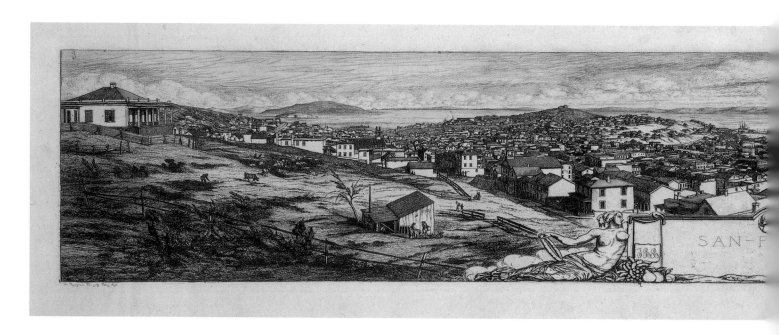

THE GOLD RUSH DECADE, 1848–1859

CITY OF HILLS

Title: View of the City of San Francisco from Rincon Point
Date: 1855
Delineator: F. N. Otis
Lithographer: C. Parsons of New York
Publisher: Endicott & Co. (New York)
Uncolored bird's-eye view, 21 ⅞ x 40 ⅞ inches
San Francisco Public Library

This map features a sweeping view over Happy Valley north to Telegraph Hill with the Clay Street Hill and Russian Hill to the left and the city below. Its title is confusing because Rincon Point does not appear to be the correct location of the viewpoint. Whereas the Marine Hospital building, drawn in the distance at the far right, was on Rincon Point, the large square building standing just to the right of the scene's center at the edge of an open field is St. Mary's Hospital on Rincon Hill. Thus the title, *View of the City of San Francisco from Rincon Hill*, rather than Rincon Point, would be more correct.

The line of small houses in the middle ground is also on Rincon Hill. The two-story wooden houses with gable roofs and front porches resemble the pre-fabricated dwellings imported from the East by William D. Howard in 1849. Beyond them is a darkened area with more buildings and another stretch of bare ground that seems to indicate the edge of the hill. The densely built up area in the distance is probably Happy Valley. Telegraph Hill is visible in the distance across the densely built-up city. An improbable park-like setting with a few strolling figures occupies the foreground.

A plausible explanation for the confusion between Rincon Point and Rincon Hill is that the delineator, F. N. Otis, never visited San Francisco and cobbled together parts of other published views of the city from this location. The high demand for views of San Francisco probably guaranteed their sale regardless of inaccuracies because the number of people known to have seen what they depicted was low.

Title: View of San Francisco
Date: 1856
Delineator and engraver: Charles Meryon
Publisher: A. Delatre, Paris
Etching, 7 ⅒ x 37 inches
Library of Congress

Francois-Louis-Alfred Pioche, a French pioneer banker, and Jules B. Bayerque, were partners in a real estate company with large holdings in the western part of San Francisco. They commissioned this etching from the prominent French artist, Charles Meryon, who never saw the city. He constructed this panoramic view from five daguerreotypes sent to him in Paris. Partial prints from the photographs were also sent pieced together to help Meryon with his composition. The surviving photographic copies of the daguerreotypes, the tracings on paper Meryon made of different sections of the panorama, and different states of the etching are preserved at the Art Institute in Chicago. To create a continuous image from the five separate images, each with a slightly different perspective, was no small challenge even for Meryon who was a highly skilled draftsman. The view is from the Clay Street Hill with Telegraph Hill left of center. The cartouche inscribed with the date 1855 in Roman numerals and portraits of Pioche and Bayerque hides what was probably a puzzling juncture between two sections of the photographs. It is difficult to follow Meryon's interpretation of the streets, and the whole scene is distorted. But these lapses from the reality do not detract from the artistic quality of the etching.

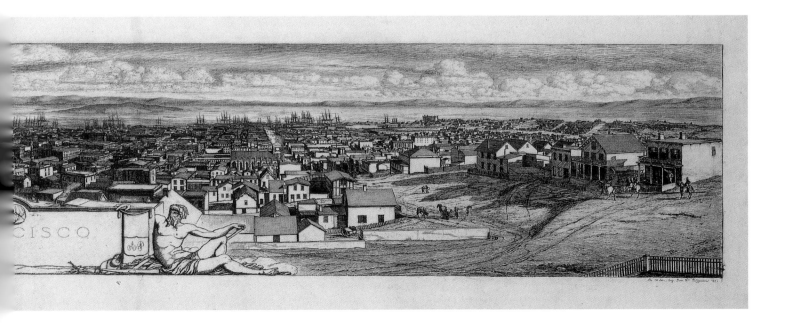

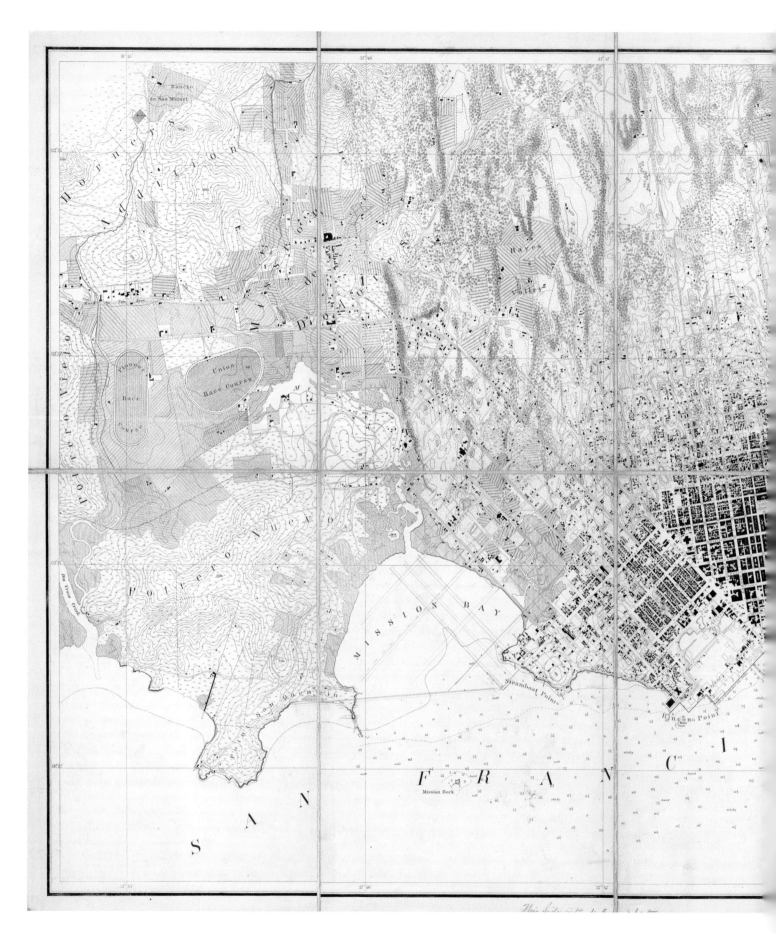

How the etching was received in San Francisco is not known. Pioche, whose investments in subdivisions in the Mission, Potrero, and Visitacion Valley districts were not profitable, committed suicide in 1875.

DEFINING RESIDENTIAL NEIGHBORHOODS AND INDUSTRIAL ZONES

Title: City of San Francisco and its Vicinity, California
Date published: 1859
Cartographer: U. S. Coast Survey, A. D. Bache, Superintendent, Topography by A. F. Rodgers. Hydrography by the Party under the command of Lieut. R. M. Cuyler, N. S. N. Assistant
Publisher: U. S. Coast Survey
Uncolored Chart map first issued in 1857, with another edition issued later in 1857 that differs from the earlier one and is apparently the same as this 1859 edition.
Measurements: 24 x 35 inches
David Rumsey Collection

By showing the footprints of buildings in black along with other graphic detail, this map permits an analysis of the city's development by 1859. Industries were concentrated around First and Howard Streets where the Donahue brothers' gas company, blacksmith shop, and foundry were located along with other factories that manufactured mining equipment and needed proximity to the wharves. Workers in these industries lived in the blocks along Mission from First to Third Streets in small houses on Annie, Jane, Jessie, and other narrow streets that had been cut through the large blocks. This was Happy Valley, formerly isolated in the sandy wastes, but now served by Omnibuses on the Yellow Line, the city's first public transit, which operated on the Mission Plank Road, beginning in 1852.

East of Fremont Street between Folsom and Market Streets, a stretch of tidal lands crossed by Steuart Street extended to a line near the bay shore identified as "the Established City Front," which would become the Embarcadero.

To the south the two 100-foot high crests of Rincon Hill rose in the vicinity of First and Harrison Streets. The hill had become, in real estate parlance, the city's first enclave of "better residence." Its homeowners were the city's leaders: the financier William Ralston; Peter Donahue, a leading industrialist; Andrew S. Hallidie, inventor of the cable car; William Tecumseh Sherman, then a banker but later to be a Civil War general; John Parrott, at one time the wealthiest man in the state; Lloyd Tevis, president of Wells Fargo & Company, and many others. Their Rincon Hill residences reflected the latest styles popular in the East.

At the base of Rincon Hill between Second and Third Streets the oval street of South Park, a 12-acre residential tract modeled on London's ovals and crescents, is indicated. George Gordon, an English entrepreneur, had purchased the land in 1852. Construction of the houses began in 1855, and by 1859 about one-quarter of the tract had been built up with attached town houses like the stylish brownstones of New York and Boston. Never completed, the row of attached houses shown on this map was later demolished; only the streets remain.

Despite the coming of public transit, travel on the Plank Road was not easy. Sand dunes 80 feet high rose above Second and Howard, and Second and Third and Market Streets. Further west, the road crossed a stretch of marshland around Mission Bay. Beyond the Yerba Buena Cemetery on Market Street (the future site of the Civic Center), a tract of land with cultivated fields is labeled Hayes Valley. Thomas Hayes, county clerk from 1853 to 1856, bought this 160-acre tract. He also acquired a franchise to build a railway line through the sand hills on Market Street to promote settlement in Hayes Valley. Although this line seems not to have been put in service at the time, by the 1860s streetcar lines ran into the Mission District and Western Addition.

North of Market Street, high rents and land prices in the city center had led to decentralization with development occurring in the lowlands around Russian Hill and what was then called the Clay Street Hill. Chinatown had started around the intersection of Dupont—later Grant—and Sacramento streets, originally a French quarter. The French soon moved to other desirable locations, and it may be that some of them sold their land to the Chinese whom they had employed as servants. Although the population of Chinatown increased exponentially, it was confined to the blocks between Keary, California, Broadway, and Stockton streets. By 1859, Stockton Street, the western edge of Chinatown, was an up-and-coming residential location for non-Chinese.

Such zoning as there was in the city had been mainly directed at regulating distasteful uses such as slaughterhouses and stockyards, but hospitals were also in this category and therefore banned from the area bounded by Filbert, McAllister, Jones, and Johnson Streets. Iron foundries, saw mills, gas works, and similar industries located south of Market Street where the large blocks could accommodate the plants and warehouses associated with them. Working class districts remained on the outer edges of the central business district. In 1855, a group of manufacturers, fearful that their operations might be prohibited, proposed that land south of Mission Creek judged to be sufficiently remote from the populated part of the city be reserved as an industrial zone. Although nothing came of the proposal, the city's growth pattern achieved the same result.

Wholesale firms moved toward the bay where business owners financed street improvements and wharf building. Although these improvements brought higher rents and land prices, surfacing streets with planks, which was relatively inexpensive because of plentiful supplies of wood, had its drawbacks. The wood planks wore out fairly quickly and burned during the terrible fires of 1851. Planking had largely ceased by 1854.

Although 100 acres of Yerba Buena Cove were filled in 1854 by leveling sand dunes, Battery Street was the only thoroughfare that connected the warehouses on the northern waterfront with the central business district where 1,500 brick buildings had been erected that year. Warehouses were concentrated on the north waterfront at the base of Telegraph Hill because the deep water around Clark's Point enabled ocean-going vessels such as the clipper ships to unload their heavy shipments on wharves located there. The most active wharves were further south. They were financed by joint stock corporations, which undertook important transportation projects. The Central Wharf Joint Stock Company had built the Long Wharf, the first really serviceable dock, in 1849. It later became Commercial Street.

A NAVIGATIONAL CHART

Title: Entrance to San Francisco Bay from a Trigonometrical Survey
Date published: 1859
Cartographer: A. D. Bache, Superintendent of the Survey of the Coast of the United States. Triangulation by R. D. Cutts Asst. and A. F. Rodgers Sub-Assts. Hydrography under the command of Lieut. Comdg. James Alden
Publisher: U. S. Coast Survey
Uncolored chart map, 23 ⅔ x 38 ⅗ inches
David Rumsey Collection

Another map of 1859 from the coastal survey encompassed the part of the bay related to its entrance, named the Golden Gate in 1847 by John Charles Fremont. Since this was a navigational chart, the inland areas were not delineated. The topography, rendered in graduated tones that produce a more realistic effect, reveals the limited amount of settlement around the bay. The City of San Francisco appears as a patch of street grid occupying a small area of the peninsula. Across the bay, the grid of Oakland is noticeable along with its railroad wharf, which stretches toward Yerba Buena Island. The Alameda railroad wharf is also shown, but, unlike the Oakland wharf later occupied by the Key Line and still later by the Bay Bridge and its attendant roadways, the Alameda wharf was not developed. The tortured coast of Marin County and the shallow inlet on the opposing shore later divided into the cities of Richmond, El Cerrito, Albany, and Berkeley have yet to attract significant settlement. Near the bottom edge of the map are three small engravings. The first on the left side is a view of the entrance to San Francisco Bay with Alcatraz Island barely visible beyond the Golden Gate and Fort Point providing a manmade element. The middle view, the bay's entrance from Yerba Buena Island, shows more human activity. A variety of boats, including a side-wheel steamer dot the waters, and the warehouses at the base of Telegraph Hill are drawn. The view to the right shows the entrance to San Pablo Bay from near Angel Island.

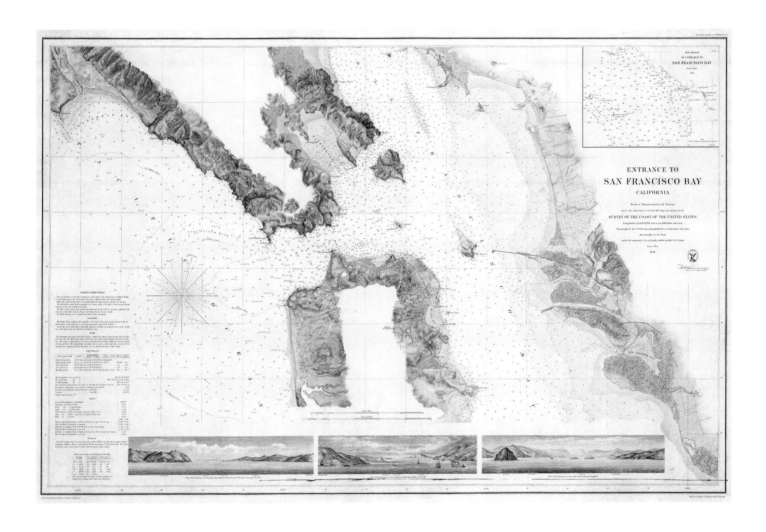

ENTRANCE TO
SAN FRANCISCO BAY
CALIFORNIA

POST-GOLD RUSH DECADES, 1860–1890

VIEWS FROM CLAY STREET HILL

Title: Map of the State of California compiled from the most recent surveys and explorations. Containing all the latest discoveries and newest towns.
Date: 1860
Author: Vincent
Engraver: S. H. Smith
Publisher: Mangeon (Paris)
Colored pocket map, 14 ⅗ x 19 ³/₁₀ inches
David Rumsey Collection

In this unusual map the state is shown horizontally with the counties colored. Set into the upper left corner is a "Panorama of San Francisco and Contra Costa." The lower right corner has a small map of San Francisco and its surrounding localities, dated 1860. The panoramic view of the city is taken from Nob Hill, then called the Clay Street Hill. The street below and slightly to the right of the hillside is Sacramento, which is traced all the way to the bay. Further to the right, although not totally opened up to the viewer, is California Street. St. Mary's Cathedral, on the corner of California and Dupont Streets (now Grant Avenue), rises above the other buildings. Stockton Street runs across the lower edge of the engraving, but because it is hidden by the hill on the left side of the view, the only indication of it is its intersection with Sacramento Street.

Several of the houses facing the viewers on the hill appear in other drawn views and in photographic panoramas taken from this popular location. An unusual house with a hipped roof and verandas on the upper and lower floors stands at the southeast corner of Sacramento and Stockton Streets.

On the northeast corner of the intersection, gable-roofed wooden houses, some with flat-sawn Gothic trim, have been carefully drawn. Between one such house on the southeast corner of Stockton and Sacramento Streets and St. Mary's stands a small house with a bowed roof that may be one of the pre-fabricated iron buildings shipped from various places in the 1850s to meet the demand for buildings. The former Jenny Lind Theatre, built in 1850 and purchased by the city to use as the city hall in 1852, is visible near the center of the view in the middle distance. Yerba Buena Island occupies the center of the bay, and Telegraph Hill, topped by its signal tower, rises near the left edge.

No explanation is given for inserting this view as part of the map of the state. However, it is nearly identical to the bird's-eye view shown in the next lithograph by Deroy.

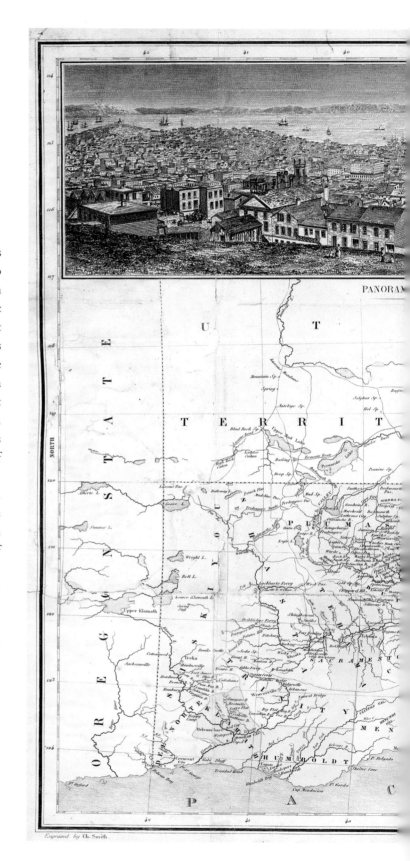

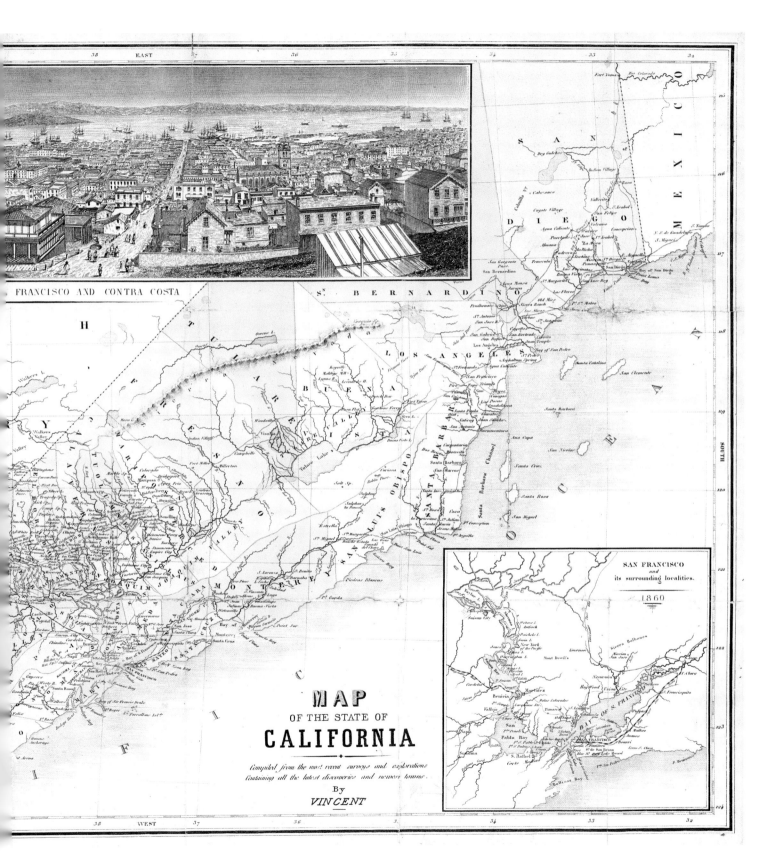

MAP

OF THE STATE OF

CALIFORNIA

Compiled from the most recent surveys and explorations
Containing all the latest discoveries and newest towns.

By

VINCENT

SAN FRANCISCO
and
its surrounding localities.

1860

FRANCISCO AND CONTRA COSTA

Title: Vue of San Francisco from the Clay St. Hill, #64 in the Ports de Mer D'Amerique, c. 1860
Date published: 1868
Delineator/lithographer: Deroy
Publisher: L. Turgis, Imp. et Editeurs (Paris)
Colored lithograph, 12 ⅜ x 18 ⅞ inches
San Francisco Public Library

Compared to Vincent's lithograph Deroy's view is slightly compressed horizontally, but that may have been determined by the page width. The colored lithograph is more painterly than Vincent's black and white image, and the festive scene in the foreground is more elaborate. The buildings below the hillside appear to have more space around them and are larger compared to those shown in the distance in Vincent's view. The upper level veranda of the pavilionlike house on the corner of Sacramento and Stockton Streets has columns in Deroy's view whereas in Vincent's view it appears fenestrated. The similarity of the compositions suggest that they were based on wood-engraved letter sheet prototypes such as Ronarque's versions of the same view published by Henry Payot, Washington St., San Francisco.

THE VAN NESS ORDINANCE

Title: City and County of San Francisco compiled from official surveys and sectioned in accordance with U. S. surveys
Date depicted and published: 1861
Cartographer: V. Wackenreuder, C. E.
Publisher: Henry G. Langley for the San Francisco Directory.
Printed by Britton & Co. (San Francisco)
Uncolored map, 19 ⅖ x 24 ⅖ inches
David Rumsey Collection

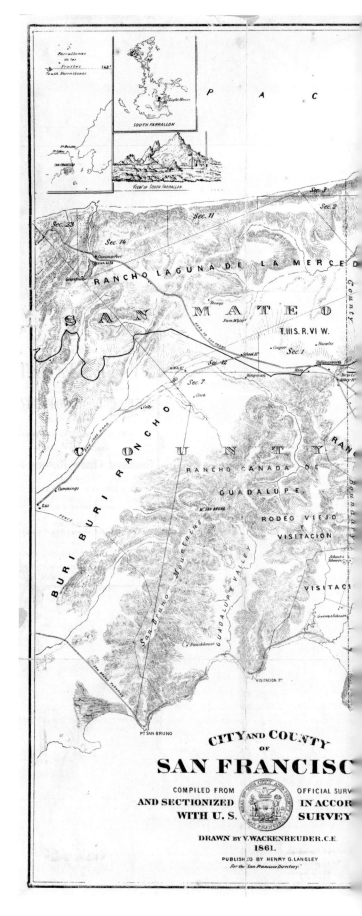

V. Wackenreuder, the San Mateo County Surveyor, drew this map, the first he published in Henry G. Langley's well-known San Francisco Directory and one of the first to extend to the western and southern parts of the peninsula's head and to show part of San Mateo County with full topography rendered with hachuring. The edge of Marin County opposite the Golden Gate is shown, and three small maps of the South Farrallone Island are set into the upper left corner. The sand hills and beach at the ocean's edge are labeled.

Features shown in this map that were not on the 1859 U. S. Coast Survey map include the path of the Spring Valley Water Works from Pilarcitos Creek to the reservoir of Laguna Honda and that of the San Francisco Water Works on the northern bay shore to reservoirs within the city grid. Names of the ranchos and of important property owners are lettered. A grid of small blocks has been laid over Horner's Addition.

By 1855, a route somewhat like today's 49 Mile Drive existed. It ran out the Plank Road to the Presidio, proceeded to Seal Rocks, and then south down the ocean beach to Lake Merced where the Lake House or Ocean House provided food, drink, boating, swinging, and bowling. The nearby San Souci House offered the same enticements.

The years of indecision about land ownership had encouraged squatters to settle on undeveloped land in the western part of the city previously granted by the Mexican *alcaldes*. Wealthy San Franciscans hired the squatters to hold land for them, but since disputes over land often became violent, "quieting" claims was desirable. To facilitate this process the city enacted, and Mayor James Van Ness signed, Ordinance 822, granting title to those who had been in actual possession of land west of Larkin and Johnson Streets from January to June of 1855. Titles to land east of these streets that had been granted by the *alcaldes* or municipal authorities of the pueblo were recognized. Disputed lands not actually in the hands of bona fide property holders reverted to the city.

Although it was ratified by the state legislature in 1858, the Van Ness Ordinance did not end the squatter warfare; it continued until 1867 when the U. S. District Court and the Congress ruled in favor of the city's claim to the lands granted to the pueblo. In the meantime, the ordinance proved to be important in planning the city because it set the pattern of streets and public squares in the area later called the Western Addition. Section No. 846 of the ordinance was a plat for the area between Larkin and Johnson Streets

and the Divisadero. Like the previous city plans, it disregarded topography. The public squares of Jefferson, Alamo, and Hamilton were approved, as was Hospital Lot, now in Duboce Park. The land was divided into blocks, and sites were reserved for 28 schools, 25 fire stations, 6 squares or plazas on 4 blocks of about 12 acres each, 4 squares of 2 blocks of 5 acres each, and a hospital of 2 blocks. The platted land resembles latticework and extends into the bay north and northeast of the Western Addition.

Portsmouth Square, popularly known as the Plaza, was landscaped, but it and the other public squares were too small to be considered parks.

A 360-DEGREE VIEW

Title: San Francisco, 1862, from Russian Hill
Date: 1862
Cartographer/Delineator: Charles B. Gifford
Printer: L. Nagel
Publisher: A. Rosenfield (San Francisco)
Uncolored lithograph, 14 ⅗ x 106 ⅔ inches
David Rumsey Collection

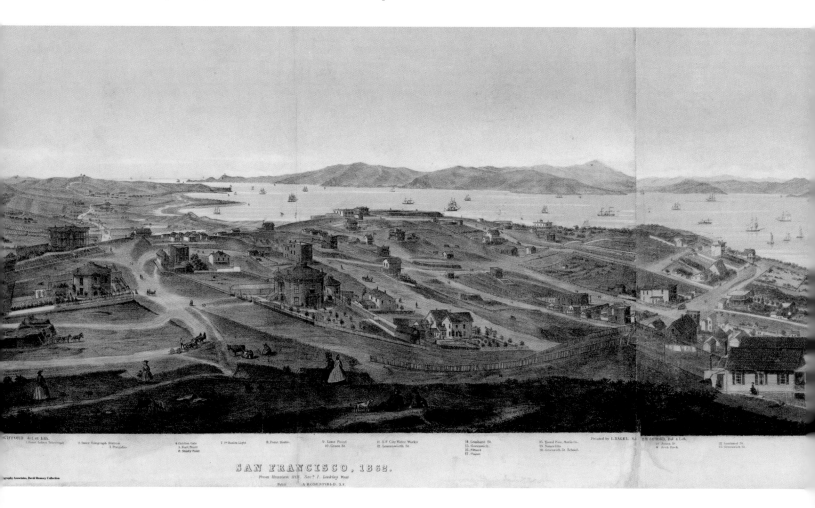

SAN FRANCISCO, 1862.
From Russian Hill Sec.ᵗ 1. Looking West
Publ.ᵈ A. ROSENFIELD, S.F.

In 1855, the clamor began for a real park, probably influenced by New York City's Central Park, then under construction.

Horse racing was popular before the Gold Rush. The Mission Dolores, the principal suburban recreation resort in early years, was the location of a Jockey Club in 1853 that supervised racing, improved breeds, and kept records. By 1857, the city had several tracks in the outside lands, which seemed to change their location as easily as the sand dunes. This map shows the Pioneer Race Track located on undeveloped land between Mission Street and Potrero Hill.

A 360-degree view of San Francisco by Charles B. Gifford, delineator and lithographer. The nine-foot long print was composed of five sheets and issued in three forms: on thin paper mounted on cloth and folded into an album with covers, on heavy paper as five separate sheets, and on heavy paper backed with linen and attached to wooden rollers for use as a wall map. The lower margin has 125 numbered references to buildings and points of interest.

The panorama begins at the Golden Gate and shows nearby Point Lobos and its signal tower—two tiny dots above the hilltop—to the left above the smattering of dark dots that indicate the Presidio. The Marin headlands are across the bay from the outer edge of Russian Hill. Mount Tamal Pais (Table Mountain) and Saucelito (sic) are marked along with Angel and Alcatraz Islands opposite Taylor Street.

The lower slopes of Russian Hill, viewed from its summit, feature Green Street on the left where two octagonal houses stand opposite each other on the street. They were inspired by Orson Fowler's 1853 tract on healthful living, *A Home for All*. Since fresh air was important to Fowler, windows on the building's eight sides provided maximum cross-ventilation. Walls made of a mixture of gravel and cement were, he claimed, porous

built at the foot of Powell Street in 1853 was described as a haven for lovers and others who wanted to get away from the crowded city streets.

The panorama's third sheet shows Washington Square visible over the brow of Russian Hill, its flagpole rising from the center of the paths crisscrossing it. Beyond it, the land begins its rise to Telegraph Hill where the observatory is shown. Although the hill is quite barren, its top was a popular tourist destination. Regardless of the problems they posed, San Franciscans appreciated the hills for the views from them of the bay and the city. Views down the streets from above revealed city life better than those on flat land.

SAN FRANCISCO, 1862.
From Russian Hill. Section 2. Looking North.
Published by A. ROSENFIELD, S.F.

L. NAGEL. Print.   C. B. GIFFORD, del et lith.

SAN FRANCIS
From Russian Hill. Section 3.
Published by A. ROSENF

enough to allow air to pass through them. Only one of the houses drawn here remains; it was given a fashionable mansard roof in the 1880s.

There are few structures and little vegetation on this sandy hill. Fences built to hold back the sand surround the properties. One of the octagonal houses has young trees planted nearby, probably as a windbreak.

Meiggs Wharf extends into the bay in the valley between Russian and Telegraph Hills. Henry Meiggs, the flamboyant developer of the wharf, came to the city in 1848 with a shipload of timber. He got rich and through a variety of investments became a civic leader. The 1,600-foot wharf he

The next four sheets show the blocks between Telegraph Hill and the eastern edge of the Clay Street Hill packed with buildings on streets ending in wharves lined with ships. These are the Broadway and Pacific Street wharves, which were constructed early because of their access to relatively level land and proximity to the deep water required for docking by the clipper ships and other ocean-going vessels. The wooden tower with a flagpole mounted on its top deck was the Jobson Observatory on Russian Hill. A figure holding a telescope pointed toward the bay stands near the flagpole. In the distance we see Mission Bay and beyond it the Potrero Nuevo.

SAN FRANCISCO, 1852.

SOUTH OF MARKET

Title: San Francisco, Bird's-Eye View
Date: 1864
Delineator/Lithographer: C. B. Gifford
Publisher: Robinson & Snow (San Francisco)
Tinted lithograph, 29 ¹/₁₀ x 46 ½ inches (sheet)
San Francisco Public Library

This view was drawn and lithographed by Charles B. Gifford, the delineator of the panorama previously discussed. A numbered map key showing 101 points of interest was published with it. Gifford's point of view directed the eye toward the newly developing blocks south of Market Street rather than the older area established north of Market Street from Portsmouth Square to Commercial Street. This vantage point shows continuous rows of business blocks lining the streets west of Yerba Buena Cove. Ships crowd the waterfront, which has become less indented though not as smooth as it will be in later views. Rincon Hill appears bisected by Bryant Street; it will be sliced through again by Second Street in 1869. The completion of the San Francisco and San Jose Railroad in 1864 improved the city's connection to the south bay and provided rail connections for the wholesale trade and light manufacturing district south of Howard Street. Its first depot was at 18th and Valencia Streets. In 1872, freight yards were opened at Third and Townsend Streets, and in 1889 a passenger station was built there.

The landscape toward the ocean is still bleak and barren, but with the settlement of the title claims in the outside lands, Golden Gate Park would begin to take shape. Frederick Law Olmsted had prepared a plan for a system of parks that was rejected in 1866, but in 1870 the city purchased the land for the park and hired William Hammond Hall to plan its 1,013 acres.

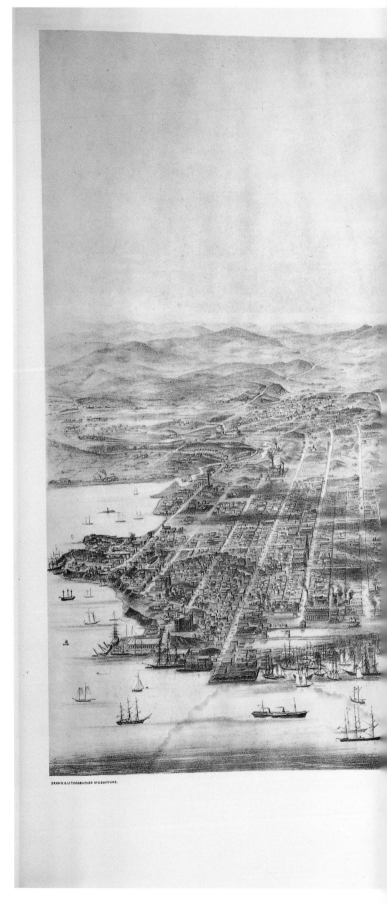

AN FRANCISCO.

BIRD'S EYE VIEW.

Published July 1st 1864, by ROBINSON & SNOW, Washington & Sansome St. S.F.

REFERENCE.

———— Market St. Rail-Road	I Summit of Telegraph Hill
———— Central R.R.	II Russian Hill
———— North Beach & Mission R.R.	III Clay St. Hill
++++ Omnibus R.R.	IIII California & Sacramento St.

Circles ¼ Mile apart. Centre PORTSMOUTH SQUARE.

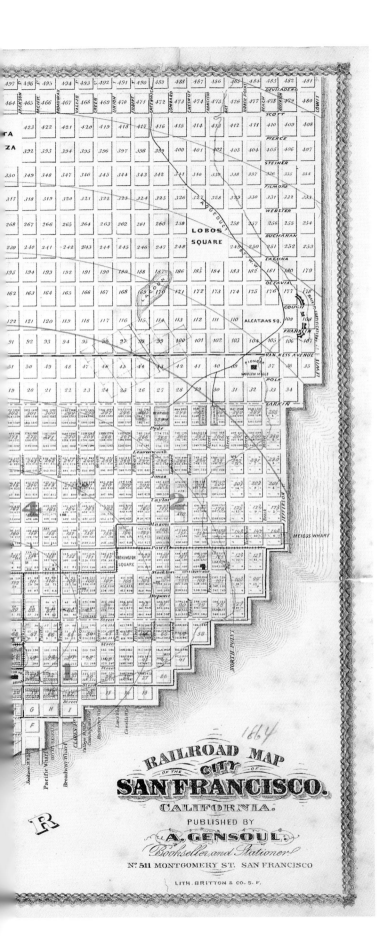

EARLY PUBLIC TRANSPORTATION

Title: The Railroad Map of the City of San Francisco
Date published: 1864
Cartographer: unknown
Lithographer: Britton & Co.
Publisher: A. Gensoul, bookseller and stationer (San Francisco)
Two-color lithograph, 13 ¾ x 15 ¼ inches
San Francisco Public Library

The map extends west to Divisadero Street and south to Alta Street. The circles, drawn at one-mile intervals, were centered on Portsmouth Square. Red numerals indicate the city's wards; their boundaries were drawn to include equal numbers of white men. Since the four streetcar lines shown on the map were horse-powered, their routes avoided the steep hills.

The Market Street Railway received the first franchise in 1857. The other three lines—the Central Railway, the North Beach & Mission Railway, and the Omnibus Railway—were franchised in 1862.

Familiar points of interest marked on the map include: the Jewish Cemetery on Dolores Street; the Orphan Asylum at Alamo, Hamilton, and O'Farrell; Alta Plaza and Lobos, Lafayette, and Jefferson Squares. Fortifications are shown at Black Point. The aqueduct extends from the west to Lombard and Larkin Street. The Pioneer Woolen Mills, designed by the prominent architect, William Mooser, and built in 1856, occupy a large site on Black Point Cove; the main building was rehabilitated in 1960s as part of the Ghirardelli Square shopping complex. In the Rincon Point area, the Marine and St. Mary's hospitals are marked.

VIEW FROM THE OCEAN EAST

Title: Bird's-Eye View of the City of San Francisco and Surrounding
Country
Date: 1868
Delineator: George H. Goddard
Publisher: Snow and May
Tinted lithograph, 28 ⅓ x 40 ⅘ inches
David Rumsey Collection

George H. Goddard was born in England in 1817 and immigrated to
California in 1850. His training in architecture and surveying led to his
employment as a government surveyor in Sacramento. He moved to San
Francisco in 1862 and died there in 1906 at the age of 89. This is one of
two panoramic maps he produced.

The view looks east from the ocean over the city, across the bay to the
East Bay, and beyond Mount Diablo as far as the distant Sierra. It also stretches
north to take in Marin County, the San Pablo Bay, and the delta, and south
past San Mateo County to the South Bay where Santa Clara and San Jose are
shown. This ambitious undertaking was the first of several large bird's-eye
views of the city looking east. The distance to the South Bay appears
compressed, but that may have been the result of the size of the plate.

The complementary shades of blue and tan make the sandy nature
of the peninsula obvious. The tone of the city grid, which has continued
to advance west and south, blends in. Familiar landmarks such as the
Cliff House and Sutro Heights are shown at the end of the long road out
of town past Lone Mountain. Ocean Beach at the western edge of the
Great Sand Bank traces a slight curve that returns inland near Ocean
House. Near a small lake east of this popular resort destination is another
small lake, and between it and the larger Lake Merced is the faint oval
outline of the Ocean Race Track. Numerous sand dunes stud the landscape
to the east where Twin Peaks is visible west of the city's edge.

In 1868 the state began construction of the bulkhead across the
inlet south of Market Street that would facilitate the filling of Yerba
Buena Cove. (The cove was not completely eliminated until 1910.) The
shoreline now ran evenly from Telegraph Hill to Rincon Hill. South of
Rincon Hill, South Beach was extended into the bay during the period
from the 1860s to the 1880s to make level ground for shipyards,
lumberyards, a gas company, and piers and repair shops for the Pacific
Mail Steamship Company. (This New York-based company dominated
transport across the Isthmus of Panama, up the west coast, and west to
Asia.) Causeways linked the land on either side of Mission Bay and the
Islais Creek inlet. The north shoreline is still scalloped with inlets that
will soon be filled in. Although the watery surroundings of San Francisco
still contribute to the city's importance, they no longer dominate the
scene as in early maps.

PUBLISHED BY **SNOW & MAY**, SAN FRANCISCO.

TY OF SAN FRANCISCO AND SURROUNDING COUNTRY

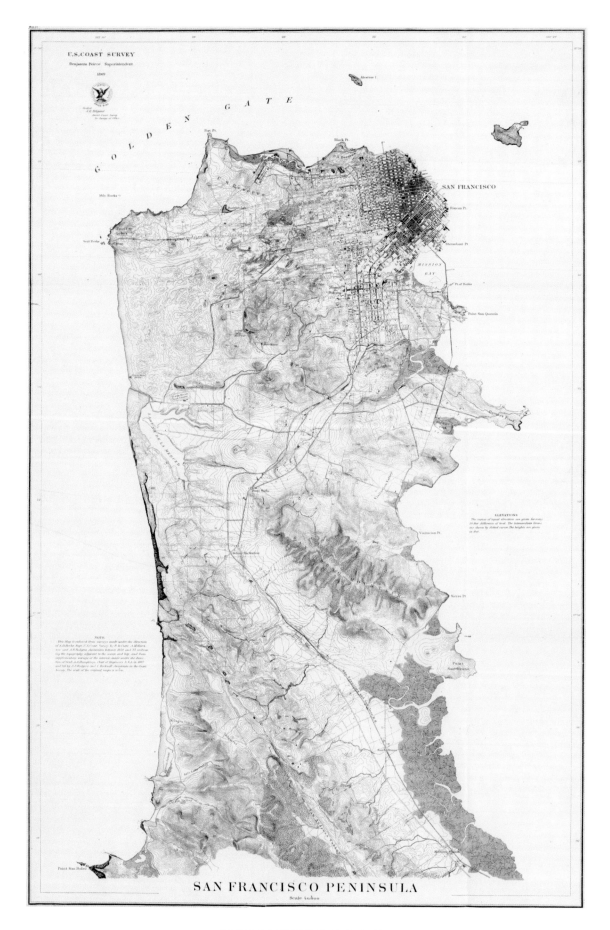

SAN FRANCISCO PENINSULA

Scale 40,000

U. S. COSTAL SURVEY MAP

Title: San Francisco Peninsula
Date: 1869
Cartography: U. S. Coast Survey, Benjamin Pierce,
Superintendent
Publisher: U. S. Coast Survey
Uncolored map, 27 ¹⁵/₁₆ x 17 ⅓ inches
David Rumsey Collection

The U. S. Coastal Survey, an arm of the Treasury Department established under Thomas Jefferson's administration, is the country's oldest scientific agency. It was well funded and became increasingly important in the 1850s and 1860s in providing scientific backing for the political agenda of westward expansion. The legend for this U. S. Coast Survey map states that it was done to show the progress of the survey during the year 1869.

The map complements Goddard's bird's-eye view of the previous year. The grid still covers a relatively small area of the city's potential size. The usual landmarks are noted, and, as in the 1859 Coast Survey map, contour lines are used to show the topography. A note titled "Elevations" states that the curves of equal elevation are given for every 20 feet difference of level. The intermediate forms are shown by dotted curves, and the heights are given in feet. The extension of the map to the south past San Mateo County allowed the depiction of prominent natural features such as San Bruno Mountain, the tidal marshes along the bay shore, and the San Andreas Valley, which would later be famous as the San Andreas Fault. The old San Jose Road runs near the San Francisco and San Jose Railroad, which first entered the city in 1864 and terminates at the Townsend Street depot. As in Goddard's bird's-eye view, sand is the dominant ground cover.

In 1869, Second Street would be cut through Rincon Hill to the industrial area of South Beach, destroying the city's first fashionable residential neighborhood on the hill. In 1892, Robert Louis Stevenson described the hill as "a new slum, a place of precarious sand cliffs, deep sandy cuttings, solitary ancient houses, and butt end of streets."

SAN FRANCISCO CITY GUIDE MAP

Title: Bancroft's Official Guide Map of City and County of San
Francisco, Compiled from Official Maps in Surveyor's Office
Date published: 1873
Cartographer: unknown
Publisher: A. L. Bancroft & Co. (San Francisco)
*Uncolored except for a blue line showing the original bay shore, pocket
map, 24 ⅔ x 29 ½ inches*
David Rumsey Collection

A. L. Bancroft & Company listed its services as: booksellers, stationers,
importers, publishers, printers, lithographers, engravers, binders, blank
book makers, etc. The company also began to produce guide maps. This
1873 Guide Map has a reference list of 376 prominent places set below
the map and keyed to it by numbers. The places are grouped in categories:
cemeteries, churches, hospitals, hotels, parks and squares, public buildings,
railroad depots, schools and colleges, theatres and halls, wharves, and
ferries. The user is instructed that "the squares formed by the horizontal
and perpendicular lines [on the map] are one mile each way and are
referred to by marginal numbers and letters." A small map "showing the
relative position of San Francisco in the surrounding country" is inset
on the right side of the map.

Developed areas of the city are shown in a darker tone. Undeveloped
areas—nearly all of the western part of the city—are blank. The original
shoreline is traced in a wide blue line and reveals the dramatic changes made
by years of filling the bay. Although this blue line appears on the 1873 and
1891 Bancroft maps of the city, it is not used on the 1887 city map, which
in other respects is the same. It seems to this writer that the inconsistent
use of the blue color indicates that it was not part of the original base map,
but was added because of special interest at the time. No explanation is
given in the map text.

LAND RECLAMATION

Title: Map exhibiting the Salt Marshes, Tide and Submerged Lands
in and adjacent to the Bays of San Francisco and San Pablo and now
Subject to Reclamation, Prepared from Maps of the U. S. Coastal
Survey and Official Records by Order of the Board of State Harbor
Commissioners and the United States Commissioners on
San Francisco Harbor
Date: 1874
Lithographers: Britton & Rey
Colored in shades of brown, 24 ⅔ x 67 ¾ inches
David Rumsey Collection
[see following pages]

This map of the bay shore shows property sold by the state to private parties,
which could now be filled. The east side of the bay including the San Pablo
Bay is at the map's top. A thin tan-colored line that encircles the bays offshore

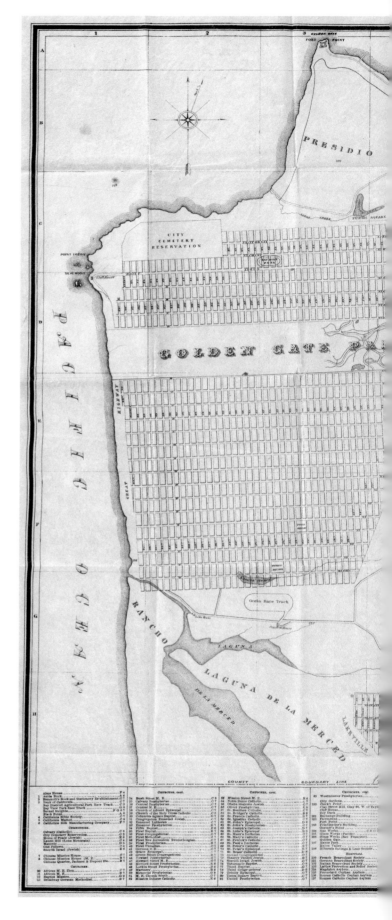

Map exhibiting the Salt Marshes, Tide and Submerged Lands in and adjacent to the Bays of San Francisco and San Pablo.

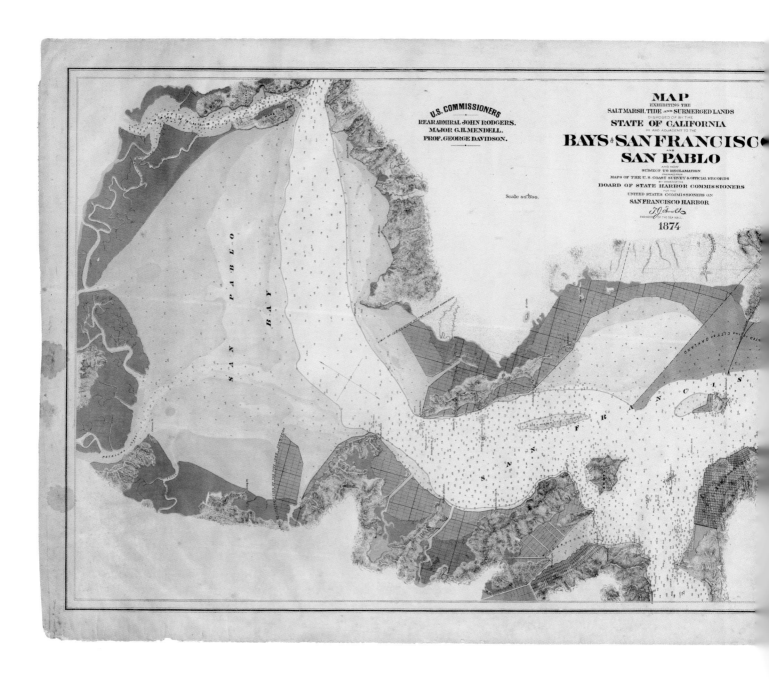

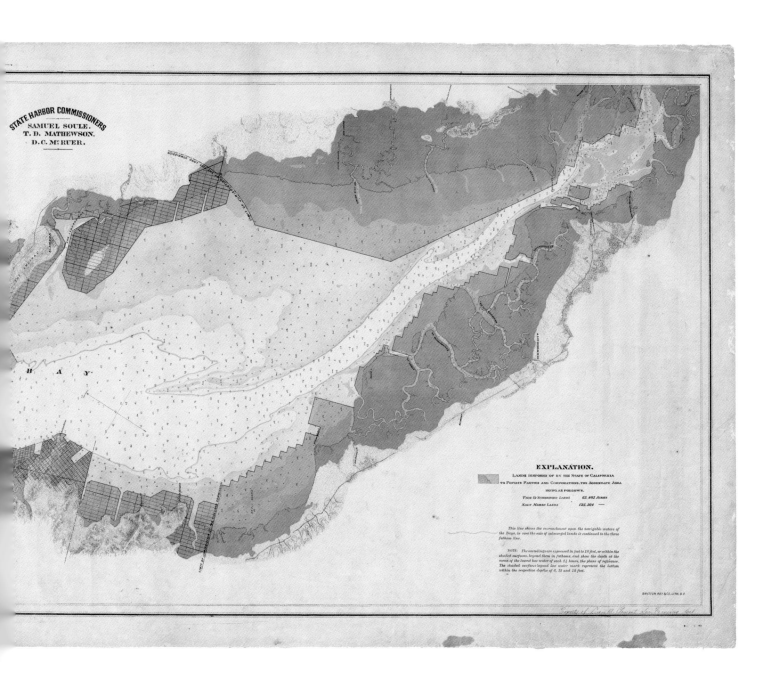

STATE HARBOR COMMISSIONERS
SAMUEL SOULE.
T. D. MATHEWSON.
D. C. McRUER.

B A Y

EXPLANATION.

LANDS DISPOSED OF BY THE STATE OF CALIFORNIA
TO PRIVATE PARTIES AND CORPORATIONS, THE AGGREGATE AREA
BEING AS FOLLOWS.

THUS IN SUBMERGED LANDS   63,863 ACRES
SALT MARSH LANDS   121,366   —

This line shows the encroachment upon the navigable waters of
the Bay, in case the sale of submerged lands is continued to the three
fathom line.

NOTE. The soundings are expressed in feet to 18 feet, or within the
shaded surfaces, beyond them in fathoms, and show the depth at the
mean of the lowest low water of each 24 hours, the plane of reference.
The shaded surfaces beyond low water mark represent the bottom
within the respective depths of 6, 12 and 18 feet.

BRITTON REY & CO. LITH. S.F.

83

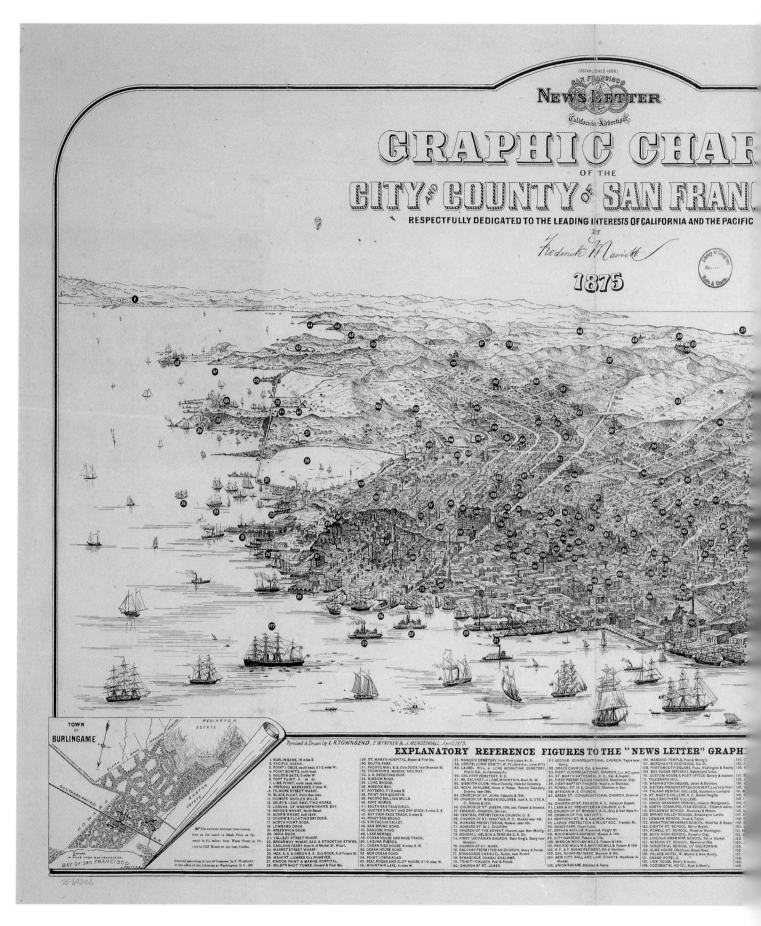

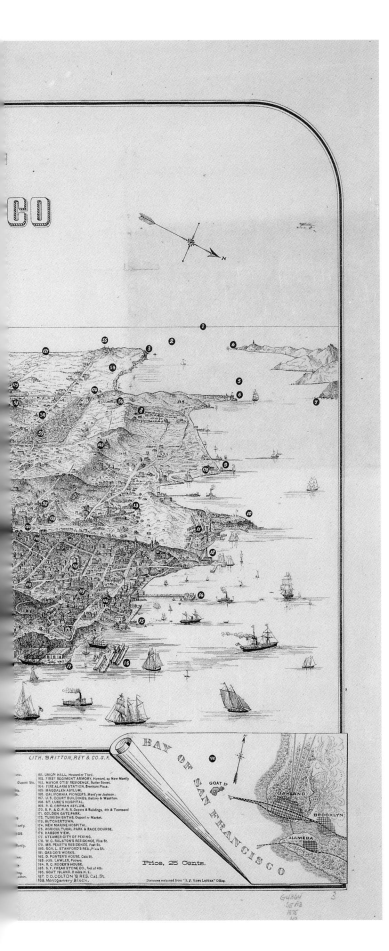

shows "the encroachment upon the navigable waters of the bays in case sale of the submerged bays is continued to the three fathom line." Clearly, waterfront property was in demand.

The orientation of this long horizontal map with north to the left gives the two bays the appearance of a rough gash in the earth. The rendering of cities around the bays reveals them as minor ports more easily connected to San Francisco by water than by roads or rail lines. The Golden Gate, placed at the bottom of the map, has the appearance of a drain. It is not clear why this unconventional orientation was used in this case, but it has the value of causing the viewer to look at the subject anew.

A COMPREHENSIVE VIEW

Title: Graphic Chart of the City and County of San Francisco, respectfully dedicated to the leading interests of California and the Pacific Coast
Date depicted: 1875
Delineator: Frederich Marriott/revised and drawn by L. R. Townsend, E. Wyneken & J. Mendenhall
Published in the San Francisco newsletter, California Advertiser
Publisher: Britton, Rey & Co., c1875
Uncolored map
Library of Congress

A simulated scroll at the bottom of the map is titled, "Explanatory Reference Figures to the Newsletter Graphic Chart." The points of interest listed below are keyed to numbers on the map.

This bird's-eye view is oriented with north toward the lower right. The Pacific Ocean at the top serves as the horizon with the Golden Gate toward the left margin. The western part of the city is compressed, and the whole map is distorted to emphasize the developed area from North Beach to Rincon Point. Ships of all kinds ply the bay; their types and destinations are given in the reference block. The numbers are set in black dots that swarm over the scene and contribute to its liveliness. Indeed, the sheer number of referenced items conveys the impression that everything worth seeing or knowing about in the city is shown.

VIEWS OF TELEGRAPH HILL

Title: San Francisco, Looking South From North Point
Date: 1877
Delineator: C. G. Gifford
Publisher: G. T. Brown & Co., Lithographers (San Francisco)
Colored lithograph, 19 3/16 x 30 7/16 inches
San Francisco Public Library

[see following pages]

85

A bird's-eye view showing Telegraph Hill prominent in the foreground, its slopes peppered with small buildings, and its rocky base carved away to create flat land for the large warehouses on Battery Street that served the clipper ships. These very large sailing vessels required deep water to dock, and Clark's Point was the closest deep water to Yerba Buena Cove where most of the wharves had been constructed. Nearby is a dry dock connected to the Fort Mason military reservation. The right hand side of the map shows part of Russian Hill and Nob Hill (formerly the Clay Street Hill) with some mansions near its top that were built following the installation of the Clay Street cable car line. In the distance south of Telegraph Hill, the Palace Hotel looms over the intersection of Montgomery and Market Streets. Uniform rows of business blocks define the central business district. Beyond the brow of Nob Hill, just visible over Leland Stanford's mansion, is the domed City Hall on the triangular site at Larkin Street and Market, formerly a park. The building had been under construction since 1871. It would not be completed for twenty more years and then would be shaken to pieces in 1906.

Title: The City of San Francisco, Birds Eye View from the Bay Looking South-West
Date: 1878
Delineator: C. R. Parsons
Publisher: Currier & Ives (New York)
Colored map, 23 ¼ x 33 ¹/₁₆ inches
David Rumsey Collection

Printed below the map are the names of 73 unnumbered buildings and geographical features. The names are listed beneath the location of the building or feature; some are accented in blue, which makes them stand out against the predominantly tan and brown tones of the city. The buildings, ships, and other features are drawn in great detail with the city foreshortened to permit a view down on the building tops and into the streets near the waterfront. The Golden Gate opens up at the top right after which the path of the ships traces the view around the bay shore to finish the panorama in the south bay at the upper left.

The city seems carpeted with buildings extending out into the Mission and Western Addition districts. Market Street, the most identifiable arterial, bisects the triangular Yerba Buena Park and ends near Golden Gate Park, which extends to the ocean. North of the park are the Agricultural Park and Race Course. The cross on its top identifies Lone Mountain. Fort Point stands on the south side of the Golden Gate beyond the Presidio. Sand dunes roll over Pacific Heights and down to the bay south of the fortified Black Point with its flagpole.

The slopes of Telegraph Hill resemble a Monopoly board game in progress. Clipper ships are docked near the stand of brick warehouses at the blasted out base of Telegraph Hill. The diagonal course of Columbus Avenue is shown cutting through the blocks from Washington and Montgomery Streets to the North Beach waterfront near the Pioneer

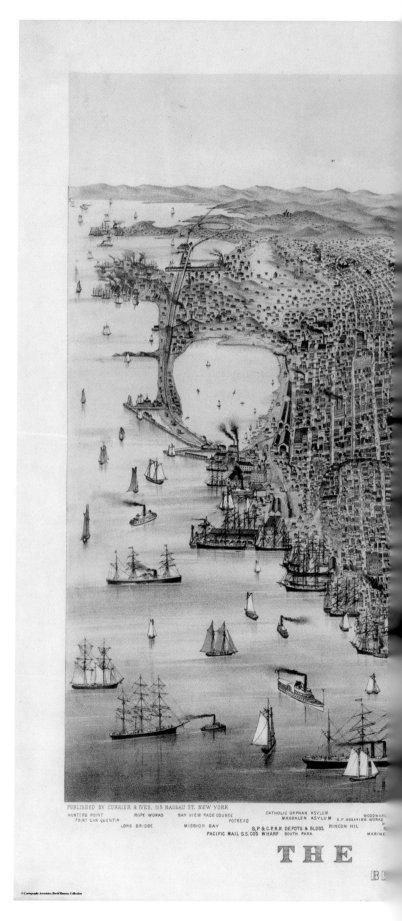

COPYRIGHT 1878, BY CURRIER & IVES, N.Y.

SKETCHED & DRAWN BY C.R. PARSONS.

RESERVOIR	ORPHAN ASYLUM	ALMS HOUSE	GOLDEN GATE PARK	AGRICULTURAL PARK & RACE COURSE	PACIFIC OCEAN, IN THE DISTANCE	CLIFF HOUSE

RESERVOIR ORPHAN ASYLUM ALMS HOUSE   GOLDEN GATE PARK   AGRICULTURAL PARK & RACE COURSE PACIFIC OCEAN, IN THE DISTANCE   CLIFF HOUSE   POINT LOBOS   PACIFIC OCEAN, IN THE DISTANCE   POINT BONITA
...ON   ST. LUKES HOSPITAL   LONE MOUNTAIN   JEWISH SYNAGOGUE   LAUREL HILL CEMETERY   MOUNTAIN LAKE PERSIDIO BARRACKS - MILITARY RESERVATION   FORT POINT GOLDEN GATE   LIME POINT
CITY HALL   TRINITY CH.   CALVARY CEMETERY   CLAY HILL   HAYES VALLEY ST. BRIDGETS CH.   FORT POINT GOLDEN GATE
...TL'A OPERA HOUSE LICK HOUSE   UNION SQ.   RES. MARK HOPKINS ESQ. RES. CHAS. CROCKER ESQ. 1ST PRESBT. CH. 1ST M.E.CHURCH.   R.C. CONVENT   TOLAND MEDICAL COLLEGE   BLACK POINT FORTIFICATION
MASONIC TEMPLE OCCIDENTAL HOTEL   BANK OF NEVADA BLDG.   RES. GOV. STANFORD PORTSMOUTH SQ.   LARKIN ST. PRESBT. CH.   WASHINGTON SQ. TELEGRAPH HILL   PIONEER MILLS
PALACE HOTEL   COSMOPOLITAN HOTEL   SAFE DEPOSIT CO'S BLDG. POST OFFICE & CUSTOM HOUSE   ST. FRANCIS CH.   SEBLY'S SMELTING WORKS
GRAND HTL. ORIENTAL BLOCK SEAMENS BETHEL   SUGAR REFINERY   INDIA DOCKS   FLOATING DRY DOCK
OAKLAND FERRY, C.P.R.R.   BAY OF SAN FRANCISCO

Y OF SAN FRANCISCO.
E VIEW FROM THE BAY LOOKING SOUTH-WEST.

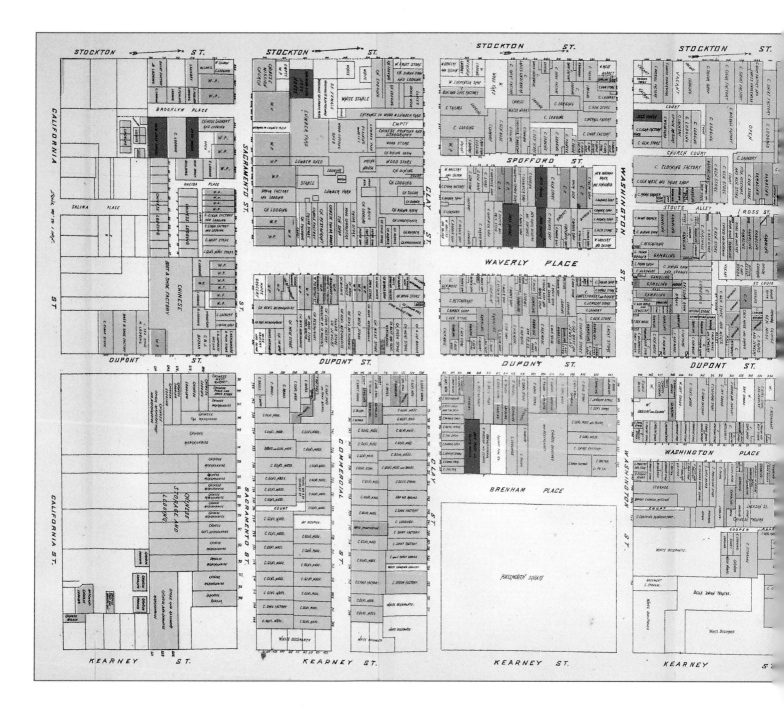

Woolen Mills. The size of St. Francis Church and other buildings is exaggerated so that it seems larger than Washington Square a few blocks to the south. Other important features such as the Selby Shot Tower near Rincon Hill are also outsized. Portsmouth Square appears less important than Union Square, the center of the city's retail shopping area. The Palace Hotel on Market Street, and the Grand Hotel next to it are visible.

The waterfront is busy. An Oakland ferry is docked at the foot-of-Market Ferry Building. The Pacific Mail Steamship Company Wharf and the Southern Pacific and Central Pacific Railroad buildings and depots occupy a large area on Mission Bay. Near the upper lefthand side of the view are Hunters Point, Point San Quentin, and the Bay View racecourse.

CHINATOWN

Title: The Official Map of Chinatown, compiled by a special committee of the Board of Supervisors
Date published: 1885
Delineator unknown
Published by the City of San Francisco in the Municipal Reports for the fiscal year, 1884–85
Colored map, variable dimensions
San Francisco Public Library

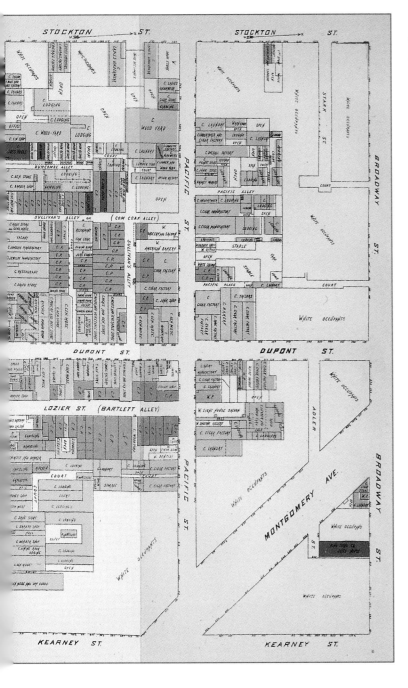

The map prepared by the Board of Supervisors' special committee focused on issues of health, safety, and morals. It documented illegal and legal activities that were packed into the district's six square blocks. Although alleys of various sizes had been cut through many of the blocks, their interiors contained enterprises that had no apparent street access. Many were labeled "barricaded gambling dens," others were opium "resorts." Houses of prostitution, colored blue for the white prostitutes and red for the Chinese, fronted on streets.

Most of Chinatown's residents—90 percent of whom were male—worked in the district in laundries or textile operations. A number of cigar and tobacco shops and warehouses along with other commercial enterprises are also indicated on the map. Legitimate commercial activities were located on the street frontages.

Chinatown was a city within the city. Its economy was diversified, and its social structure was regulated by clan and district associations, such as the powerful Chinese Consolidated Benevolent Association called the "Six Companies." This was the only city area where the buildings had a color scheme: red, yellow, and green, symbolizing health, wealth, and happiness. The shops and temples were festooned with colorful lanterns and pendants with inscriptions in Chinese. A non-western calendar determined the holidays. Both San Franciscans and out-of-towners were at once attracted to and repelled by the bizarre appearance of the streets and alleys and the dress of the residents. An ambience of exoticism made Chinatown a tourist attraction before and after the 1906 earthquake, when it was rebuilt much as it had been but with more Chinese-style bric-a-brac applied to the buildings.

Chinatown was the city's most congested area. Within the boundaries of Broadway, Stockton, Kearny, and California Streets estimates of the population density given in the Municipal Reports ranged from 200 to 300 persons per acre. Crowding in this ghetto had intensified in the depressed economy that followed the completion of the transcontinental railroad in 1869 and continued through the financial crises of the 1870s. The depression intensified the jingoism associated with the Workingmen's Party, founded in 1877 by Denis Kearney. This animosity was expressed on the national level when congress made Chinese immigration illegal by passing the Chinese Exclusion Act in 1882.

THE PROGRESSIVE MOVEMENT

The Progressive era in San Francisco dawned in the 1880s after the 1870s depression ended. The ideas of the reform-minded citizens focused on the city, a showcase for the best and worst of urban developments. Municipal corruption had produced a strong reaction against redistributing tax revenues to pay for urban needs. This reaction in turn forced the city to find other ways to raise money for such things as transit. A solution was to court the favors of large corporations such as the Southern Pacific Railway Company with franchises that would enable the expansion of its lines throughout the city. The "Big Four"— Charles Crocker, Mark Hopkins, Collis P. Huntington, and Leland Stanford— had acquired the SP in 1868. (In 1899 the SP absorbed the Central Pacific Railroad, originally the western part of the transcontinental railroad, and became one of the largest railroad companies in the west.)

In 1879, the city granted twenty-six franchises to the SP, which began its city-wide expansion and thus fueled a huge building boom in the west and southwest parts of San Francisco. The Sunset and Richmond districts and the outer reaches of the South-of-Market, the Mission, and the Noe Valley districts became accessible through streetcar lines and were rapidly developed by individuals and realty companies that had in-house building contractors. The development of these suburbs depended on the availability of water, gas, and street railways, which enhanced real estate values. In 1884, the SP combined its franchises under the name, the Market Street Railway Company.

Although the following map does not show the street railways, the city is entirely platted, and various homestead association tracts are labeled, indicating the path of future settlement.

REAL ESTATE CITY

Title: Guide Map of the City of San Francisco Compiled from the Official
Surveys and Engraved Expressedly for Langley's San Francisco Directory
Date copyrighted: 1890
Cartographer: George B. Wilbur of Painter & Co.
Publisher: Henry Langley
Colored map, 21 ¼ x 26 ¾ inches
David Rumsey Collection

McAfee, Baldwin & Hammon, Real Estate Agents and Auctioneers, located at 10 Montgomery Street, appear to have commissioned the map. Their services, which are listed outside the map's borders, include "lots for sale in all parts of the city" and "improved and unimproved property at public or private sale."

The practice of naming different parts of the city and coloring them to make them easier for the user to identify was typical of real estate maps, but what the colors signify here, if anything, is not clear.

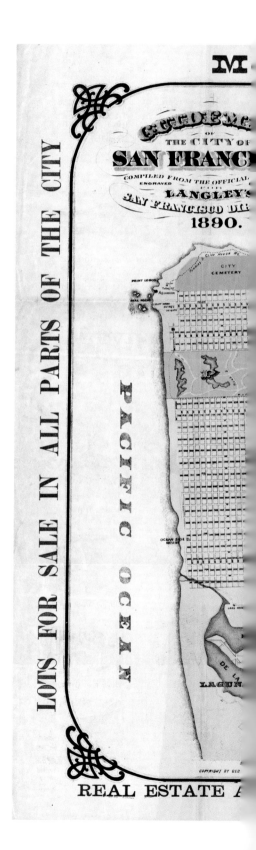

Among the important destinations lettered on the map are the cemeteries: City Cemetery near Land's End; Laurel Hill, Odd Fellows, Calvary, and Masonic, all located near Golden Gate Park in the Outside Lands. The park has roads and water elements, but no structures. Nearby is the Golden Gate Race Course. Six public squares are indicated, but only four, Alta Plaza, Alamo Square, Lafayette Park, and Jefferson Square, exist today. Lobos and Hamilton Squares were privatized.

Shoreline features such as the many wharves, ferry slips, the Pacific Mail Steamship Company Wharf, the Oriental Dock, the Central Pacific Railroad wharf are noted. The official waterfront line, established in 1877 is drawn past Hunters Point to the county line.

In reality, the outlying suburbs were still sandy wastes. The Central Ocean Road from Lake and Ocean Houses past the Ocean Race Course appears as a ghostly trace under the Sunset district plat. Rising above Seal Rocks and Point Lobos, the Cliff House and Sutro Heights were popular tourist destinations on weekends as were the cemeteries and the Agricultural Park. They were all served by the Ferries & Cliff House Railway, which ran out California Street nearly to Point Lobos.

The map is useful in showing how the neighborhoods had become defined by 1890. Although the early districts are not labeled, they are colored differently. Downtown, bounded by the South-of-Market area, the western Addition, and the waterfront, abutted Nob and Russian Hill and included North Beach, the Barbary Coast vice district, the warehouse-wholesale district along the waterfront, the financial district, the central shopping area, and the hotel district.

The South-of-Market area was the most populated after Chinatown; it was packed with houses and lodgings that served families and transients. Most residents worked in the foundries and machine shops along Howard Street between Main and First Streets and in the district's many factories. The "slot," as Market Street was called, referred to the channel for the cables that powered the streetcars, but it aptly described the division between the wealthy, who stayed in the Palace and the Grand Hotels on Market, and the blue-color workers and indigents who lived "south of the slot."

The Potrero district, originally the Mission Dolores pastureland, was also dedicated to manufacturing along the bay shore. Claus Spreckels's California Sugar Refinery, estimated to be worth $17 million in 1890, occupied a huge complex in the Potrero district. The other companies that composed this heavy industry sector were the Union Iron Works and Pacific Rolling Mills on Potrero Point. The Union Iron Works employed 1,200 workers and occupied 15 acres. It comprised a complete shipyard, rolling mill, machine shops, foundries, pattern shops and one of the country's largest hydraulic lift docks. The Pacific Rolling Mills produced 30,000 tons of iron and 10,000 tons of steel a year. Its 800 workers operated six trains of rollers, 25 furnaces, 54 boilers, and 15 engines. The company made the tracks for the Market Street cable railroad system.

The nearby workers' housing centered on Dogpatch, an area bounded by 3rd, Tubbs, Indiana, and Mariposa Streets, where churches, schools and stores served the community far from downtown. Although Potrero Hill offered sweeping views of the bay, it never became an elite residential area like Rincon Hill because the railroad yards and factories at the base of the hill were not a desirable prospect for the hill dwellers who could afford more convenient hilltop properties in other parts of the city.

The Mission district, also south of Market Street, is shown

beginning around 9th Street; it followed the curve of Market that extended further south to encompass what is now the Outer Mission district, the Bayview district, and Visitation Valley. By 1880, streetcar lines ran on Valencia, Mission, Howard, Folsom, and Harrison. Families followed, and, in fact, the area grew to house the greatest number of families in the city by the century's turning. One or two families occupied houses or flats on major thoroughfares and the narrow side streets in the district's many neighborhoods. The population density was much lower than that south of Market. Commercial strips served the predominantly Irish and German population. Although the district was heavily Roman Catholic, major Protestant denominations were represented by large wooden churches scattered throughout the district.

Like the South-of-Market district, the Mission was a working-class neighborhood with many of the skilled workers employed in the factories near the bay. However, businessmen and professionally trained workers also lived in the district along with contractors, politicians, and lawyers. Although only one park served the area before the conversion of a cemetery at 18th and Dolores Streets into Dolores Park, Woodward Gardens, a private amusement park located between 13th and 14th and Mission and Valencia Streets, had been welcoming the public with an art museum, an amphitheater, live and stuffed animals, and extensive gardens since 1866.

To the south the map shows more remnants of the colonial era, the Potrero Viejo, the Rancho Canada de Guadalupe Rodeo Viejo y Visitacion, and the Rancho Rincon de las Salinas. Each of these sections

had homestead association tracts, but the degree of development is not clear. Southwest of the Mission the Sunset and Richmond districts, though platted, are not named.

The Western Addition extended officially from Larkin to Divisadero Streets, north to the bay and south to what is now Duboce Street. It was the city's solidly upper middle class neighborhood until the aftermath of the 1906 earthquake and fire. The dynamiting of Van Ness Avenue, which stopped the fire, left the rest of the Western Addition intact and habitable. Predominantly German, the area also had a significant percentage of the Jewish population.

Pacific Heights and Presidio Heights stretched westward along a high ridge that began its rise at Van Ness Avenue and California Street. Although this high land was technically part of the Western Addition, it gained its own cachet when the city's wealthy began to congregate there. After the 1906 calamity destroyed the precinct of millionaires on Nob Hill, many of its denizens moved westward to these new heights.

1893 MIDWINTER FAIR IN MAPS

Title: Bird's-eye view of Golden Gate Park, San Francisco 1892
Date: 1892
Delineator: H. B. Elliott
Printer: Bosqui Eng.[graving] Co. (San Francisco)
Publisher: A.M. Freeman & Co. (San Francisco)
Colored lithograph, 17 ⅛ x 24 ⅞ inches
San Francisco Public Library
[see following page]

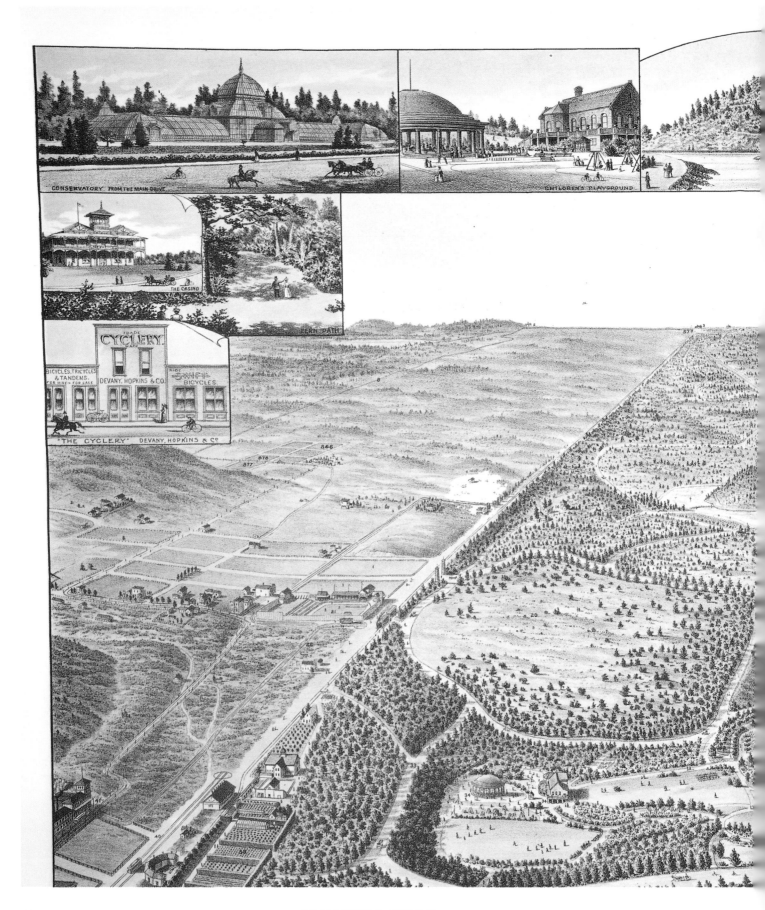

CONSERVATORY FROM THE MAIN DRIVE

CHILDREN'S PLAYGROUND

THE CASINO

FERN PATH

TRADE CYCLERY MARK

BICYCLES, TRICYCLES & TANDEMS. FOR HIRE FOR SALE

DEVANY, HOPKINS & CO.

RIDE SWIFT BICYCLES

"THE CYCLERY" DEVANY, HOPKINS & C°

STRAWBERRY HILL FROM THE LAKE

MUSIC STAND

J. R. DICKEY

This bird's-eye-view of Golden Gate Park dramatizes its length and its topography. Although sand dunes are shown on both sides, the park itself appears verdant with hundreds of trees lining its curving roadways. While the grounds of the 1893 Midwinter Fair are visible on the right hand side of the park, it is not the main focus of the scene. A band of vignettes across the top of the sheet displays the park's major attractions: the Conservatory, the Children's Playground, Stow Lake with Strawberry Hill, the Music stand, J. R. Dickey's building, the Casino, the Fern Path, and Devany, Hopkins & Co.'s Cyclery, which may have commissioned the map.

Title: View of Midwinter Fair in Golden Gate Park San Francisco, Looking Northwest, Showing Property of R. W. Tansill. To be sold at Auction, Thursday November 2nd 1893 at 12 o'clock by Baldwin & Hammon
Date: 1893
Delineator: unknown
Publisher: Baldwin and Hamilton
Colored lithograph
Bancroft Library map collection

The foreground of this bird's-eye view shows the section of Golden Gate Park where the 1893–94 Midwinter Fair was located. Beyond the park R. W. Tansill's lots are shown and further to the northwest we see the Golden Gate and the bay. Across Fulton Street at its intersection with 8th and 10th Avenues are several houses, and in the distance other buildings indicate that although most of it is still bare land, the Richmond district is being developed.

In the margin above the map a telegram from the R. W. Tansill Co.,1st Ave. and 38th St. in New York, begins, "FOR THE MIDWINTER FAIR!" and goes on to state that R. W. Tansill will donate the proceeds of the lot that sells for the highest price to the Midwinter Fair "with our compliments and best wishes for its success." The sale price of the lot and the amount of the gift are not known at this point, but the offer makes it clear that the Midwinter Fair was already having a positive impact on an area. Indeed, by the early 1890s the price of lots on Stanyan Street around the park's eastern edge had quadrupled to more than $100.

Michael H. de Young, owner and publisher of the *Chronicle* newspaper, conceived the exposition, not because a civic celebration was in order, but to provide an antidote to the hard times created by the national depression that began in 1893 and affected San Francisco's economy until 1897. De Young's experience as a commissioner and vice-president of the 1893 Columbian Exposition in Chicago persuaded him that a midwinter fair in San Francisco would be an opportunity to advertise the city's benign climate and scenic attractions. He headed an organizing committee of business and professional leaders that mounted a fund-raising drive. When the campaign raised $361,000, the committee elected de Young head of the fair.

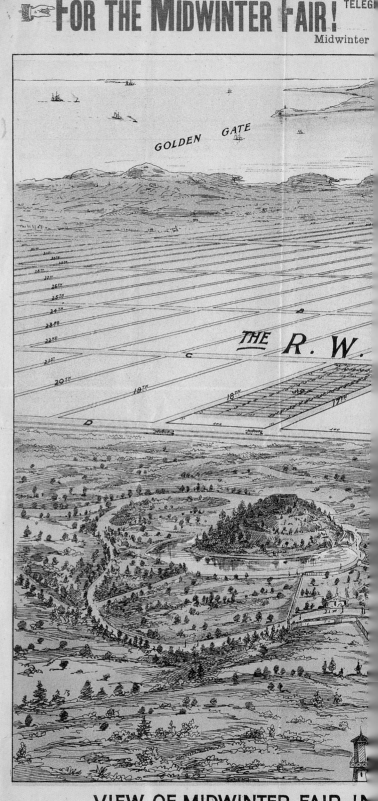

FOR THE MIDWINTER FAIR!
GOLDEN GATE
THE R. W.

VIEW OF MIDWINTER FAIR IN
SHOWING PROPERTY OF R. W. TANSILL, TO

. W. TANSILL CO., Ist Ave. and 38th St., New York:

"New York City, Oct. 17th, 1893.

R. W. TANSILL, Palace Hotel, San Francisco : Donate the entire proceeds of the lot that sells for the highest price to the
our compliments, and best wishes for its success, and charge same to us.   R. W. TANSILL CO."

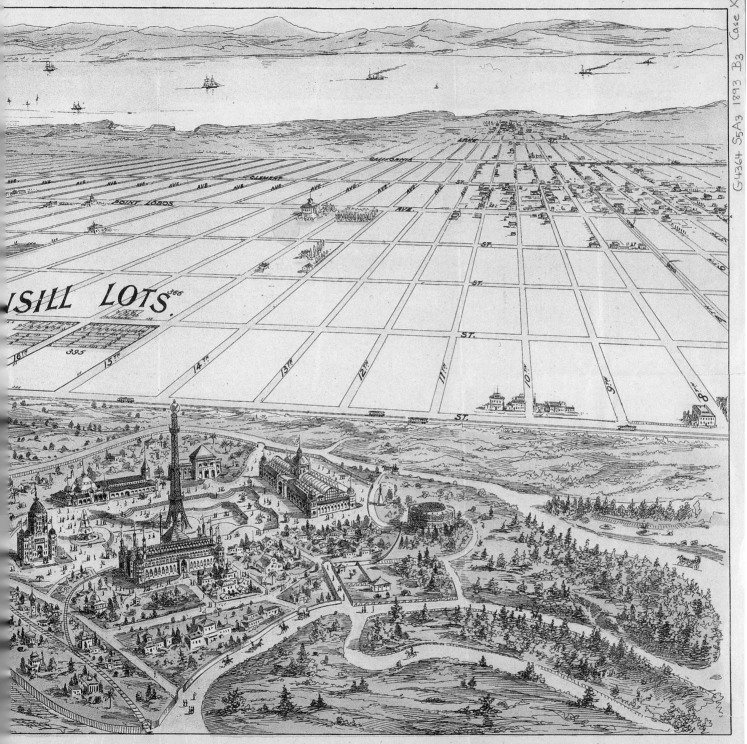

TANSILL LOTS.

DEN GATE PARK SAN FRANCISCO, LOOKING NORTH-WEST.

AT AUCTION, THURSDAY NOV. 2ND 1893 AT 12 O'CLOCK BY BALDWIN & HAMMOND.

The Illustrated D

VOL. I, NO. 2

PUBLISHED BY THE ILLUSTRATED DIRECTORY CO.
12 Flood Building, San Francisco, Cal.
E. S. GLOVER, MANAGER

A MONTHLY MAGAZINE OF AMERICAN CIT

MARKET ST., SAN FRANCISCO, FROM WATER FRONT T

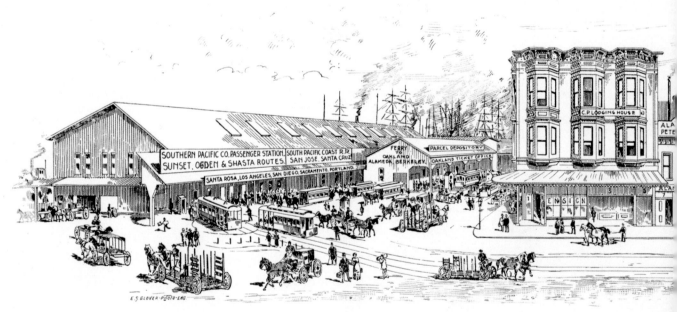

Ferry Bldg   I

S. P. PASSENGER STATION AND FERRY LINES   EAST ST.   MARKET

FERRY PARCEL DEPOSITORY, Ferry B'ldg
    Foster & Orear, Proprietors
    General News Depot, etc.

1 Market Street. ENSIGN SALOON,
    C Schwartz, R. Rusing, A. Mayer, Props.
5. THE C. P. LODGING HOUSE,
    N. B. Thayer, Proprietor

7. "ALAMEDA CAFE," Coffee
    Jacob Pet
7. "ALAMEDA EXCHANGE"
    Peter H

I

ectory;

JAN. 1895

Yearly Subscription, Five Dollars
Single Copies, Fifty Cents
COPYRIGHTED 1894, BY ELI S. GLOVER

ND ST.

9–11   17

SIDE   STEUART ST.

9–11. **L. FOARD**, Ship Chandler and Naval Stores
17. **MARINE DRUG STORE**,
        N. S. Thompson, Druggist

Two hundred acres of Golden Gate Park were dedicated to the fair grounds. But unlike the "White City" created for the Chicago Exposition, the Midwinter Fair's major buildings were designed in an assortment of styles and framed an open space called the Grand Court centered on a weak imitation of the Eiffel Tower in Paris.

By the time the fair ended in July 1894, its attendance had exceeded two million people. The profit of $126,991 financed the conversion of the Fine and Decorative Arts Building (which de Young donated to the city) and the adjacent Royal Bavarian Pavilion into a permanent museum. It opened in 1895 as the Memorial Museum, which commemorated the fair and housed its benefactor's potpourri of artifacts and artworks along with relics of the fair. The Egyptian Revival-style edifice stood until 1926, when it was judged unsafe and demolished. The only other surviving components of the fair were the Grand Court, now the Music Concourse, and the Japanese Tea Garden, which is as popular today as it was during the fair. The roads shown on the map through and around the fairgrounds do not exist today.

In 1924, a city charter amendment officially named a new building designed by Louis Christian Mullgardt and constructed next to the old Memorial Museum the M. H. de Young Memorial Museum. (Mullgardt had designed the famous Tower of Jewels for the 1915 Panama Pacific International Exposition.) In the fall of 2005, a new de Young museum opened. Designed by the Swiss architects, Herzog and de Meuron, the new museum is clad with perforated copper plates that will turn green over time and blend into the park setting unlike the previous museum buildings, which were designed to stand out.

THE ILLUSTRATED DIRECTORY;
A MONTHLY MAGAZINE OF AMERICAN CITIES

Title: Title Page: The Illustrated Directory: a Monthly Magazine of American Cities,
Vol. 1, No. 2, Market St., San Francisco, Page 1. from Water Front to Second St. Page 5. Market St.—North Side—Corner Geary and Kearny Sts.
Date: Jan. 1895
Photo. Engraver: E. S. Glover
Published by the Illustrated Directory Co., 12 Flood Building, E. S. Glover, Manager
Copyrighted 1894 by Eli S. Glover.
Uncolored, 9 7/8 x 13 3/4 inches
David Rumsey Collection

The Illustrated Directory published drawings of the street fronts of every building on the blocks of the downtown area of San Francisco. Almost all of these buildings were destroyed by the 1906 fire. The businesses occupying the buildings are identified, the architectural detail is carefully rendered, and the streets are filled with appropriate activities.

Page 1 of Vol. 1 shows the waterfront buildings on the left: the

Southern Pacific Railroad Company's passenger station and next to it the station for ferries to Oakland, Alameda, and Berkeley. The south side of the next Market Street block from East Street to Steuart Street has a variety of enterprises including a lodging house, a ship chandlery, a candy factory, and a druggist and apothecary. The buildings are identified and their proprietors named in the space below.

Title: The Illustrated Directory, a Monthly Magazine of American Cities,
Vol. 1, No. 2, Market St., San Francisco, Page 5. Market St.—
North Side—Corner Geary and Kearny Sts.
Date: Jan. 1895
Photo. Engraver: E. S. Glover
Published by the Illustrated Directory Co., 12 Flood Building, E. S. Glover, Manager
Copyrighted 1894 by Eli S. Glover.
Uncolored, 9 ⅞ x 13 ¾ inches
David Rumsey Collection

Page 5 of Vol. 1 of the *Illustrated Directory* shows the intersection of Market Street with Geary and Kearny Streets. The 1890 Chronicle Building dominates the scene as it did the city skyline. Designed in the fashionable Romanesque Revival-style, it was the first San Francisco building by the well-known architecture firm Burnham & Root, whose office was in Chicago, home of the skyscraper. The word "elevator" follows the building's name in the directory listing, and is proof of the building's modernity despite its centuries-old style. The neighboring structures do not exceed four stories; their floors were reached the old fashioned way by flights of stairs.

This was not the last building that Daniel H. Burnham would design for San Francisco; the Mills Building followed in 1891. In 1904–1905 Burnham's office would create a sweeping plan for the city just in time for the 1906 earthquake.

It would be difficult to exaggerate the importance of newspapers in San Francisco at the time of this image. The U. S. Census's national survey of the periodical press in 1880 found that San Francisco, the nation's ninth-largest city, had the third-highest circulation rate per capita. San Francisco ranked second nationwide with 21 daily newspapers; New York had 29; and Philadelphia had 24.

Competition among the city's three major newspapers: the *Chronicle* owned by Michael H. de Young, the *Examiner* owned by William Randolph Hearst, and the *Call* owned by Claus Spreckels, was fierce. Under Hearst's direction the *Examiner* had increased its circulation by five times to 50,000 in four years. Ten years later its circulation of nearly 80,000 led the *Chronicle*. It is probable that the *Examiner*'s success motivated the construction of de Young's skyscraper in 1890. Spreckels topped the Chronicle Building with the Call Building on a site diagonally across Market Street in 1904, and Hearst erected his building for the *Examiner* in 1909. (It is the only one still standing unaltered.) For many years this intersection was known as "newspaper corner."

702   700   GEARY ST.   KEAR

MAR

700. **PACIFIC TELEPHONE & TELEGRAPH CO.**
SUNSET TELEPHONE & TELEGRAPH CO.,
Connecting all towns in California with Long Distance Telephones and Metallic Copper Loop Lines.

702. **THOS. MORFFEW, D.D.S.,** 2d Floor, Dentist

702. **DRS. CARVER & LEANER,** 3d Floor, Chiropodists—Pedicure & Manicure Parlors

702. **L. MONACO,** 4th Floor. Photographer

5½ Kearny St. **B. J. BUR**
Successors to Burr &

9 Geary St. **S. W. WOLF,**
Merchant Tailor, Clea

10 Geary St. **LUCAS DE**
A. E. Lucas & Co., Pro
of U. S., Canada and

12 Geary St. **JOHN NOR**
and Valises. Travele
Offices Chronicle Building,
OREIAN B. BURNS,

CHRONICLE BUILDING, ELEVATOR 652   640 638   634 632 630 628   624

—NORTH SIDE — CORNER GEARY AND KEARNY STS.

oor,
Tailors

**MERCHANTS' RETAIL COMMERCIAL
AGENCY,** of Chicago, Ill., Rooms 31 and 32

epairing

MORAGA LAND ASS'N, J. A. Burton, Sec.
The Moraga Rancho. Choice Fruit Lands

NCY,
all parts

FRED. S. WILLIAMS, Steam Power Plants,
Constructing and Mechanical Engineer

Trunks

J. P. McELROY, Room 91
Attorney and Counsellor at Law

Dentist

M. M. HEINEMAN, Rooms 81 to 84
Importer of Diamonds, Watches, Jewelry,
Jewelry Sold on Installments.

634. **THE BOUQUET,** Thos. W. Shaw

638. **EASTON, ELDRIDGE & CO.** Corporation
Real Estate Agents and Auctioneers
House and Insurance Brokers

638. **NORTHERN PACIFIC R. R.,**
T. K. Stateler, General Agent
The Only All-Rail Line to Yellowstone Park

540. **T. ELLSWORTH,** General Agent of the
Preferred Accident Insurance Co., and
Manager of Hartford Life and Annuity Ins. Co·

628. **CHICAGO & ALTON R. R.**
Union Overland Ticket Office
Frank G. High, General Passenger Agent

628. **J. W. WRIGHT,** Loans
Real Estate and Financial Agent

630. **MORRIS & MERSHON,** Real Estate and Ins.
Agts. Palo Alto Property at Stanford University

632. **MERCHANT'S PUBLISHING CO.**
Pacific Coast Business Directory

632. **T. P. RIORDAN,**
Real Estate Agent and Insurance Broker

5

103

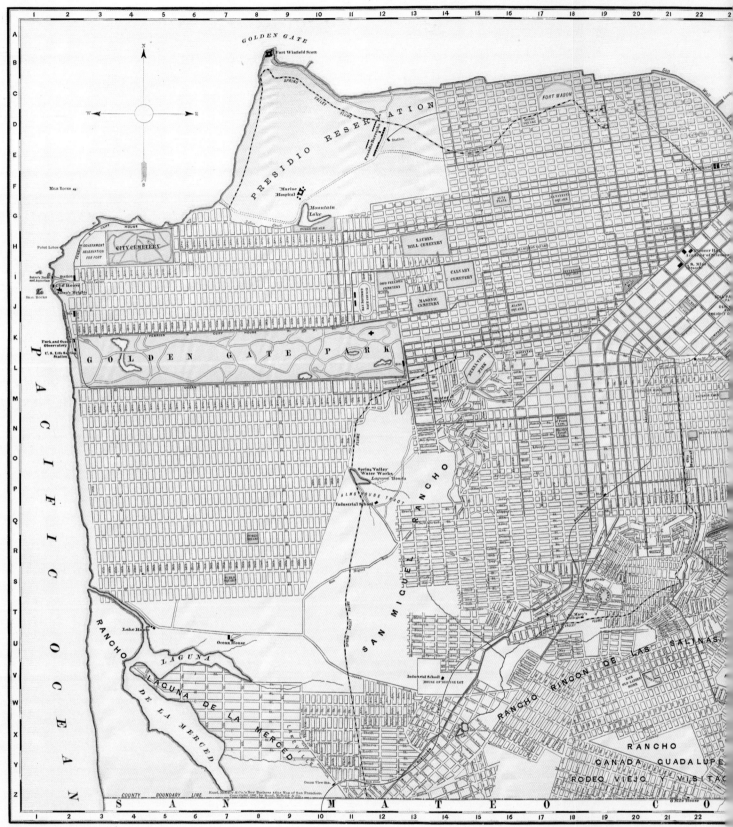

MAP OF SAN FRANCISCO AND VICINITY.
Scale of Statute Miles.
Scale of Kilometres.

RAND, MCNALLY & COMPANY'S MAP OF SAN FRANCISCO

Title: Rand, McNally & Company's Indexed Atlas of the World,
Map of San Francisco
Date issued: 1897
Publishers: Rand, McNally & Co.
Colored map, 10 ¼ x 14 ⅙ inches
David Rumsey Collection

Rand McNally & Company's map of San Francisco appeared in their *Indexed Atlas of the World* that they advertised as "containing large scale maps of every country and civil division upon the face of the globe, together with historical, descriptive, and statistical matter relative to each." The atlas was engraved, printed and published by Rand, McNally & Co., Chicago and New York.

This was the high point of Rand McNally's nineteenth-century atlases. The map's uniform pink coloring may have been used to complement the pale green of the public parks and other open spaces. With the exception of some undeveloped former colonial ranches the city has been platted. However, the lack of topographical information nullifies the impact of the now famous hills on the city's character.

The network of red colored streetcar lines ties the city together in ways that explain how the neighborhoods noted in the1890 guide map (pp. 92-93), published for Langley's San Francisco Directory, were identified.[1] Most of the lines followed the grid of streets in the northeastern part of the city where the population was concentrated. Land use had intensified around the central business district in the 1880s with buildings of two and three stories of flats and apartment houses constructed in response to increasing demand for downtown housing.

In 1883, Leland Stanford began to convert the Market Street Railroad Company's lines to a cable system that made travel away from the central business district faster and encouraged families to move out to the suburbs. The lines radiated from the ferry slips and the Southern Pacific Railroad's main depot at 3rd and Townsend Streets. The main line out from Market Street to 28th and Valencia Streets contributed to the growth of the outer Mission district; the branch lines on Haight and McAllister Streets promoted growth in the Western Addition and around the eastern end of Golden Gate Park. Cable car lines on Geary, California, and Sacramento Streets also encouraged development of the Western Addition. The Omnibus Company and the City Railroad Company took riders deep into the North-of-Market area, and the Central and Sutter Street lines served Russian Hill, the Western Addition, and Pacific Heights.

RAND, McNALLY & CO'S
INDEXED
ATLAS OF THE WORLD
MAP OF
SAN FRANCISCO
SCALES.
Statute Miles, 69.16 = 1 Degree.
Kilometres, 111.307 = 1 Degree.
Rand, McNally & Co., Engravers, Chicago.

EXPLANATION:
Street Car Lines

---

1. The city also had cable car lines, which first ran on Clay Street from Kearny to Leavenworth Street in 1873. Andrew S. Hallidie had invented this transportation form to enable traversing the city's steep hills. Nob Hill was conquered first because it had become fashionable, but many other lines were soon in operation. The cars were moved by gripping a motorized endless cable sunk in a slot below the street level and between the car tracks. The device that gripped the cable was operated by the car's motorman.

The Map of San Francisco and Vicinity set in upper right corner of the Rand McNally map sheet shows the network of railways dominated by the Southern Pacific that now ties the nine counties of the Bay Area's metropolitan region together. The inset map also presents the region's topography in a meaningful way.

The map shown here was included in the *Indexed Atlas of the World*, a series published in two- and four-volume editions from 1894 to 1908. These atlases were very popular and appeared in enlarged folio formats.

A CHART MAP IN FATHOMS AND FEET

Title: San Francisco Entrance, California
Date issued: 1905
Publisher: U. S. Coast and Geodetic Survey, published in Washington, D. C.
Chart map colored in sepia tones, 33 ½ x 41 ⅓ inches
David Rumsey Collection

A chart map with soundings in fathoms and feet. Areas of forbidden anchorage in the bay are indicated by bands of darker tone. Topographic relief is shown in contours and spot heights. The legend states that additions to the topography have come from other sources along with corrections taken from surveys by the Corps of Engineers. The triangulation was taken in 1852 and 1899; the topography in 1851 and 1901; and the hydrography from 1853 and 1901.

The cities around the bay are shown platted, and in the case of San Francisco, dark tones reveal the degree of development. The East Bay cities of Richmond, Berkeley, Oakland, and Alameda appear completely platted. Although Richmond and Berkeley had not attracted a large population, Oakland had been a bedroom community for San Francisco since the 1850s when the trans-bay ferries began to operate. Affordable housing in a rural setting attracted those who could not pay San Francisco's exorbitant rents.

The Key Route Mole extends into the bay from the foot of 40th Street to a pier and ferry slip near Yerba Buena Island. It was an interurban system of electric trains in the East Bay that real estate magnates Francis M. Smith and Frank C. Havens acquired in 1893. By 1901 they controlled about 75 miles of track, and in 1903 connected their lines to San Francisco with ferry service. The Key Route Mole shown on this map extended into the bay from the foot of 40th Street to a pier and ferry slip not far from Yerba Buena Island, then called Goat Island.

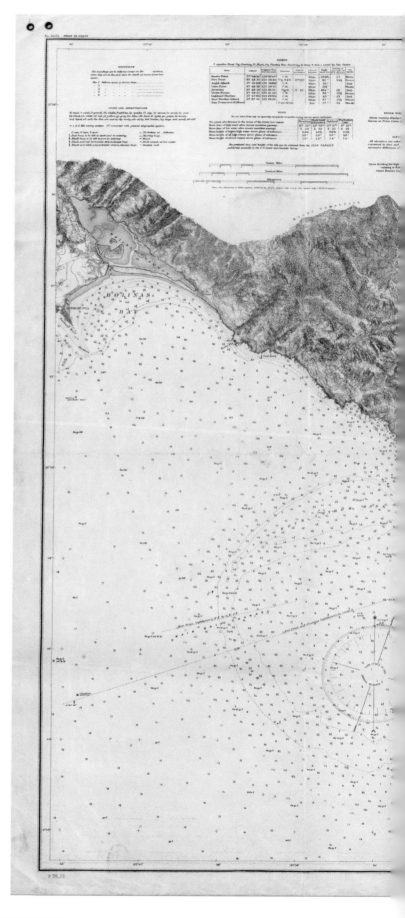

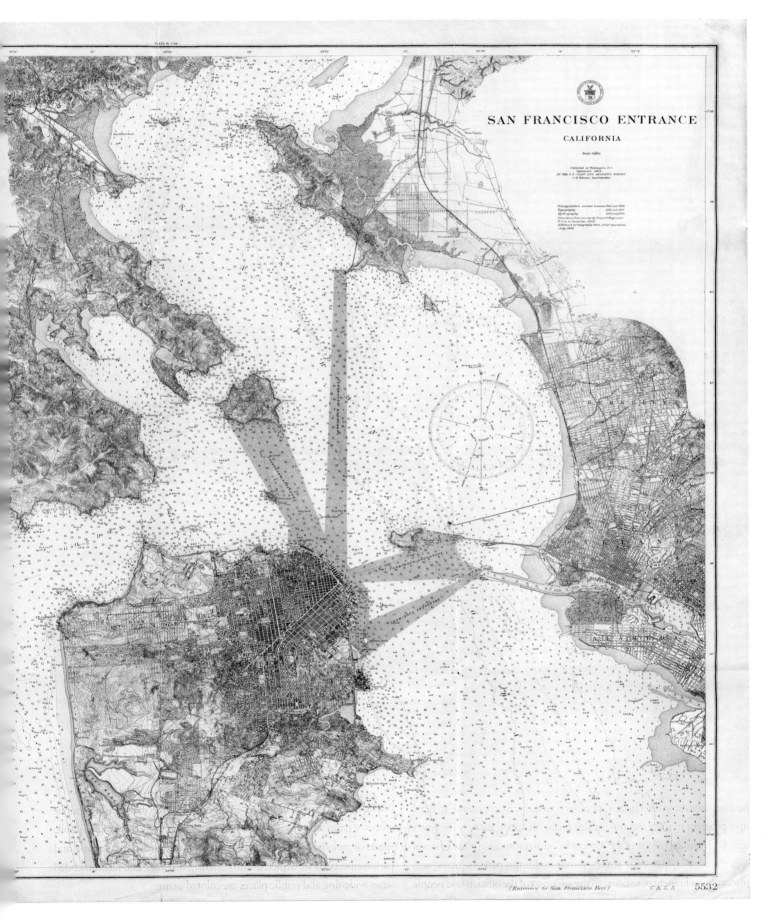

SAN FRANCISCO ENTRANCE

CALIFORNIA

Scale 1:40000

Published at Washington, D.C.
September, 1903.
BY THE U.S COAST AND GEODETIC SURVEY
O. H. Tittmann, Superintendent.

Triangulation executed between 1851 and 1899.
Topography   "   1852 and 1901.
Hydrography   "   1853 and 1901.
Corrections from survey by Corps of Engineers
U.S.A. to November, 1902.
Additions to topography from other documents
July, 1903.

(Entrance to San Francisco Bay)

C & G S   5532

107

BEFORE THE QUAKE: PLANNING FOR BEAUTFICATION

THE BURNHAM PLAN FOR SAN FRANCISCO, 1904–05

Recovery from the depression years of the 1890s offered a bright future for San Francisco at the beginning of the twentieth century. This was certainly the case in real estate where sales in 1902 and 1903 more than doubled those in 1900. Luxury hotels such as the St. Francis on Union Square and the Fairmont on Nob Hill were under construction, and new office buildings were publicized. For example, the Flood Building on Market at Powell Street was reported to have 600 offices. The people who would rent them filled the city's many new apartment buildings as soon as they were finished.

The brightest future prospect was the completion of the Panama Canal, slated for 1915. Leading citizens who embraced the idea that San Francisco should hold an international exposition to celebrate the canal's completion met on January 15, 1904 and formed the Association for Improvement and Adornment of San Francisco. They elected the former mayor, James Duval Phelan, president of the association. Improvement referred to such things as securing a bountiful water supply for the city from the Sierra, as well as addressing street and sidewalk problems. Problems with the latter adversely affected the city's image. For example, along lower Market Street (the location of many of the city's important enterprises), the sidewalks were four feet above the street in some places and well below the curb in others. The city's cultural institutions had also been slighted in the boom times; a new opera house and a public auditorium among other civic buildings were needed to show San Francisco as a place of refinement.

Urban design was uppermost in the minds of Phelan and his colleagues in the association. Priorities included lining major streets such as Van Ness Avenue with trees and extending the panhandle of Golden Gate Park to the intersection of Van Ness and Market Street where a proper civic center would be located.

Phelan also felt that this agenda required a plan prepared by someone with experience in such undertakings. Through his consultations with Willis Polk, the local architect who was Daniel H. Burnham's west coast representative, Phelan had approached the Chicago architect about a plan for San Francisco. It was not Burnham's previous local work designing the Chronicle and the Mills Buildings that attracted Phelan's attention; it was the grand plan he had prepared in 1901 for Washington, D. C. Burnham's positive response led to Phelan's appointing an executive committee to draw up a program to meet the association's goals. An appeal for new members stated: "The main objects of the Association are to promote in every practical way the beautifying of the streets, public buildings, parks, squares, and places of San Francisco; to bring to the attention of the officials and people

of the city the best methods for instituting artistic municipal betterments … in short, to make San Francisco a more agreeable city in which to live."

In April 1904 the Association prepared a formal invitation to Burnham to draft a plan for the city, and on May 4, Burnham arrived from Chicago to attend a dinner in his honor at the St. Francis Hotel. At the conclusion of an eloquent speech about the possibilities for the city's enhancement, the Association adopted a resolution inviting Burnham to prepare a plan.

Burnham then solicited and received suggestions from over two hundred representatives of civic groups, who attended a conference on improvements to the city held two nights later at the Palace Hotel. But a commitment made to President Theodore Roosevelt's Secretary of War, William Howard Taft, to prepare plans for Manila and Baguio, the summer capitol of the Philippines, postponed Burnham's return to San Francisco to begin work on the plan until September 22. When he did return, he brought with him his young associate, Edward Bennett, whose role in designing the plan was bigger than Burnham's.

To satisfy Burnham's desire for a vantage point high above the city from which to formulate the plan, Willis Polk designed a small wooden studio he called "the shanty" for a spur of Twin Peaks. On September 27, 1905, the completed Burnham Plan was presented to the board of supervisors. In the report that accompanied his plan, Burnham defended his grand plan, noting that it would yield large results even if it were never fully realized.

Title: Map of the City and County of San Francisco showing Areas Recommended as Necessary for Public Places, Parks, Park Connections, and Highways. Report of D. H. Burnham, Sept. 1905
Date published: 1905
Publication Author: D. H. Burnham; Edward Bennett
Publisher: City of San Francisco
Engraver: Edward O'Day
Colored map, 17 ⁷⁄₁₀ x 21 ¼ inches
David Rumsey Collection

The title block in the upper right corner states that the map shows areas recommended as necessary for public places, parks, park connections, and highways. The colors used to designate the existing and recommended public spaces, parks, and streets are listed below the title. Existing public spaces or parks are indicated with a light gray tone, and existing semi-public spaces or parks have light diagonal lines. Areas recommended for parks and park connections are depicted with dark diagonal lines, and recommended street widening and public places are colored orange.

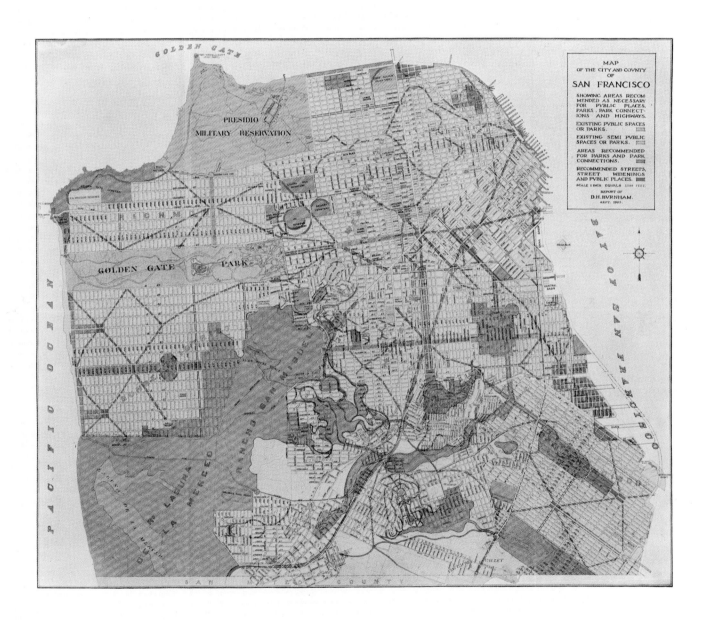

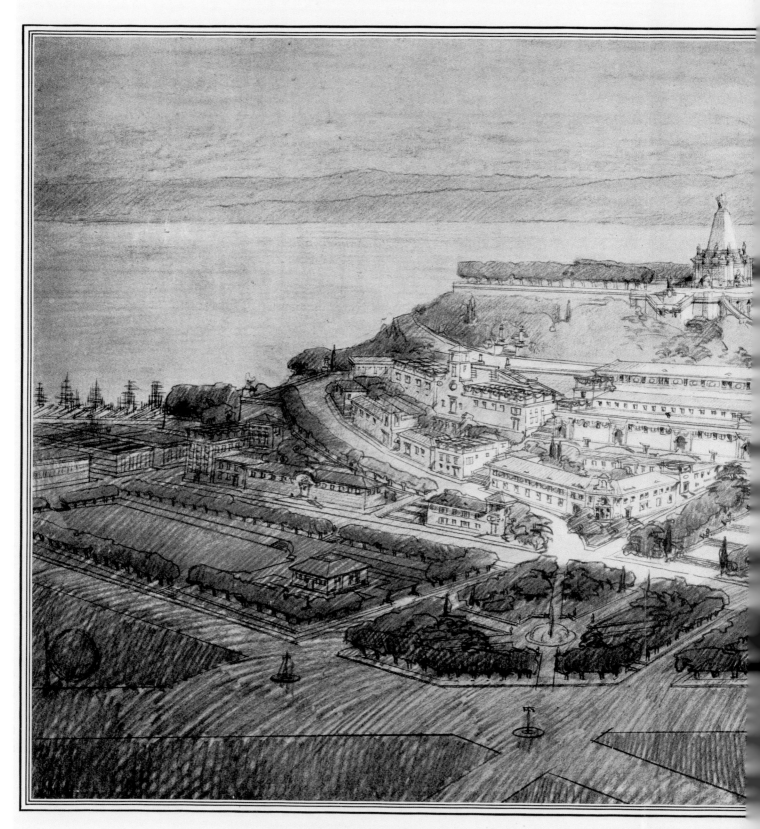

TELEGRAPH HILL, LOOKING EAST, SHOWING SUGGESTED ARCHIT

Burnham's admiration for Paris is reflected in his plan for San Francisco with its system of parks and boulevards radiating from traffic circles. The panhandle of Golden Gate Park is shown cutting through the South-of-Market district to the Pacific Mail Steamship company's docks on the bay at 2nd and King Streets. At its intersection with Van Ness Avenue and Market Street, a spacious traffic circle—a *rond point* similar to the Place de la Concorde—would be the location of the civic center. Diagonal streets radiating from nodes occur in other parts of the city, particularly in areas where the land was level.

The city's lack of recreational space inspired the addition of tracts of land to the park system that were inappropriate for private use because of steep grades and difficulty of access. A park several times larger than Golden Gate Park included Twin Peaks, the Rancho San Miguel, and the oceanside Rancho Laguna de la Merced. Located on the city's outskirts, it was to San Francisco what the Bois de Boulogne was to Paris. The working class districts of Bernal and Potrero Heights would have parks connected by greenways. A bay shore park following the meander of Islais Creek perhaps recalled Rock Creek Park in Washington, D. C., for which Burnham had completed a plan prior to the one for San Francisco.

Burnham and Bennett valued the hills and devoted a section of the report to their treatment. The bases of the hills were to have circuit roads that followed the contours of their slopes. Points of interest would be enhanced with terraces oriented toward views. Most hilltops were to be left in a natural state according to their character with trees planted on their slopes. However, the Twin Peaks were to be leveled to make room for a large plaza with a huge statue personifying San Francisco.

Title: Telegraph Hill, Looking East, from the Report of D. H. Burnham on the Improvement and Adornment of San Francisco
Date published: September 27, 1905
Delineator: Edward Bennett team
Publisher: City of San Francisco
Date distributed: August 1906
Uncolored pencil drawing, 8 ¼ x 12 ²/₁₀ inches
David Rumsey Collection

The suggested architectural treatment for Telegraph Hill shows the hill decapitated and crowned with a neo-classical monument. Allées of shaped trees frame a walled terrace, and a grand branching stair descends to a lower terrace on the hill's south side. Another terraced stair descends to the base of the hill at Washington Square. Monumental buildings line the streets that ascend the hill following its contours. While it is true that the hill introduces the city in an important way, the changes required to make this visionary prospectus real boggle the mind. It is doubtful that the "treatment" was ever taken seriously.

L TREATMENT

Title: View of Civic Center, looking from the south side of
Market Street, from the Report of D. H. Burnham on the
Improvement and Adornment of San Francisco
Date published: September 27, 1905
Delineator: Edward Bennett team
Publisher: City of San Francisco
Date distributed: August 1906
Uncolored pencil drawing, 8 ⅔ x 10 ¼ inches
David Rumsey Collection

VIEW OF CIV

TER, LOOKING FROM THE SOUTH SIDE OF MARKET STREET

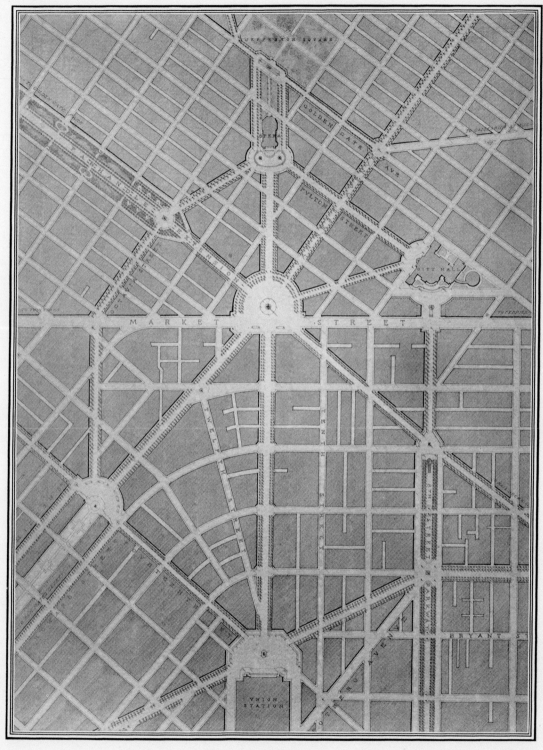

PLAN OF CIVIC CENTER

Title: Plan of the Civic Center, from the Report of D. H.
Burnham on the Improvement and Adornment of San Francisco
Date published: September 27, 1905
Delineator: Edward Bennett team
Publisher: City of San Francisco
Date distributed: August 1906
Uncolored pencil drawing, 11 x 8 ¼ inches
David Rumsey Collection

On the other hand, the proposals for the Civic Center deserved more serious consideration. The bird's-eye view drawing of its plan clearly show how the existing street grid would be altered to accommodate the proposed extension of the panhandle and the other radiating streets shown framing City Hall.

The immense place with its obelisk in the center recalls the Place de la Concorde in Paris. Market Street crosses its south side. A new avenue leads from Market Street straight to a proposed Union Station. North of Market, Fulton Street leads from a public square near the opera house to the City Hall sited across Market at the intersection with 8th Street. Many other existing streets are threaded through this spider web of landscaped arterials.

As in the case of the proposed treatment of Telegraph Hill, the adoption of the Civic Center plan was unlikely because of the costly disruption of streets and the necessary condemnation of private property.

Implementation of the plan was vague. Burnham recommended a city charter amendment to establish an art commission to take control of civic art matters. Doubtless he thought the association would continue to influence city policy and advocate funding. Estimation of the cost of the plan was about $50 million, but Burnham suggested that it would pay for itself through trade brought about by the modernization of transportation and port facilities and by the increased tourism that the beautiful city would encourage.

Following the presentation of the plan at the St. Francis Hotel, the board of supervisors ordered Burnham's report printed as a municipal document, including photographs of the city and reproductions of the maps, perspective drawings, and plans executed by Edward Bennett and his team of artists and draftsmen. In mid-April 1906, bound copies were delivered to City Hall and an exhibition of originals of the drawings and plans was installed there. A few copies of the report were released to members of the association. The rest were buried at 5:13 in the morning of April 18 when an earthquake with a magnitude of 7.9 toppled the dome and most of the roof of City Hall.

THE RISE OF THE PHOENIX: POST-1906-EARTHQUAKE SAN FRANCISCO

AFTER THE QUAKE

Title: Map of the Fire Area
Date published: c.1906
Publisher: R. J. Waters and Co., San Francisco
Printed linear map with the fire area colored in red,
variable measurements
U. C. Berkeley Earth Sciences Map Library

A charred wasteland of 512 blocks, more than four-square miles, marked the area destroyed by the earthquake and fire. The skeletal remains of buildings—some of them steel-framed and structurally sound—were what was left of the oldest part of the city. Van Ness Avenue, the western edge of the fire area had been dynamited to create a firebreak, and scores of refugees occupied tents in the public squares of Pacific Heights. More than 3,000 people were dead, and 225,000 people—over half the population—were homeless. The Southern Pacific Railroad evacuated a great number of them from the city free of charge. Some never returned.

The city's business leaders responded heroically to the challenge of restoration. Although James Phelan and others who had joined him in the Association for Improvement and Adornment of San Francisco contributed generously to the post-earthquake recovery, William H. Crocker is credited as having led the recovery effort by personally securing millions of dollars in loans through his contacts in the U.S. and abroad.

Despite the devastating economic effects of the catastrophe, new opportunities soon arose for profitable investment. Fillmore Street, for example, changed from a modest commercial artery into the city's principal business thoroughfare. An undamaged streetcar line that connected the street to the Mission district was its main advantage. But the vacant lots that could be rapidly built up with stores, restaurants, saloons, and hotels were soon sold. The adjacent Western Addition, a middle- to upper-middle-class residential neighborhood, was transformed into to a dense mixed-use district with many property owners living over the stores they had created by raising their houses up a story.

Van Ness Avenue, formerly lined with mansions that were destroyed when the boulevard was dynamited, became a fashionable shopping street and replaced Market Street as the setting for weekend promenades.

Underpopulated areas such as the outer Mission and the Richmond district attracted developers who built houses in new tracts, which, unlike the South-of-Market and North Beach areas, had private front yards. On the other hand, the housing demand permitted the rebuilding

of cheap boarding houses and tenements that city reformers had hoped to do away with through better building codes.

The high hopes of the sponsors of the Burnham Plan soon faded. The citizenry opposed any imposition of codes that might delay reconstruction. Burnham was urged to come to San Francisco immediately to defend his work. Dignitaries such as Benjamin Ide Wheeler, president of the University of California, endorsed his vision prior to Burnham's arrival. Wheeler expressed enthusiasm for contouring the hills, saying that he would like to see Nob Hill turned into a park with its glorious view preserved for the people.

However, at the first full meeting of the Committee for Reconstruction on May 3, 1906, Mayor Eugene Schmitz was not sanguine about the future of the plan. He said that the city was less able to implement the plan after the fire than it had been before. He believed that Burnham's recommendations would increase the expense of reconstruction beyond justification, and while street improvements and new public buildings were necessary, he thought utility should be the order of the day.

Burnham arrived in San Francisco and met tirelessly with subcommittees, particularly those charged with studying the widening, extending, and grading of streets, restoring pavements and creating parks, reservoirs, and boulevards. After lengthy deliberations the committees' reports recommended the immediate execution of some of the recommendations and the postponement of others for five to ten years. Widening some streets and creating new diagonal routes were deemed immediate improvements. Nob and Russian Hills, which had been burned over, were to be encircled with contour streets. Deferred improvements included the widening of streets such as Columbus Avenue and Geary, Pacific, Powell, and Pine Streets, and the extension of the Golden Gate Park panhandle to the waterfront.

The board of supervisors approved the subcommittees' report on May 21 to the delight of Burnham and the reformers. But M. H. de Young, publisher of the *Chronicle* led an attack on the Committee of Forty, saying that what the city needed was business, not parks and boulevards. The *San Francisco Bulletin* joined in on May 24, reporting violent opposition from some of the landowners to the proposed street widenings. As the uproar continued the issues became entangled with investigations of corruption that resulted in the indictment in November of Mayor Eugene Schmitz and his powerful henchman, "Boss" Abe Ruef.

In spite of the political maelstrom that engulfed the city leaders, reconstruction proceeded at a rapid pace—but not in accordance with the Burnham Plan. The central business district was rebuilt in the same location, which was, in fact, the best possible in respect to relations with other

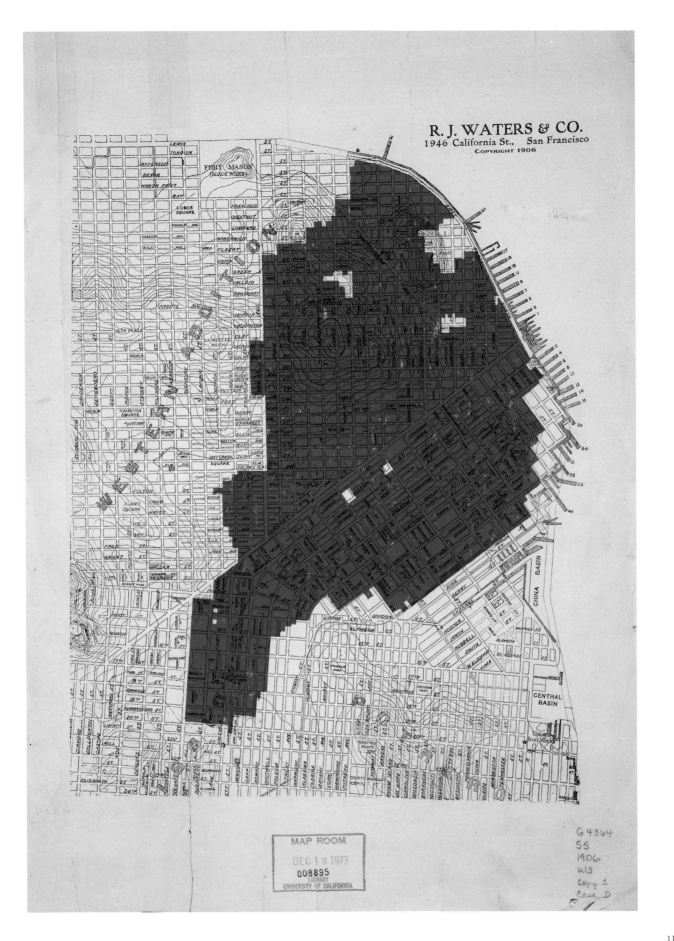

R. J. WATERS & CO.
1946 California St.,   San Francisco
COPYRIGHT 1906

117

important bay area cities. Major buildings not damaged structurally were under reconstruction, and within three months 18 of them, including the St. Francis and Fairmont Hotels, the Merchants' Exchange, and the office buildings named for millionaires William Crocker, Claus Spreckels, James Flood, and Darius O. Mills, were partially occupied. Work on other office buildings continued.

While wholesale businesses moved from the waterfront area north of Market Street to locations near the railroad yards at 4th and Townsend Streets, other enterprises stayed where they were. Chinatown was rebuilt with larger, more substantial structures along Grant Avenue. The southern slope of Nob Hill was densely rebuilt with apartment houses. Within three years 20,500 buildings were completed, and 40,000 workers in the building trades had been hired, more than double the number employed before the fire.

The Burnham Plan seemed destined to vanish without a trace; important civic needs it included remained unaddressed in the reconstruction thus far. The most important was a new City Hall. The wreckage of the jerry-built pile that crumbled in 1906 had been cleared away except for one wing, which served the city treasurer, the auditor, and the registrar of voters.

In April 1909, the board of supervisors decided to take up the matter of a new city hall and consulted none other than Daniel H. Burnham. On April 14, 1909, Burnham was once again in San Francisco, proposing to city officials the creation of a civic center at the intersection of Van Ness Avenue and Market Street. Burnham argued that, unlike the site formerly slated for the city hall at the intersection of Larkin and McAllister Streets, the new site would accommodate a courthouse, state and federal buildings, a library, and an auditorium in addition to the city hall. The Golden Gate Park panhandle could be extended to the civic center, initiating the reorganization of the city's circulation system advocated in the 1905 plan.

The board of supervisors approved a civic center bond issue of $8,480,000 for the land and the city hall. Residents in various parts of the city successfully lobbied the supervisors to add other measures to the ballot. These included funds for a polytechnic high school, a detention home,

parks on Telegraph Hill, in the Potrero, Bayview, and Glen Park districts as well as an aquatic park for the north waterfront and three playgrounds in the southern part of the city. Ironically, the parks and playgrounds were now advocated by the conservative taxpayers who had rejected Burnham's 1905 plan. The chorus of approval for the civic center bond issue was disrupted by M. H. de Young, who mounted the same fiery opposition to it that he had to the 1905 plan, insisting that its extravagance would endanger the city's economy. As it turned out, the only bonds the voters approved were those for the polytechnic high school. Only one-third of the registered voters came out to vote, an indication of the lack of interest in city planning despite the attention Burnham's efforts had received in 1905 and again in 1909 for his revised plan.

Still, Burnham's return to planning the city was one of many signs that the idea of hosting an international exposition to create permanent improvements had surfaced again. Yet, the motivation in 1909 did not spring from a climate of confidence as in 1904, but rather from the ongoing necessity for economic recovery from the 1906 disaster.

The Burnham Plan had failed to win public approval in 1905 mainly because it was deemed impractical. Patrick Calhoun, President of the United Railroads, opined that Burnham's urban transportation system would not be possible to operate. Property owners voted down the legislation needed to enact the street widening proposals. Finally, the so-called graft trials that followed the indictments of Abe Ruef and Mayor Schmitz ended consideration of the plan.

THE PANAMA PACIFIC INTERNATIONAL EXPOSITION

In contrast to 1905, comprehensive design did not arouse opposition when its use was proposed for the Panama Pacific International Exposition (PPIE) doubtless because the PPIE was a temporary installation of an artificial city dedicated to commerce.

To test the potential appeal of the exposition, the city planned a festival honoring the Spanish explorer, Don Gaspar de Portolá, from October 19–23, 1909. The five days of revelry in the streets were really about celebrating the city's phoenixlike rise from the ashes. The nearly 500,000 visitors it attracted convinced the festival sponsors that a worldwide attraction would be beneficial. The anticipated completion of the Panama Canal in 1915 seemed certain to make San Francisco the center of Pacific Ocean trade. The board of directors that took charge of planning for the PPIE was not a continuation of the board of the Association for the Adornment and Improvement of San Francisco. The PPIE board's president, Charles Moore, was the head of the Chamber of Commerce; civic-minded reformers such as James D. Phelan and Rudolph Spreckels were notably absent.

While San Francisco debated plans for the exposition, San Diego promoted its plan to hold a 1915 Panama Exposition. By 1910, the two cities were competing for the necessary Congressional approval of the exposition site. They were not alone. New Orleans argued that its location near the country's center was more appropriate for an international exposition than that of a western outpost. Moreover, proximity to South America and Europe insured a huge attendance. San Francisco countered this argument by claiming that, as the gateway to the Orient, it would attract twice as many people as New Orleans. Funds poured into the campaign to lobby the congress for approval of its site, and in January 1911 the lobbying was rewarded when congressional approval came for San Francisco to host the exposition. On January 31, its citizens celebrated the first day of Carnival Week.

Choosing a site in the city for the exposition was the next task for the exposition's directors. Although virtually the whole city was considered, strong support soon emerged for three proposed locations. William B, Bourne, president of the Spring Valley Water Company, suggested the first one: 1,300 acres on the western side of the city next to the water company's land at Lake Merced. The argument in favor of the proposal focused on its potential for permanent improvement in the city's transportation system through the construction of a tunnel under Twin Peaks that would provide a convenient route to the exposition. The long-term result would be the development of the western part of the city. Since most of the wealth generated by Bourne's proposal would accrue to his corporation, his fellow board members rejected it right away.

M. H. de Young envisioned the exposition as the successor to the 1893–94 Midwinter Fair he had organized in Golden Gate Park. The 1915 exposition would have a 562-acre site in the western part of the park beyond 20th Avenue, 150 acres of Lincoln Park's oceanfront, and 200 acres dedicated to a grand boulevard connecting the two sites. The park would inherit the permanent exposition buildings devoted to art, manufacturing, and horticulture, along with any others that might be useful. The rest of the park would be made into gardens with statuary, fountains, and promenades.

Meanwhile a plan that combined elements of all the sites followed the waterfront to North Beach, Harbor View, the Presidio, Lincoln Park, and Golden Gate Park. This composite plan entailed so many permanent improvements and was so inclusive that it was soon viewed as having the same impracticality that had defeated the Burnham Plan, which it recalled. Finally, in 1912, a site of 635 acres that combined Harbor View with part of the Presidio, was selected. Over 100 acres of marshy submerged land within the Presidio reservation was filled so that by February 1913 a two-and-a-half-mile stretch of land on the northern waterfront was ready for building operations. The site comprised 287 acres of the Presidio, 330 acres of Harbor View, and 18 acres of Fort Mason.

In addition to mounting an advertising campaign designed to counter the bad news of the previous years, the Board of Directors' publicity department—named with remarkable candor the Office of Exploitation—vowed to take its message, *Come to California!*, everywhere that publicity could go.

For its part the Southern Pacific Railroad company designated March 1, 1911, as California Invitation Day and distributed four million post cards on that day with the request that receivers send them to friends in the East. The cards listed bargain train fares for those traveling to the exposition and announced that, "California wants people like you." When the cards vanished almost immediately, four million more were ordered, depleting the west coast's supply of cardboard. For its part, the state carried out a program of waterfront improvements that included the present line of piers on the Embarcadero.

The exposition board also surveyed the overall state of San Francisco's industry to prepare for meetings with important capitalists who might be persuaded to open a branch office or even to move their headquarters to the city. So convinced were the directors by their own propaganda that even the approaching world war could not move them to cancel the exposition. As it turned out, Germany, France, and Great Britain did not want the exposition canceled either.

Planning for the fair grounds began immediately. Edward Bennett, who had played a major role in preparing Burnham's 1905 plan, designed the site plan; it departed significantly from those of previous world fairs. Instead of ensembles of Neo-Classical buildings grouped around major and minor axes, the eight major exhibition palaces formed one large building that enclosed three inner courts introduced by forecourts. Architects designed the courts instead of separate buildings. The utilitarian structures inside the walls of the courts were designed by the exposition's engineering department to house the exhibitions and were not lavishly appointed, as had been the case in the Chicago and St. Louis expositions.

Title: Map of San Francisco and Bird's-Eye-View of the Panama-Pacific International Exposition Grounds
Date published: 1915
Cartographer: unknown
Publisher: International Harvester Co. of America (Chicago)
Colored map and bird's-eye-view, 15 x 8 ⁹⁄₁₀
U. C. Berkeley Earth Sciences Map Collection

Title: The Grounds of the Panama Pacific International Exposition Grounds
Date: 1915
Delineator: unknown
Publisher: The Tourist Association of Central California (San Francisco)
Uncolored, 13 ¼ x 15 ½
U.C. Berkeley, Earth Sciences Map Collection
[see following pages]

A well-drawn plan of the exposition grounds extending south to Fort Mason and The Zone, and north into the Presidio grounds. The plan may serve as a guide to the following description of the fair.

Three separate buildings devoted to horticulture, machinery, and the festival hall were located outside the system of courtyards. Their designs were not coordinated like those in the inner walled core. The Palace of Fine Arts and the Machinery Palace stood at either end of the major north-south axis. State and national pavilions were located west of the Palace of Fine Arts on the Presidio grounds along with athletic fields, racetracks, and livestock pavilions. The Zone, also called the Joy Zone, filled the area around Fort Mason.

The Tower of Jewels, the fair's centerpiece, introduced the Court of the Universe. The 432-foot-tall tower rose above an entrance arch that was larger than the Arc de Triomphe in Paris. The tower was the masterwork of Louis Christian Mullgardt, known as an architect of houses, which, although distinctive, gave no hints of the sheer exoticism of the tower's design. Encrusted with military trophies, the tower advanced the concept of ornament further through the display of 102,000 glass Novagems made of faceted, colored glass and backed with mirrors. These jewels were attached to wires and hung from the tower so that they constantly turned and sparkled.

Another departure from precedent was the fair's color scheme, created by Jules Guerin, known nationally for the elegant architectural renderings he had made for Daniel Burnham's many plans. Guerin's challenge was to harmonize the colors used by architects, artists, landscape gardeners, and lighting engineers. The colors were chosen to represent the golden tones of the California landscape, which in turn evoked the Golden Gate, named by John C. Fremont for Constantinople's Golden Horn, and also for the gold that had contributed so dramatically to the city's wealth.

To give the lath and plaster buildings a warm tone rather than the cold white of Chicago's fair, the New York designer Paul Denivelle created a fake travertine limestone that was used throughout the walled core of the fair. Guerin supervised the use of the color and even had the sand from Monterey used for the pedestrian paths of the compound toasted to a brown hue.

Still, the fair was not monochromatic. For example, the Palace of Fine Arts, designed by Bernard Maybeck, was described by the exposition historian, Frank Morton Todd, as having pale green peristyle columns, a gallery wall of Pompeian red, and a burnt orange dome with a turquoise-green border.

The most dramatic use of color was in the indirect lighting that also distinguished the fair from its predecessors. William D'Arcy Ryan, director of General Electric's illuminating laboratory in Schenectady, New York, supervised the lighting. Astonishing night-lighting effects were achieved with arc lights set on tall masts that illuminated the building walls and with searchlights on their roofs that raked the sky. A company of marines operated a battery of 48 searchlights called the Scintillator, which, among other effects, was used to create artificial auroras on foggy nights.

Perhaps the most unforgettable display was called "The Burning of the Tower" in which concealed ruby lights in pans behind the colonnades on the different levels created red fire. The huge structure appeared to turn into incandescent metal that seemed about to melt. "Yet it did not melt," wrote Frank Morton Todd, "but stood and burned like some sentient thing doomed to eternal torment."[1]

The fair closed on December 4. The Palace of Fine Arts, the fair's most popular building, was the only thing saved. Although its partisans had mounted a campaign to save it before the fair ended, its preservation probably resulted more from its location on the Presidio grounds, which were not subject to the development pressures of the rest of the site. The Exposition Corporation gave the Marina Green and the Yacht Harbor to the city.

Surprisingly, Maybeck did not join the protest over the destruction of his palace. He made plans—never carried out—to remodel the complex in the contemporary Mission Revival mode and to convert the rotunda into an auditorium. Perhaps he was not motivated to preserve his popular creation because of its celebration of a bygone time that vanished with the approach of war. When both Maybeck and the palace had attained old age, he was asked to suggest a treatment for the nearly ruinous building. His answer was: "I think the main building should be torn down and redwoods planted around—completely around—the rotunda…. As they grow, the columns would slowly crumble at approximately the same speed…. I should like my palace to die behind those great trees of its own accord and become its cemetery."[2]

Although only the Palace survived the clearing of the exposition grounds, developments initiated by the fair enriched other parts of the city. Alma de Bretteville Spreckels reclaimed the August Rodin statues exhibited in the French Pavilion at the fair. She had intended that her husband use the pavilion (a copy of the Palace of the Legion of Honor in Paris) as a model for the museum he would build in San Francisco to house the many works of art they had acquired in France. Adolph died in 1924, the year the California Palace of the Legion of Honor opened in Lincoln Park, not far from the former exposition grounds. The architect, George Applegarth, adhered to the design of the French Pavilion and thus created a copy of a copy.

The most important project related to the PPIE was the Civic Center, which had first been proposed in 1899 to incorporate the recently completed City Hall. After the building's collapse in the 1906 earthquake, a new one was certainly in order, but a bond issue in 1909 that would have funded it failed to win voters' approval.

In 1912, under provisions of the new city charter enacted in 1900, James Rolph became the first mayor elected to a four-year term. In his inaugural address he declared that three important measures deserved immediate attention: a new city hall, a public water system, and improved streetcar transportation. To plan the city hall and supervise its construction, he appointed a board of three consulting architects. John Galen Howard, president of the local chapter of the American Institute of Architects and the supervising architect for the University of California's campus in Berkeley, was head of the board. The other members were Frederick H. Meyer and John Reid, Jr.

A bond issue was put before the city in March 1912, for which Rolph campaigned and won approval. The funds provided for acquiring the land and constructing the city hall. The PPIE Corporation, established in 1906, contributed the funds for a civic auditorium, designed by its consulting architects, Howard, Meyer, and Reid. The auditorium was important because it allowed the board to offer free meeting rooms to visiting commercial associations if they agreed to hold their annual conventions in San Francisco during the exposition.

1. Todd, Frank Morton. The Story of the Exposition. New York: Putnum's Sons, 1921, 2:383
2. Newhall, Ruth Waldo. San Francisco's Enchanted Palace. Berkeley: 1967, 75.

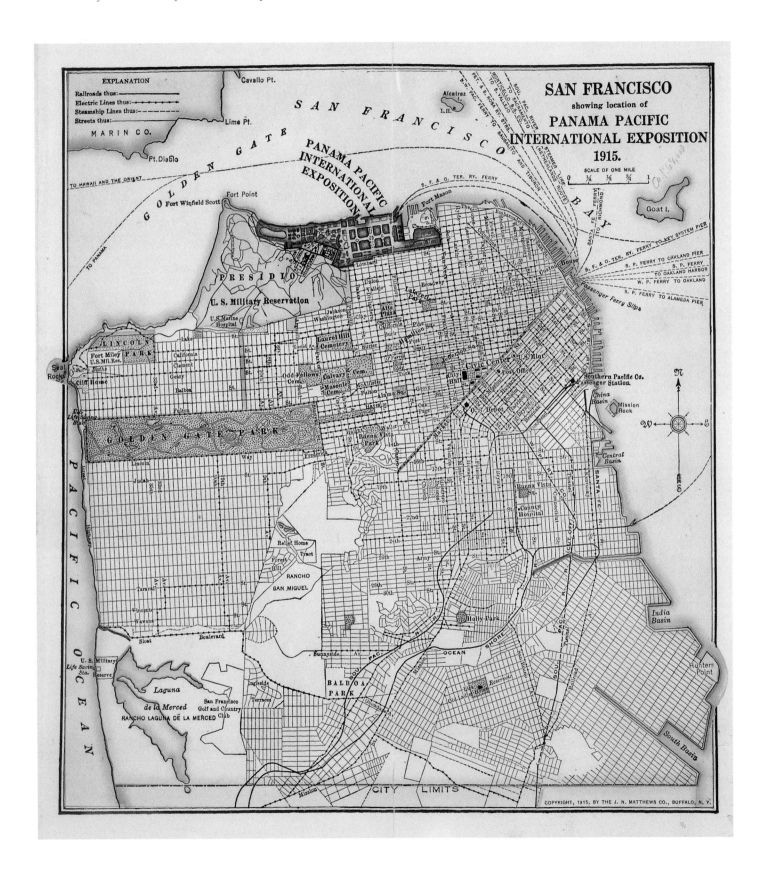

As a vice-president of the PPIE, Rolph seized every opportunity to boost the exposition as a harbinger of great achievements in the city. However, it was the PPIE Corporation, established in 1906, which controlled the planning, construction, and operation of the exposition. The city raised $5 million for the fair, but had no further involvement.

The civic auditorium, which opened in January 1915, was the first civic center building to be completed. Groundbreaking for the City Hall took place in the spring of 1913; it was dedicated late in December of 1915. Rolph presided over both occasions. The new City Hall was designed by Arthur Brown, Jr., and John Bakewell, Jr., whose firm won the competition for it. It did not open officially until after the fair closed in 1915.

The architect George Kelham won the 1915 competition for the Main Public Library, for which Andrew Carnegie gave $750,000. It was dedicated early in 1917. World War I delayed action on other civic center buildings: The opera house, veteran's building, and federal building were not built until the 1930s. They were designed by Bakewell and Brown, with G. Albert Lansburgh associating with Arthur Brown, Jr. on the opera house design.

CITY PLANNING

Burnham had been accused of neglecting commerce and industry in favor of civic art in formulating his 1905 plan. He had defended his emphasis on beautification by saying that if the city were beautiful, people would come there to spend their money no matter where they made it. However, city planning as an integral part of local government was not accepted until the case was made that it was a means of improving municipal economies and saving taxpayers' money.

Burnham's 1905 and 1909 plans advanced the idea of relying on experts to plan the city's development. Increasing interest in formalizing the city's role in the planning process led to the first city plan-enabling act, passed by the state legislature on May 21, 1915. The act did not mandate planning for cities, but it authorized the legislative bodies of municipalities to create advisory, unpaid citizens' commissions that would plan the physical development of the city. The act also authorized the city councils to zone their cities, designating areas for residence, commerce, and industry based on the advice of the city planning commission. In 1917, the legislature approved legislation authorizing cities to enact zoning regulations.

The second measure Mayor Rolph cited in 1912 as deserving immediate attention was a publicly owned water system. In 1905, the city had requested the federal government's permission to dam the Tuolumne River at the head of the Hetch Hetchy Valley in the Sierra in order to supplement the supply of water San Francisco received from the Spring Valley Water Company. This privately owned utility, chartered by the state in 1858, had been delivering water to the city since 1862. The name came from a reservoir located between the

streets of Mason and Taylor and Washington and Broadway, but the main source was the chain of lakes called Crystal Springs Lakes and their surrounding watershed on the peninsula south of San Francisco. Although the purchase of the water system had long been part of the city's agenda, it was not accomplished until 1929. By then it was part of the Hetch Hetchy project because, with President Wilson's signing of the Raker Act in December 1913, San Francisco gained the right to construct the dam. It was completed in 1923, and the system, designed by the city engineer, Michael M. O'Shaughnessy, was in operation in 1934.

In contrast to the water system's slow progress, the extension of the Municipal Railway that Mayor Rolph had championed took place before the end of his first term. The city charter of 1900 included municipal ownership of public utilities. In 1912, the Geary Street line was extended 3.5 miles. The next campaign involved dealing with the monopoly the United Railroads held on Market Street. In 1913, Rolph negotiated an agreement with the United Railroads that allowed the Municipal Railway access to Market Street. Another campaign succeeded in gaining voter support for a huge bond issue to build Municipal Railway lines to serve the PPIE.

Title: The Chevalier Commercial, Pictorial, and Tourist map of San Francisco from latest U. S. Gov. and Official Surveys
Date issued: 1911
Designed, engraved and copyrighted by Aug.[uste] Chevalier, Lithographer and Publisher (San Francisco)
Colored map, 63 x 57 $^1/_{10}$ inches
David Rumsey Collection

A wall map with rollers at both ends, in warm ochre tones with blue-green used for water and green for vegetation. The map extends south of the city/county line to include Sierra Point and San Bruno Mountain. Buildings and natural features are drawn isometrically. New landmarks and points of interest starting from the Golden Gate include Harbor Basin, the future site of the Panama Pacific International Exposition, the U. S. Army Transport Docks at Black Point, and Fisherman's Wharf. The northeast shore bristles with wharves; among them is the Key Route pier that completed the combination rail and ferry line from the East Bay.

The 1903 Ferry Building at the foot of Market Street begins a procession of important buildings that line Market Street from 1st to 7th Streets; Most of them were built after the 1906 earthquake and fire. The U. S. Court of Appeals Building at Mission and 7th Streets was completed in 1905.

The dry docks at Hunters Point are drawn, and Candlestick Park is indicated. Proceeding west to the Pacific Ocean we find Balboa Park with the House of Refuge, and the Oceanview tract. Ocean Avenue and Sloat Boulevard are in place with the Ingleside Race Track between them. The Ocean Shore Railroad to Ingleside is traced.

Sloat Boulevard connects to Dewey Boulevard and to the Great Highway; this route would become Portola Drive. Buildings are drawn in Golden Gate Park and the Odd Fellows Cemetery and crematorium building are shown just outside the park at the beginning of the panhandle. Although the map does not appear radically different from its predecessors, there are indications of developments that will be completed in the years after the PPIE.

Title: Map of City and County of San Francisco showing [the] Location of Wells, to accompany [a] Report on [the] Underground Water Supply of San Francisco
Date issued: May 1913
Cartographer: Produced under [the] Direction of M. M. O'Shaughnessy, city engineer
Colored map, 15 ⅝ x 13 ¼
San Francisco Public Library

Like Mayor Rolph, Michael M. O'Shaughnessy, the city engineer from 1912–1934, was dedicated to the success of public projects such as the municipal railway and securing a water system for the city. This map shows locations of the city's underground water supply, which was conceded to be inadequate. After years of inaction, San Francisco finally purchased the Spring Valley Water Company's properties in 1930.

O'Shaughnessy's vision for the railway took it to parts of the city that had previously been underserved by public transit. These included the areas west of Twin Peaks, the Richmond and Marina districts, and the far reaches of North Beach and the Mission district. For example, from 1912 to 1919, the Geary Street transit line was extended from three to 63 miles of track; the Stockton Street Tunnel was completed in 1914, and the Twin Peaks Tunnel Railway was operating in February 1918.

The 11,750-foot-long Twin Peaks Tunnel allowed development of residential tracts west of the barrier of hills in the city's geographical center. The tracts had been included in the San Miguel Rancho property acquired by Adolph Sutro and sold to developers by his heirs in 1911. Among these subdivisions was the exclusive St. Francis Wood subdivision, opened in 1912 and planned by the Olmsted Brothers. The Mason McDuffie realty company developed St. Francis Wood; the gates and fountains were designed by John Galen Howard. A central boulevard with a landscaped median strip was interrupted midway by a circle with a fountain; the boulevard terminated at the top of the rise in a terrace and another fountain. Tree-lined streets following the land contours and sidewalks separated from them by planting echoed the "Garden-City" model advocated at the time.

Although designed to appeal to those who wanted to escape urban life in the dense inner city neighborhoods, the lots did not sell well before the tunnel's opening. That most of the houses in St. Francis Wood were built in the 1920s was proof of the tunnel's success in promoting development. Many of the new residents were Irish and came from the Mission district. Nearby Forest Hill was planned by Mark Daniels, a

landscape architect, in 1912–13. Like St. Francis Wood it was given a formal entrance (never completed) and a street plan that reflected the hill's contours.

Ingleside Terrace and Westwood Park were two other subdivisions that depended on the tunnel. The first traced the loop of the Ingleside Race Track, in operation from 1885 to 1909. Developer Joseph Leonard acquired 148 acres of the track's property, created the parklike subdivision, and managed the tract until 1924 when it was largely built out. The neighboring Westwood Park, built up from 1917 to 1927, was planned by an engineer John Punnett and mimicked Ingleside Terrace's street plan of concentric loops.

O'Shaughnessy also planned Portola Drive, a scenic route that connected the circle at the St. Francis Wood entrance to the west end of Market Street. The drive followed the old San Miguel Road, built in the 1860s as a toll road to Ocean House and the Ocean Race Track. It was also part of the boulevard system created from 1916 to 1920 that included the Marina Boulevard and El Camino Real, which connected the Presidio with the Great Highway and the Esplanade along Ocean Beach. The system more or less followed Burnham's proposed Outer Drive. Sloat Boulevard, another O'Shaughnessy project, defined the southern boundary of the Sunset District, which extended from the western terminus of Portola Drive to the great Highway.

49 Mile Drive, the designated tourist route around San Francisco, was another result of O'Shaughnessy's vision for a greater San Francisco. Automobile use, which accelerated the growth of the Sunset and Richmond districts, could not be enjoyed as freely in the old areas of the city. Just as the cable car had made the heights overlooking the downtown accessible in the 1870s, the automobile exploited the geography of the "Outside Lands" in the 1920s and 1930s.

Title: Official Map of San Francisco and the San Francisco Bay Metropolitan Area
Date: 1931
Cartographer: unknown
Distributed by the San Francisco Chamber of Commerce
Publisher: W. C. Eubank Co. (San Francisco)
Uncolored map with automobile routes traced in red, variable measurements
U. C. Berkeley Earth Sciences Map Library
[see page 128]

The effect of the post-World War I economic boom in the 1920s was most obvious in San Francisco's downtown district where a strand of new skyscrapers changed the city's skyline. It was the best of times that would become the worst of times when this map was created at the height of the Great Depression. Yet modernism had gained partisans. The automobile was one harbinger of change. Van Ness Avenue, no longer an exclusive residential area, was now lined with palatial showrooms for Pierced Arrows, Cadillacs, and Packards.

In 1921, the San Francisco Motorcar Dealers Association campaigned for bridges across the bay to alleviate the traffic jams caused by motorists waiting to board ferries to other parts of the bay. This map reveals that ten years later automobiles had become as important as transit lines to getting around the city.

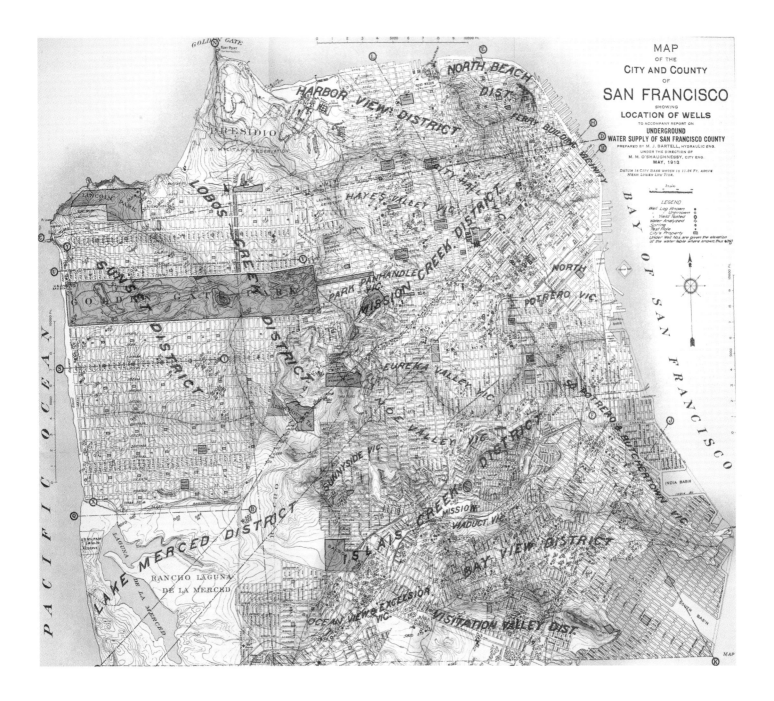

Civic leaders pushed for urban planning as a way to make San Francisco the heart of the regional metropolis taking shape around the bay. James Duval Phelan, now a state senator, joined Frederick Dohrmann, a prominent business leader, in organizing the Regional Plan Association in 1924. Although the association was only active for about three years, it took steps toward a comprehensive plan for the development of the nine San Francisco Bay Counties that would bridge the bay, create a coordinated system of highways and scenic boulevards, unify port and harbor development, connect the bay cities with rapid transit, create recreational areas, and institute regional zoning. Continued prosperity and growth would attend these measures.

No one plan resulted from this ambitious agenda, but in 1926–27 Dohrmann's interest in making San Francisco the Bay Area's center of commercial aviation prompted a proposal that the State Board of Harbor Commissioners be authorized to construct an aviation landing platform one million feet square and 150 to 200 feet above the bay's high water mark on a site on the Embarcadero near the Ferry Building. A two-tiered street extended north and south from the platform along the Embarcadero to handle the traffic that future bay bridges would create. It was a preview of the freeway constructed in the 1950s. The architect, Louis P. Hobart, drew up the concept, and for a while it was publicized. But the San Francisco Board of Supervisors was more

Official Map of San Francisco and the San Francisco Bay Metropolitan Area

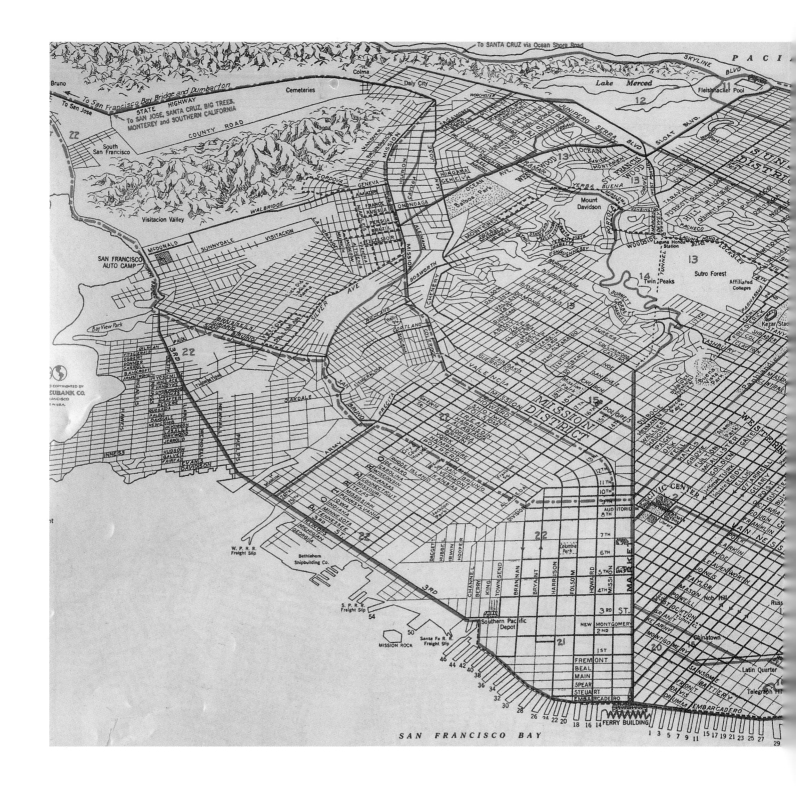

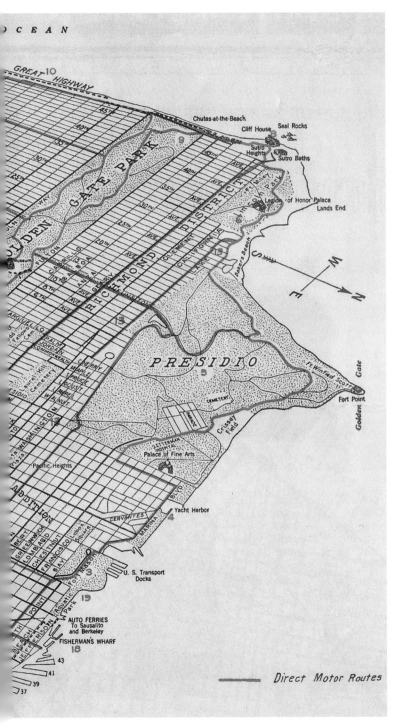

realistic about airport sites and in 1927 decided in favor of Mills Field south of San Bruno, the present location of the airport.

In the 1930s, two long-envisioned bridges across the bay were constructed. The Bay Bridge connecting the city to the east bay was dedicated in 1936, and the Golden Gate Bridge in 1937. These were by far the most dramatic construction projects Bay Area residents had even been privileged to watch.

The Bay Bridge is eight and a quarter miles long from Rincon Hill to the Oakland toll plaza. When completed it was the world's longest steel bridge built on two levels for vehicles only. Originally trucks and the Key Route trains ran on the lower level; the trains ceased to run in the late 1950s. The bridge's western section has twin suspension bridges joined at a central point; the eastern segment had a 1,400-foot cantilevered span followed by a truss bridge. Although the Bay Bridge site was less problematic than that of the Golden Gate Bridge, bedrock was at a deeper level. One of the western piers had to be sunk 220 feet before bedrock was reached.

Studies of trans-bay automobile traffic forecast that the Bay Bridge would divert four-fifths of the vehicular ferry traffic. A San Francisco Bay Bridge Commission was appointed in September 1929 to oversee plans for bay bridges; the U. S. Army and Navy also reviewed the Rincon Hill/Yerba Buena crossing. Approval of the chosen route came in July, but the commission also predicted that additional bay bridges would be required in the future.

The Golden Gate Bridge, a steel suspension bridge, which serves pedestrians as well as vehicles, crosses the nine-mile wide Golden Gate from Fort Point to Marin County. The central span is 4,200 feet long; the twin towers are 746 high. Joseph B. Strauss, an engineer whose specialty was bridges, designed the bridge. He had advocated its construction since 1917. Irving Morrow who often wrote about architecture is said to have chosen the color, one of the bridge's famous aspects.

Opposition to the Golden Gate Bridge came from a variety of sources, among them private citizens who said it would spoil the scenic beauty of the entrance to the bay. Some engineers and geologists doubted that the bridge could be constructed. However, the strongest opposition came from the railroads and ferry companies. In 1930, 43 ferry boats carried some 47 million passengers and over six million vehicles across the bay. In the years after the bridges were opened to automobile traffic, most of the ferry service was discontinued.

POST-WAR SAN FRANCISCO

TOWARD THE CONTEMPORARY CITY

Title: San Francisco and Vicinity
Date: 1954
Cartographers and Publishers: U. S. Geodetic Survey
Polyconic projection, colored map, 63 ⁴/₁₀ x 36 ¼ inches
John Woodbridge Collection

This 1954 map shows San Francisco apparently settled into a more or less permanent form; its major automobile routes are traced in red, including the Golden Gate and Bay Bridges that linked the city to its vicinity. The developed area of the city is shown in light red, and the open spaces and parks in complementary green.

FREEWAYS

Plans had been underway since the 1940s to construct the Embarcadero Freeway. An agreement in June 1953 between the city and the state highway department approved the freeway route parallel to the Ferry Building. Under construction in the mid-1950s, the freeway visually altered the city's waterfront until the 1989 earthquake damaged the structure and led to its removal and the roadway's return, more or less, to its 1954 state.

The James Lick Freeway, completed in 1950, took traffic from the Bay Bridge and sent it to downtown locations south of Market Street and further south to the Bayshore Highway. The goal of the Embarcadero Freeway was to connect automobile traffic to the Golden Gate Bridge. Another route to the bridge was projected through the panhandle of Golden Gate Park, across 19th Avenue, and through the Presidio.

Anti-freeway sentiment began with the planning of the Embarcadeo Freeway and gained strength with the planning of the panhandle route in the late 1950s. The issue was so politically sensitive that the board of supervisors asked the state Department of Highways to engage the prominent landscape architect, Lawrence Halprin, to make an urban design study of the freeway. In 1962, Halprin presented his design, which used landscaping, a sculptural handling of sunken corridors for the streets on either side of the panhandle, and a tunnel under the park to make the freeway as unobtrusive as possible. But the *San Francisco Chronicle*'s anti-freeway editorials, backed by public opinion, rejected any freeway through the park. In 1966, the city rejected federal funds to build the proposed route. With that action, all planning for freeway construction within the city ceased.

URBAN RENEWAL AND REDEVELOPMENT

While freeways intended to link San Francisco more effectively to the Bay Area were being alternately approved and contested, areas of the city were proposed for renewal, a process justified by the use of words from the vocabulary of disease such as blight and cancer. Heart disease was a particularly useful metaphor for what ailed cities that were dying at their core, their health eroded by the post-World War II exodus to the suburbs. Yet, just like surgery used to remove cancerous tissue might have post-operative problems, the sweeping removal of substandard buildings resulted more often than not in scarred landscapes that remained wastelands for years. The redevelopment agency's power of eminent domain in the postwar era permitted large-scale razing of areas but could not guarantee that private developers would rush to rebuild them and heal the wounds.

Concurrent with the publication of the city's 1948 master plan, the board of supervisors designated 280 blocks of the Western Addition a blighted area. (A certain percentage of properties within a district had to be determined blighted before an area could be designated for redevelopment.) The Redevelopment Agency was then established to administer a program for its reconstruction. Such large-scale projects strained the capabilities of the city's staff. Since little thought had been given to the relocation of residents of largely poor minority groups, relocation programs for displaced people provided neither adequate counseling nor alternative housing. This inadequacy persisted despite the fact that the 1949 National Housing Act had pledged "a decent home and a suitable living environment for every American family."

Other redevelopment areas included Diamond Heights, with 325 acres, parts of which lacked street access because the grades were too steep to meet the city's criteria for streets. Instead of a densely settled area like the Western Addition, Diamond Heights had few residents or property owners. The 1954 U. S. Geodetic Survey shows the area very sparsely developed. In addition to its lack of transportation, it was quite remote from parts of the city that were deemed desirable.

In spite of federal grants from the Housing and Home Finance Agency for the 28-block Area 1 of the Western Addition (finally approved in 1956) and for Diamond Heights, the redevelopment process was so fragmented by delays that by the 1960s virtually nothing had been accomplished. Not until the 1970s did apartment houses, townhouses, and single-family houses cover the slopes of Diamond Heights.

An area of the city that promised an easier path for redevelopment was bounded by Clay and Battery Streets, Broadway, and the Embarcadero; it was called Area E. The site, 78 acres adjacent to the financial district, was occupied

by the old and picturesque produce market. Vehicular circulation around the market area was congested; its infrastructure was old and crumbling, and, moreover, the bayside site with its splendid views seemed wasted on such a mundane use. It was argued that moving the market to an area south of Market Street more easily accessible to delivery trucks would improve the efficiency of its operation and make way for a prime residential area. The architectural firm of Skidmore, Owings & Merrill prepared a plan that was published in 1957, which showed distribution of office buildings and parking. In 1959, a prospectus for an architectural competition for the newly christened Golden Gateway was issued, and in 1960, nine eligible developers bid for the right to develop the site. It was the largest number of bids for any of the nation's redevelopment projects up to that time and proved that San Francisco could attract serious developers for practical projects.

The project area was cleared and Phase 1 of the residential development was built between 1961 and 1963; the office buildings and the mixed-use development called Embarcadero Center was completed by 1981. The last phase of residential development was completed in 1982.

Title: The Yerba Buena Redevelopment Area and Vicinity
Date: 2005
Designer: Robin Chiang, Robin Chiang and Company
Unpublished bird's-eye view of the built-out YBC redevelopment area, colored drawing in pen and ink, flow pen, and colored pencils, 11 x 10 ¼ inches
Robin Chiang

The redevelopment area most publicized over its long history is the 1,100-acre site, originally called Area D, south of Market Street. The year after its designation in 1954, real estate and hotel entrepreneur Ben Swig promoted a so-called "prosperity plan" that featured a convention center, sports stadium, high-rise office buildings, and a 7,000-car parking garage for the four blocks bounded by 4th, 5th, Mission, and Folsom streets. The four blocks were outside the designated redevelopment area and closer to Market Street. After studying the area, Planning Director Paul Oppermann found that it did not meet federal standards for blight; it was not designated; and Swig withdrew his plan for of lack of support. The city then proposed that 12 blocks of the original 19 be targeted for project study under the 1954 amendment to the 1949 National Housing Act, which permitted financial assistance for non-residential projects. The planners also recommended spot clearance of deteriorated industrial properties rather than total razing of the area.

The South-of-Market redevelopment area was located near the Happy Valley settlement of workers' housing of the 1850s, which had grown and consolidated until the 1906 earthquake and fire destroyed the blocks of small wooden houses and commercial buildings. The area was then rebuilt with modest hotels, and institutions and businesses that served the largely single, male population. Although the 1930s Great Depression adversely affected the population, the area remained more or less stable, if seedy, until targeted by the redevelopment agency for clearance. Arguably, the area's blight was in the eyes of the outsiders; for most of the residents it was the best neighborhood they could find.

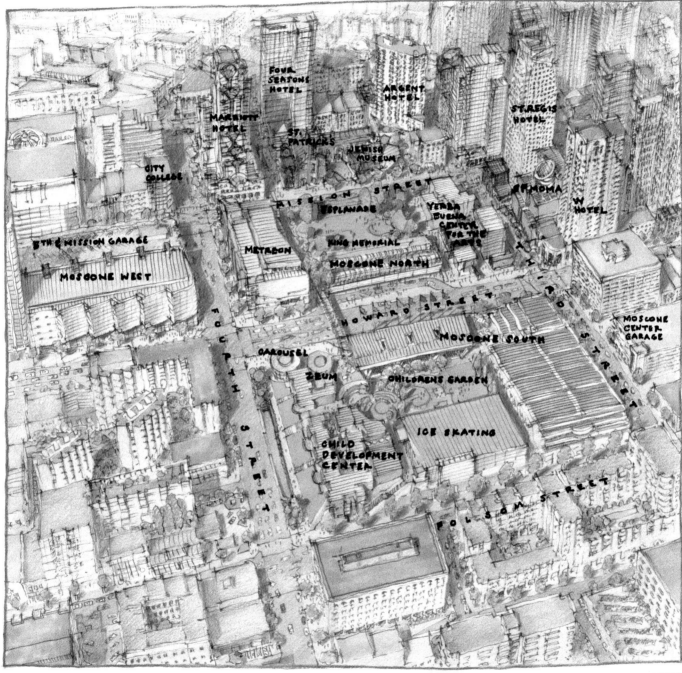

San Francisco
Yerba Buena District
San Francisco Redevelopment Agency

Four Seasons Hotel
Argent Hotel
St. Regis Hotel
Marriott Hotel
St. Patrick's
Jewish Museum
City College
MISSION STREET
Esplanade
Yerba Buena Center for the Arts
SF MOMA
W Hotel
5th & Mission Garage
Metreon
King Memorial
Moscone North
Moscone West
HOWARD STREET
Moscone South
3RD STREET
Moscone Center Garage
Carousel
Zeum
Children's Garden
FOURTH STREET
Ice Skating
Child Development Center
FOLSOM STREET

To facilitate private development south of Market Street the city re-designated Area D after reducing its size to 156 acres. In 1964, the redevelopment agency proposed beginning development on 96 acres, thereafter called Yerba Buena Center (YBC) in memory of the name first given to the city by its founders. The focal area was further narrowed to three central blocks, approximately 25 acres, for mixed-use development including office and retail, two theaters, a museum, a convention center, and a sports center. Although the project area was cleared in the late 1960s, the rebuilding process became one of the longest board games in the city's history. But if the players changed over the years, the pieces remained remarkably constant after they were established in 1965. Although grand schemes were proposed, including one by Kenzo Tange, famous for his designs of the two gymnasiums for the 1964 Olympic Games in Tokyo, the requirement for a single developer for the three-block project did not attract bidders.

Meanwhile the Neighborhood Legal Assistance Foundation joined with the Tenants and Owners in Opposition to Redevelopment (TOOR) organization of 1969, to file suits against the project in the federal courts because of its inadequate relocation plan for the 3,000 to 4,000 residents who would be displaced from the area. The TOOR lawsuit halted the project.

Justin Herman's untimely death in August 1971 was another setback. Herman had been head of the redevelopment agency since 1956. Before that he headed the San Francisco Regional Office of the Housing and Home Finance Agency. Herman was both experienced and effective as an administrator, a believer in redevelopment as a means to build a great city, and a master builder who advocated architectural excellence. Often compared to New York City's Robert Moses, Herman was acknowledged even by his detractors as a financial wizard and a perfectionist who never shunned controversy.

In 1976, George Moscone became mayor of the city and moved to activate the YBC project by appointing a select committee to produce recommendations for a plan that voters would approve. Important issues such as the balance between housing and open space and historic preservation were aired in subcommittees known as the "warring tribes." After five months and 50 or so meetings, 17 recommendations were made. In 1978, following acceptance of the environmental impact report, the board of supervisors approved the project and bond issuance for the convention center. Completed in 1981, the convention center was named for George Moscone, who had been assassinated in November 1978.

In 1984, a master plan for a 10-acre park, Yerba Buena Gardens, was approved, and the project area was cleared. The bird's-eye view shown here presents the present state of the city's new cultural center. Although some 50 years were consumed in its making, the results, if still tied to memories of the inequities of redevelopment, have given the South-of-Market area the vitality that William Ralston and Ashbury Harpending hoped for when they created the two blocks of New Montgomery Street south of the Market Street "slot" in the expectation that successful commercial development would follow the erection in 1873 of Ralston's Palace Hotel.[1]

It is worth noting that multiple versions of the components first proposed in the 1964 YBC plan were built so that today the area has several convention center buildings, museums, theaters, hotels, office buildings, and retail stores. The "sports center," now called SBC Park, was finally built in 2000 on a bayside site further south at 2nd and King streets. TOOR formed a development corporation and was able to build affordable housing on four sites in the vicinity of the Yerba Buena Gardens. Market-rate housing was built throughout the SOMA district.

---

1. *Ralston's original goal was to extend Montgomery Street across Market Street and through Rincon Hill to the Pacific Mail Steamship Company's docks and warehouses on the waterfront between First and Second Streets. Ralston and Harpending's New Montgomery Real Estate Company bought up properties from Market to Howard Street, ensuring the development of the new street that far, but the refusal of property owners south of Howard Street to sell ended the street's progress.*

THE MANHATTANIZATION OF SAN FRANCISCO

Opposition to high-rise development in the city's financial district began in the 1960s following the completion of the Bank of America headquarters in 1969 and the construction of the Transamerica Tower, completed in 1971. Planning Director Allan Jacobs had published an urban design plan that year, which established guidelines for building height, bulk, shape, orientation, color, and views and clarified the goals of San Franciscans who feared that pressures for development in the financial district would transform it into an unwanted version of Manhattan. Alvin Duskin, a local businessman, sponsored two initiatives, one in 1971 and the other in 1972, that proposed limiting the height of downtown buildings to 72 feet, less than that of the skyscrapers that had been built in the 1890s. Both initiatives lost, but the campaigns around them activated an anti-high-rise movement. Pro- and anti-development forces mobilized over the next years, and in 1983 planning director Dean Macris put forward the Downtown Plan, adopted in 1985. The plan called for a reduction in permitted building heights and floor-area ratios, preservation for 266 architecturally significant buildings, mandatory shadow studies of designs for new buildings to insure sunlight access, and the promotion of an architectural design for new buildings that would avoid the so-called "refrigerator" tops typical of the postwar Modern buildings. The plan was criticized for being more about architecture than limiting office growth; in fact, such growth was simply shifted from the financial district north of Market Street to the South of Market area. Another anti-growth initiative, Proposition M, passed in 1986, but the amount of office space built by that time resulted in a high vacancy rate that slowed growth pressures until the end of the decade when the so-called Dot Com invasion created an estimated 55,000 jobs mainly in the South of Market (SOMA) and Mission districts.

The Dot Com companies did not create the forest of high-rise towers so feared in the 1980s. Rather, it was the conversion to offices of the industrial buildings and warehouses so common in the SOMA and outer Mission districts that characterized the changed environment of the turn of the twentieth century. There were also blocks of new four-story Live/Work loft buildings, made possible by a code originally intended to protect artists living next to their studios in the SOMA. The new code defined a building type subject to lower taxes that allowed individuals to combine their home and office space.

THE CONTEMPORARY CITY

CONTEMPORARY MAPS

Title: Downtown San Francisco, An Axonometric View of the
City by the Bay
Date issued: 1998
Design: mapPoster, a division of Ludington Ltd.
Publisher: Ludington Ltd (Hastings-on-Hudson, N. Y.)
*Axonometric rendering based on aerial photographs taken by Alex
McLean, ground photography, and records of footprints of the
buildings*, 23 x 35 inches
mapPoster.com, a division of Ludington Ltd.

The view is taken from above the downtown area, focusing on the financial district north of Market Street and the blocks south of Market Street that were developed from the 1970s to the 1990s. The forest of high-rise towers shows the effect of the economic boom that produced what was then called the Manhattanization of San Francisco. Another notable change from previous maps and views of the city is the absence of the Embarcadero Freeway, demolished in 1991 as a result of damage it sustained in the 1989 earthquake. Among the benefits of the freeway's removal was the rehabilitation of the Ferry Building, completed in 2003, to create an indoor public market hall on the ground floor and office space on the upper level. Ferries to and from Oakland use the Golden Gate Transit Ferry terminal on the building's bayside.

The mapmakers who work for mapPoster.com used Apple's Adobe Illustrator program to create the lines and shapes that compose this map. After a decision was reached on how to delineate the buildings, a team of people took charge of the colors and types of buildings and proceeded to draw the map street by street. This map took from six months to one year to create. The company mapPoster.com grew out of a graphics services company, Graphic Chart and Map Company, Inc., which creates custom maps for customers world wide.

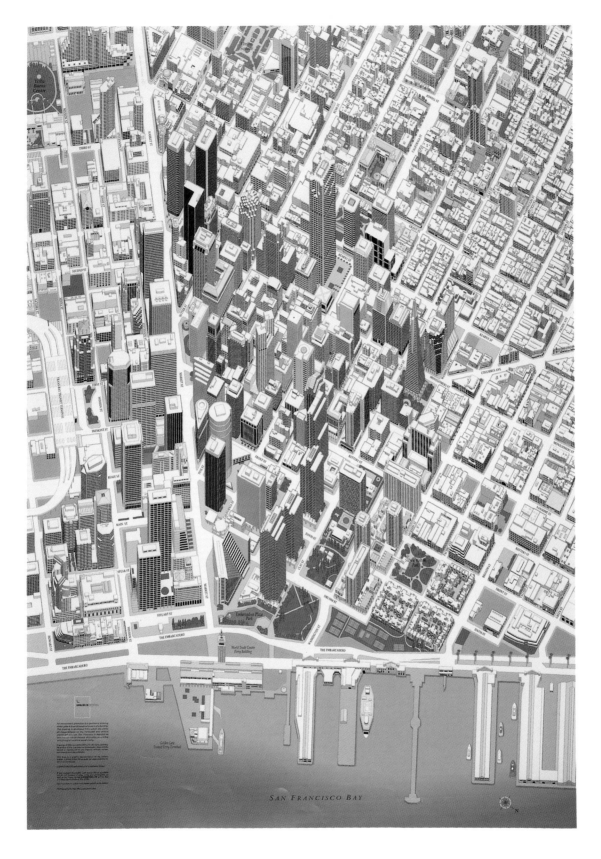

DOWNTOWN SAN FRANCISCO

An Axonometric View of the City by the Bay

Title: San Francisco Business Times Downtown San Francisco
Commercial Real Estate Map
Date issued: 2003
Graphic Design: Reineck & Reineck
Publisher: San Francisco Business Times
Colored map, 39 ½ x 24 inches
Reineck & Reineck

Three organizations commissioned the original version of this map: Colliers International Commercial Realtors, the *San Francisco Business Times*, and the San Francisco Association of Realtors. The map covers both the North of Market (NOMA) and SOMA areas and has been reprinted several times. Among the useful kinds of information it conveys are linear wireframe 3D depictions of major buildings constructed during and since the 1970s boom times. The drawings are superimposed on their site. A range of light to dark purple tones is used to indicate the decades of construction from the 1960s to the 2000s. Commercial building types are shown in warm tones; parks and large developments such as Yerba Buena Gardens in pale green. Thus the downtown building cycles are chronicled by color.

49–MILE SCENIC DRIVE

The 49-Mile Scenic Drive indicated by the heavy blue line is a planned route within San Francisco. Driving in the congested downtown area is not recommended during commute hours. Portions of the route may be affected by construction projects, especially in the downtown area. For the latest routing, check with the San Francisco Visitor Information Center.

This citywide map is designed to show the route of the 49-Mile Scenic Drive and major points of interest and thoroughfares. The "Downtown San Francisco" map (reverse side) shows all the streets within that area. Both maps show bus lines to popular visitor destinations. Please refer to the scale of miles and kilometers to estimate distances.

If you are planning a walking tour, check with the Visitor Information Center or your hotel or motel regarding distances and other factors. In some cases public or vehicular transportation is advisable.

1 Civic Center includes City Hall, Federal and State Office Buildings, Bill Graham Civic Auditorium, new Main Library and the Performing Arts Center's handsome components: Davies Symphony Hall, War Memorial Opera House and Veterans Building/Herbst Theatre where the U.N. charter was signed. A permanent memorial commemorating the 50th anniversary of the United Nations is located in United Nations Plaza. H-5

2 Cathedral Hill is dominated by the strikingly contemporary St. Mary's Cathedral. H-4

3 Japan Center and Japantown have many shops, restaurants, several theaters and two hotels. The Peace Plaza of the Japan Center is the focal point for Japanese festivals. H-4

4 Haas-Lilienthal House, an 1886 Victorian at 2007 Franklin, is open Sundays, as well as Wednesday afternoons. H-3

5 Union Square is the heart of the downtown shopping and hotel district. Many civic events are held in the square. I-4

6 Chinatown evokes all the exotic sights and sounds of Hong Kong or Canton beginning at the Chinatown Gate, Grant Avenue at Bush Street. I-3

7 Nob Hill is the elegant hilltop area of hotels and apartments with Gothic Grace Cathedral, Huntington Park and the Nob Hill Masonic Center at its crest. I-3

8 Cable Car Barn, Mason and Washington Streets, has a visitors gallery and a museum with 19th century photos of cable car operations and scale models. I-3

9 Portsmouth Square, a small historic park in Chinatown where the U.S. flag was raised in July 1846, is a gathering place for the community. I-3

10 Jackson Square has preserved handsome 19th century buildings occupied by antique dealers, art galleries, gift and apparel shops. Enter the square on Jackson Street at Montgomery. J-3

11 North Beach is a neon-studded nightlife area clustered around Broadway and Columbus. Three blocks north is Washington Square, the piazza of the city's Italian sector. I-2

12 Telegraph Hill has Coit Tower, a 210-foot (64 m) landmark, plus one of the city's best views. (Congested area best visited on foot or via public transportation.) I-2

13 PIER 39 is a waterfront festival marketplace. Built on a 1,000-foot-long pier and flanked by small boat marinas, it offers sweeping views of the bay and city. I-1,2

14 Fisherman's Wharf is the center for seafood restaurants, fishing boats, harbor cruise boats, gift shops and numerous attractions. H, I-2

15 Alcatraz, infamous former Federal prison, is an island a mile and a half (2.4 km) off Fisherman's Wharf. Alcatraz tours leave from Pier 41. (Reservations suggested.) I-1

16 Aquatic Park, three blocks west of Fisherman's Wharf, has Hyde Street Pier with old-time exhibition ships and ship-shaped Maritime Museum. Municipal Pier is a popular spot for fishing. H-2

17 The Cannery, an inviting three-level restoration that was once a canning factory, is now filled with a spectrum of shops, galleries and restaurants. A nearby center, the nautically-inspired **Anchorage,** offers shopping, dining and lodging as well. H-2

18 Ghirardelli Square, a collection of red brick buildings that served as a chocolate factory, now is a charming restaurant and shopping center with open-air plazas and waterfront views. Across the street is landscaped Victorian Park. H-2

19 Russian Hill has country-like lanes and terraces and panoramic bay views. **Lombard Street** descends the hill from Hyde—with nine hairpin turns in a single block. H-2

20 Union Street's Victorian buildings, from Van Ness to Steiner, now house art galleries, antique shops, specialty stores, restaurants, coffee houses and pubs. G, H-3

21 Fort Mason Center, hub of the world's largest urban park—the Golden Gate National Recreation Area, anchors a number of museums, theaters and galleries and is a staging area for special events. H-2

22 Marina Green, a grassy waterfront recreational area, is a good place to watch yachting activities. **Crissy Field** also offers bayside vantage points. G-2

23 Palace of Fine Arts, built for the 1915 Panama-Pacific International Exposition, has been restored to its original glory. Contains the **Exploratorium** science museum and the Palace of Fine Arts Theatre. F-2

24 Presidio of San Francisco, a unit of the Golden Gate National Recreation Area, offers 1,500 acres (16 sq. km) of parklike hills and ocean vistas. D, E, F-2,3

25 Fort Point National Historic Site lies beneath the structure of the Golden Gate Bridge and offers an unusual view of the bridge and the bay's shifting tides. D-1

26 Golden Gate Bridge, the world's most beautiful suspension bridge, links The City with Marin County and the area to the north. Auto toll collected southbound; pedestrians free. D-1

27 China Beach at 28th and Sea Cliff Avenue has 600 feet (183 m) of sandy beach frontage for sunbathing and picnicking. C-4

28 California Palace of the Legion of Honor, a replica of its Paris namesake, has masterpieces of European art from Medieval times into the 20th century, many Rodin bronzes, period rooms, prints and drawings. B-4

29 Ocean Beach has plenty of sand and surf—and a view of the small, stony islands called Seal Rocks. Swimming and wading at this beach are strongly discouraged; immediately offshore are unpredictable currents which can take even the strongest swimmer by surprise. A-5, 6

30 The Zoo contains Primate Discovery Center, Gorilla World, Little Puffer steam train and a thousand fascinating animals and birds from all over the world. A-9

31 Lake Merced's fresh waters offer boating and trout fishing within the city limits. B-10, 11

32 Sigmund Stern Grove rings with the sounds of musical entertainment, free for all on summer Sundays. C-9

33 Golden Gate Park, originally 1,017 acres (4 sq. km) of sand dunes, has National AIDS Memorial Grove, miles of drives, green lawns, playfields, bridle paths, lakes and flowers. Facilities in the park are shown in detail. A/F-5, 6

34 Japanese Tea Garden, an authentic Japanese garden dating back to 1894, has a tea house, pagoda ponds, bridges and bonsai. In the spring the cherry blossoms and flowering shrubs create a rare floral spectacle. **Strybing Arboretum,** a "living library," nurtures over 7,000 species of plants. D-5

35 Museums: Asian Art Museum (closing Oct. 2001) the Avery Brundage Collection, is top-rated internationally for its jades, porcelains, bronzes and ceramics. **M.H. de Young Memorial Museum** (closed until 2005). D-5

36 California Academy of Sciences encompasses many fascinating halls devoted to the natural sciences. Outstanding are Steinhart Aquarium, Fish Roundabout, Planetarium, Wild California, Earth and Space Hall. E-5

37 Twin Peaks has a scenic drive to its 910-foot (227 m) summit, and offers a 360° panoramic view of the city. F-7

38 Mission Dolores, Dolores and 16th Streets. Father Serra established this Spanish Mission in 1776; the historic church was completed in 1791. H-6

39 San Francisco-Oakland Bay Bridge is one of the world's longest (8 1/4 miles/13.3 km) steel bridges. Toll collected westbound. K-3

40 Ferry Building, a terminal for commuters before the bridges were built, is one of the city's landmarks. J-3

41 Embarcadero Center, an eight-building complex, embraces shops and restaurants. Justin Herman Plaza is framed by Vaillancourt Fountain. J-3

42 Montgomery Street is the center of an expanding Financial District. Major buildings are often distinguished by landscaped plazas and art works. J-3

43 San Francisco Visitor Information Center is operated by the Convention & Visitors Bureau. Multilingual personnel are there to assist with brochures and information. The Center is located at Hallidie Plaza (lower level), Powell and Market Streets. Open 9 a.m. to 5 p.m. Monday-Friday, 9-3 Saturday-Sunday. Closed major holidays. I-4

44 Old Mint, an impressive 1873 building, is a virtually unique example of Federal Greek Revival architecture; starting point for Barbary Coast Trail. Closed to the public. I-4

45 The Moscone Center, offers 442,000 square feet of show space, and the biggest column-free exhibit hall in the United Sates. Located in the central blocks of **Yerba Buena Gardens** are Martin Luther King, Jr. Memorial, the **Yerba Buena Center for the Arts** and **The Rooftop** children's area. J-4

46 San Francisco Museum of Modern Art housed in an impressive new building, is the principal center for modern art in the Bay Area. J-4

47 Pacific Bell Park, home of the San Francisco Giants, evokes the intimate feeling of classic ball parks across the land. K-5

48 Sports Arenas: 3Com Park is the home of the San Francisco 49ers (football). K-11. Cow Palace, an indoor arena, hosts sports contests, trade shows and entertainment events. H-12

49 San Francisco International Airport, 14 miles (24 km) south via the freeway, is San Francisco's gateway to the Pacific and to the world. J-12

Event Phone Information

A daily summary of special events and activities is available by dialing 283-0176.

Similar information available:

Francais	283-0172
Deutsch	283-0173
Español	283-0175
Italiano	283-0171
日本語	283-0174

For more information on San Francisco, visit the Web site of the San Francisco Convention and Visitors Bureau at www.sfvisitor.org

Title: San Francisco Visitors Map
Date issued: 2001
Graphic Design: Reineck & Reineck
Publisher: San Francisco Convention and Visitors Bureau
Colored map, 24 x 17 inches
Reineck & Reineck

A map of San Francisco that shows 49 points of interest keyed to blue numbers on the map and described in blocks of text on the right hand side of the sheet. The 49-Mile Scenic Drive, which motorists can follow around the city, is indicated by a blue line. Signs posted along the route inscribed with "49 mile" in the upper right corner and a dove's head above SCENIC DRIVE serve to guide motorists along the route. This route was first designated in 1938 by the Downtown Association as a way to publicize the city's attractions to mobile tourists. Amended several times, this is the current version.

PERSONAL AND PUBLIC TRANSPORTATION

Title: San Francisco Bike Map & Walking Guide
Date issued: 2004
Graphic Design: Reineck & Reineck
Publisher: Rufus Graphics (San Francisco)
Colored map, 24 x 18 inches
Reineck & Reineck

Biking and walking are popular recreational activities in San Francisco in spite of the many steep hills. In the early 1980s, Spencer Chase, a bicycle enthusiast, rode most of the city's streets and recorded the steepness of the hills as percentages in four categories. The street grades are shown in a legend in the map's lower righthand corner; the grade percentages are indicated in colors ranging from white for 0 to 5 percent to red for grades over 18 percent. In 1985, Reineck & Reineck expanded this information to create the San Francisco Bike Map & Walking Guide. The map has been improved, updated, and reprinted nine times with the help of the San Francisco Bicycle Coalition and San Francisco's City Bicycle Program.

Numbered routes shown on the map are the official San Francisco Bike Routes. Unnumbered routes—paths, lanes, and shared roadway/wide curb lanes as well as hiking trails and the San Francisco Bay Trail—are indicated with different colors. Street signs with a bicycle logo are shown on a legend in the map's upper left corner along with information about the Official San Francisco Bike Route System. A small map set in the upper right corner indicates the location of bicycle parking in the downtown area.

This is the most comprehensive biking map for San Francisco. The reverse side (not shown here) has a detailed biking map for the Presidio and another map with scenic bike routes.

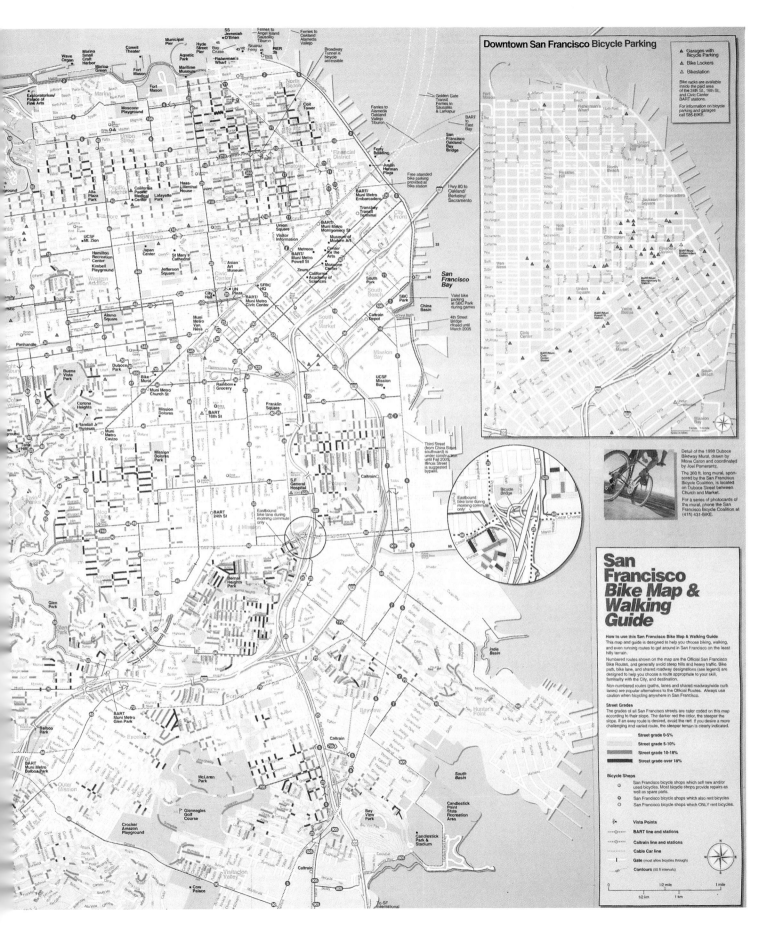

▲ Garages with Bicycle Parking
▲ Bike Lockers
△ Bikestation

Bike racks are available inside the paid area of the 24th St., 16th St. and Civic Center BART stations.

For information on bicycle parking and garages call 585-BIKE.

Detail of the 1998 Duboce Bikeway Mural, drawn by Mona Caron and coordinated by Joel Pomerantz.

The 360 ft. long mural, sponsored by the San Francisco Bicycle Coalition, is located on Duboce Street between Church and Market.

For a series of photocards of the mural, phone the San Francisco Bicycle Coalition at (415) 431-BIKE.

San Francisco Bike Map & Walking Guide

How to use this San Francisco Bike Map & Walking Guide
This map and guide is designed to help you choose biking, walking, and even running routes to get around in San Francisco on the least hilly terrain.

Numbered routes shown on the map are the Official San Francisco Bike Routes, and generally avoid steep hills and heavy traffic. Bike path, bike lane, and shared roadway designations (see legend) are designed to help you choose a route appropriate to your skill, familiarity with the City, and destination.

Non-numbered routes (paths, lanes and shared roadway/wide curb lanes) are popular alternatives to the Official Routes. Always use caution when bicycling anywhere in San Francisco.

Street Grades
The grades of all San Francisco streets are color coded on this map according to their slope. The darker red the color, the steeper the slope. If an easy route is desired, avoid the red. If you desire a more challenging and varied route, the steeper terrain is clearly indicated.

Street grade 0-5%
Street grade 5-10%
Street grade 10-18%
Street grade over 18%

Bicycle Shops
○ San Francisco bicycle shops which sell new and/or used bicycles. Most bicycle shops provide repairs as well as spare parts.
⊙ San Francisco bicycle shops which also rent bicycles.
● San Francisco bicycle shops which ONLY rent bicycles.

Vista Points
BART line and stations
Caltrain line and stations
Cable Car line
Gate (most allow bicycles through)
Contours (50 ft intervals)

0   1/2 mile   1 mile
1/2 km   1 km

143

Title: The Bay Area Rapid Transit System
Date published: September 2005
Designer: Reineck & Reineck
Variable measurements
The BART System

The BART was the first entirely new rapid transit system undertaken in the United States in over 50 years. It was also the largest urban design project then underway in the country and the first land-use plan ever developed for the Bay Area. As of this writing, 104 of the 385 miles of the rail called for in the original plan for the BART have been completed along with 43 stations in four counties. This map is the latest of three for the system.

Interest in a rapid transit system for the San Francisco Bay Area gained momentum in the post-World War II period. The Bay Area Rapid Transportation Commission, established by the state legislature in 1951, approved the first plan for the system in 1956. The BART District, drawn up in 1957, comprised the five inner-bay counties: San Francisco, Alameda, Contra Costa, Marin, and San Mateo. Following the withdrawal from the plan of Marin and San Mateo counties, the three remaining counties authorized construction of a 75-mile system. Voters then passed a $792 million bond issue, to which $180 million in surplus Bay Bridge tolls, $71 million in revenue bonds, and $8 million in federal grants were added. The first construction contract was let in 1965 for the Oakland-Fremont line, which began operation in 1972. By 1973, 16 stations in the East Bay and 10 for the San Francisco/Daly City line were completed.

The next phase of construction ended in 1996 with the extension of the East Bay Concord line to Pittsburg/Bay Point and the opening of the Dublin/Pleasanton line. The line to the San Francisco International Airport and the peninsula city of Millbrae began operation in 2000. Planning for the extension of the Fremont line to San Jose is in progress.

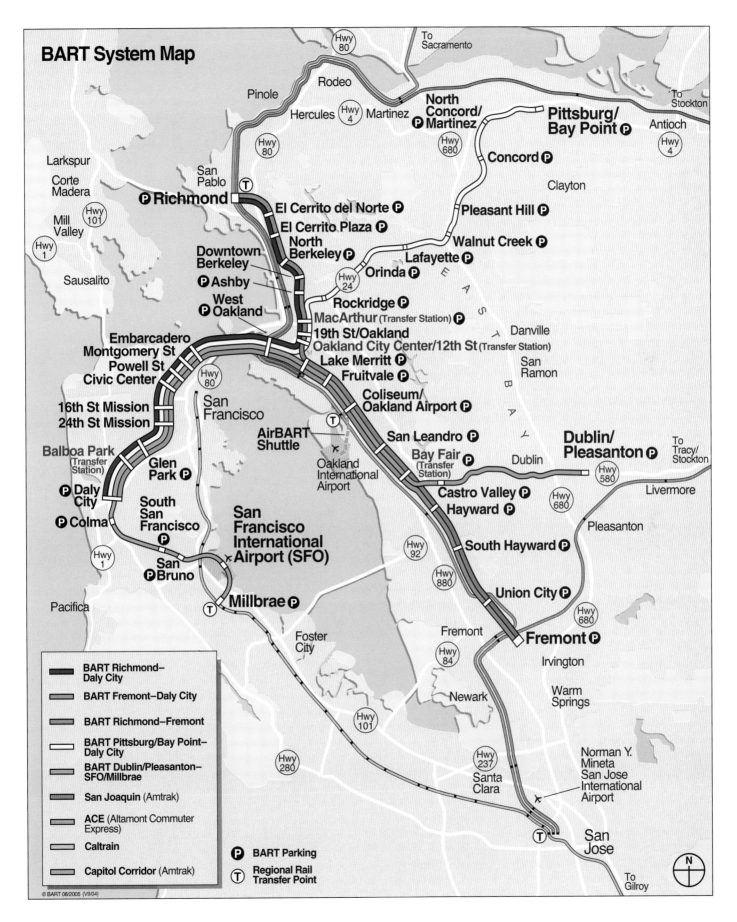

BART System Map

Larkspur
Corte Madera
Mill Valley
Sausalito
Pacifica

P Richmond
San Pablo **T**
El Cerrito del Norte P
El Cerrito Plaza P
North Berkeley **P**
Downtown Berkeley
P Ashby
West Oakland P

Rodeo
Pinole
Hercules **Hwy 4** Martinez
North Concord/ Martinez P
Pittsburg/ Bay Point P
Antioch
Concord P
Clayton
Pleasant Hill P
Walnut Creek P
Lafayette P
Orinda P
Danville
San Ramon

To Sacramento
To Stockton

Embarcadero
Montgomery St
Powell St
Civic Center
16th St Mission
24th St Mission
Balboa Park (Transfer Station)
P Daly City
Glen Park P
P Colma
South San Francisco P
San Bruno P
Millbrae P T

Rockridge P
MacArthur (Transfer Station) **P**
19th St/Oakland
Oakland City Center/12th St (Transfer Station)
Lake Merritt P
Fruitvale P
Coliseum/ Oakland Airport P
San Leandro P
Bay Fair (Transfer Station) **P**
Castro Valley P
Hayward P
South Hayward P
Union City P
Fremont P

San Francisco
AirBART Shuttle
Oakland International Airport
San Francisco International Airport (SFO)
Foster City

Dublin/ Pleasanton P
To Tracy/ Stockton
Livermore
Dublin
Pleasanton
Fremont
Irvington
Warm Springs
Newark
Norman Y. Mineta San Jose International Airport
Santa Clara
San Jose
To Gilroy

Legend

- BART Richmond–Daly City
- BART Fremont–Daly City
- BART Richmond–Fremont
- BART Pittsburg/Bay Point–Daly City
- BART Dublin/Pleasanton–SFO/Millbrae
- San Joaquin (Amtrak)
- ACE (Altamont Commuter Express)
- Caltrain
- Capitol Corridor (Amtrak)

P BART Parking
T Regional Rail Transfer Point

© BART 08/2005 (V9/04)

145

RECREATION

Title: Map and Guide to Golden Gate Park
Date issued: 2005
Graphic Design: Reineck & Reineck
Publisher: Rufus Graphics
Colored map illustrative with drawings of points of interest,
34 ½ x 5 ¼ inches
Reineck & Reineck

This map of Golden Gate Park as it is today should be compared with the 1892 bird's-eye view (pp. 96-97). Perhaps the most significant additions to the park are the new de Young Museum, opened in 2005, and the California Academy of Sciences slated to open by 2008. Other changes include the restoration of the Beach Chalet in 1997 and the Conservatory in 2003. The park's points of interest are numbered on the map and keyed to drawings below. The reverse side of the map has histories of its buildings and biographical sketches of its creators, William Hammond Hall and John McLaren.

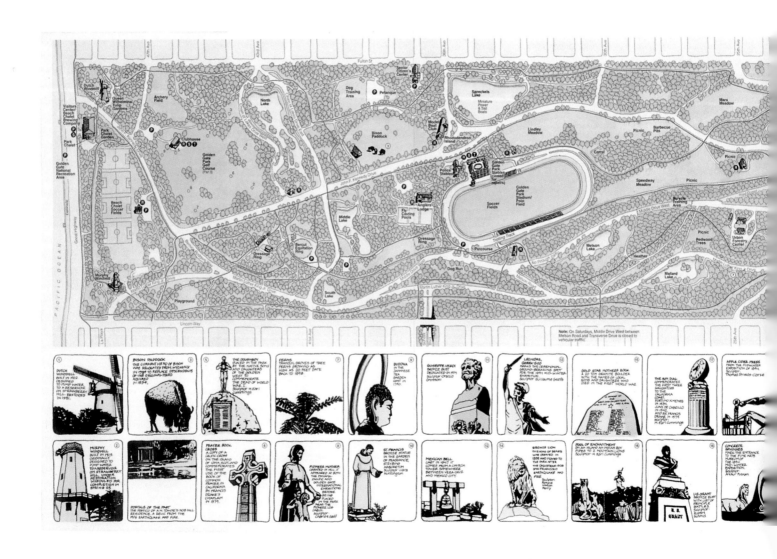

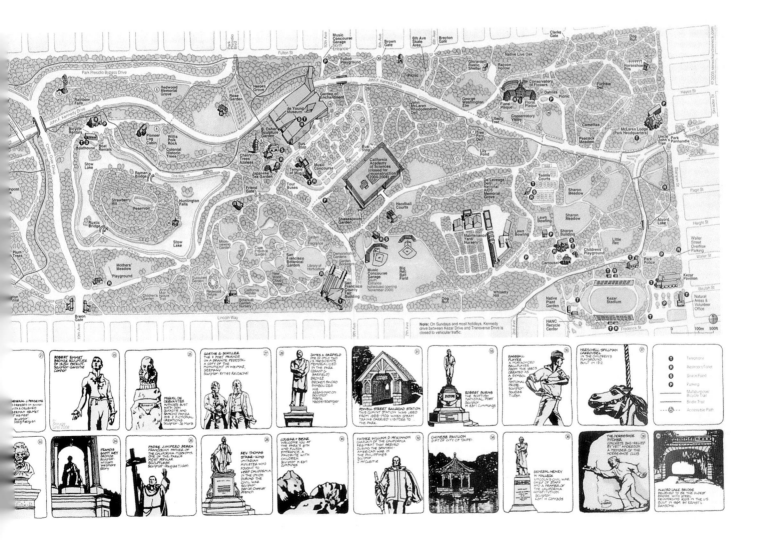

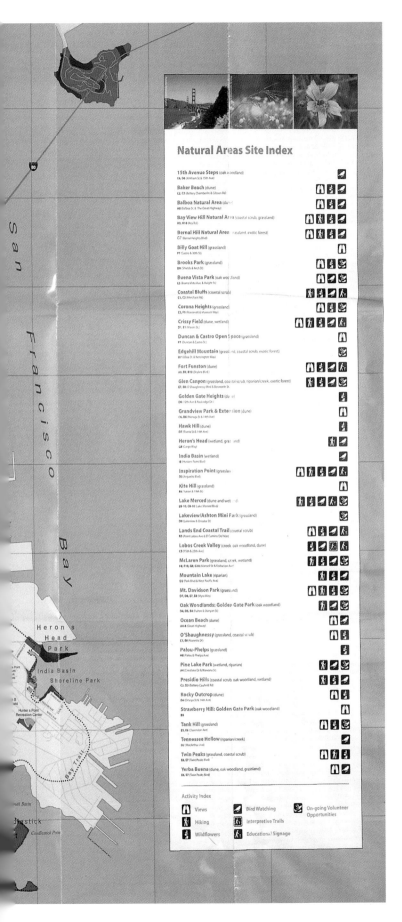

Title: Nature in the City, a Guide to
San Francisco's Natural Heritage
Date issued: 2005
Design: Peter Brastow, Suzanna Buehl, Damien Raffa,
Sean Stasio, and Lisa Wayne
Publisher: San Francisco Recreation and Parks Department
Colored map, 35 x 23 inches
San Francisco Recreation and Parks Department

Although its residents may not be aware of it, San Francisco abounds with remarkable natural resources. This unusual map was created to give San Franciscans a deeper sense of place through ways of exploring, as its title states, *Nature in the City*. San Francisco is one of the few cities that boasts national park lands within its borders as well as internationally recognized ecological areas. Many of these are part of the United Nations' World Network of Biosphere Reserves and serve as living laboratories for the management of land, water, and biodiversity. The map also helps to recruit volunteers for programs that take place on park sites throughout the city.

Colors and symbols that indicate the map's features are listed in a title block in the upper lefthand corner of the map sheet. A sidebar with a natural areas site index for the different zones of coastal scrub, dunes, riparian/creek, exotic forest, wetlands, grasslands, and oak woodlands is on the righthand side of the map sheet. An activity index has symbols for views, hiking, wildflowers, bird watching, interpretive trails, educational signage, and on-going volunteer opportunities accompanies the site index. The map itself has a white ground with the natural areas indicated by shades of green.

The back of the map has color photographs of the natural areas and other information. It is hard to imagine a more seductive invitation to explore San Francisco's from nature's point of view.

HOME BUYER'S REFERENCE MAP

Title: Site Suitability Analysis
Date produced: 2004
Unpublished colored map, variable measurements
Rick Waterman

This map shows a range of suitability for use in purchasing a home in San Francisco based on specific physical criteria. The criteria consider elevation and slope of the terrain as well as the proximity to open space, public schools, bicycle networks, and selected roadways.

This map represents the cartographic output of a site-suitability model created in a Geographic Information System (GIS). GIS is a recent tool being applied to the art and science of cartography. Its capacity to analyze and display complex sets of spatial data and their related attributes gives the contemporary cartographer the ability to represent the growing complexities of our dynamically changing world. The map attempts to reveal elements of this modern cartographic revolution while retaining established conventions in map design. Although the map permits readability within the realm of traditional design, features such as a digital terrain model and seamless classification color ramping allow the eye to visualize the topography of the geographically unique city in much greater detail.

Site Suitability Analysis
Home purchase in San Francisco

This map shows a range of suitability for the purchasing of a home in San Francisco based on specific physical criteria. These criteria consider elevation and slope, as well as the proximity to open space areas, public schools, bicycle networks and select roadways.

Suitability Index

1 = Low
3 = High

Bike Network

Neighborhood

Public School

Open Space

1

2

3

0   2 Miles

Rick Waterman SFSU 2004

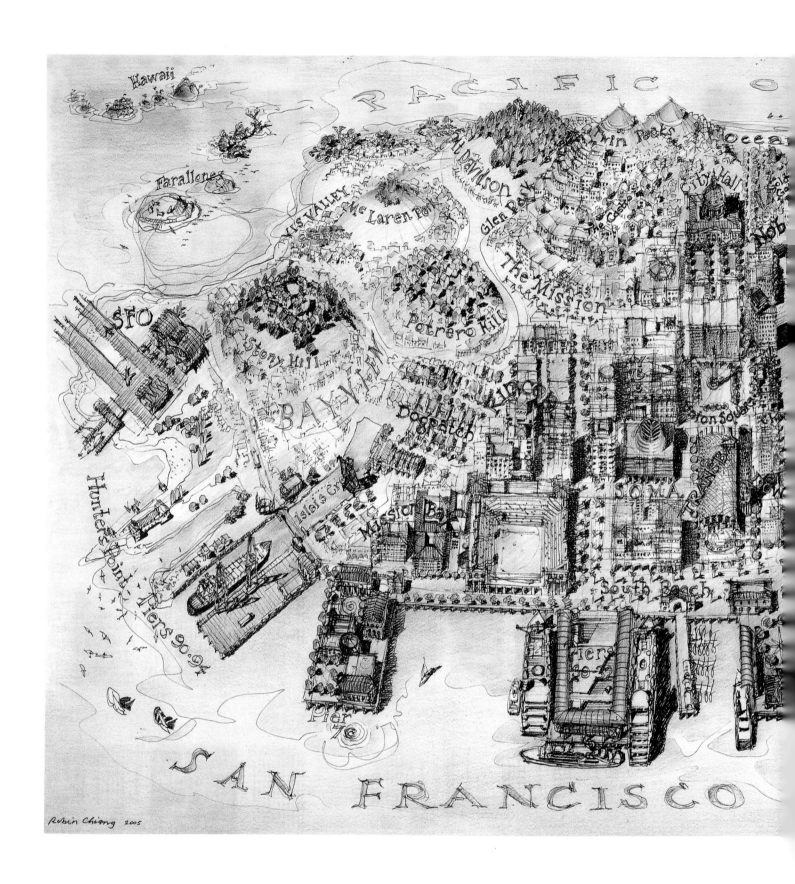

Robin Chiang 2005

TOWARD THE FUTURE CITY

Title: Bird's-eye view of San Francisco from the Waterfront
Date: 2005
Delineator: Robin Chiang
Unpublished colored drawing, 36 x 23 inches
Robin Chiang, Robin Chiang & Company, architects

This imaginary view of the city shows the possibilities for development of the piers along the Embarcadero that were constructed at the time of the 1915 Panama-Pacific International Exposition. The piers were originally intended for the publics-trust use of cargo shipping. For many years the waterfront bustled with trade and commerce; countless vessels were serviced at port facilities. But with the advent of intermodal container shipping, San Francisco's viability as a cargo port declined, largely because of the lack of land adjacent to the piers to reuse for the containers and their attendant machinery. The focus of the city's shrinking cargo handling activity has shifted to the waterfront south of China Basin.

Piers and associated facilities no longer needed for maritime use have stood as empty deteriorating monuments to a bygone era, their use confined to non-maritime interim functions such as parking, warehousing, and offices. Conversion to permanent new uses has been constrained by policies of previous acts such as the 1965 McAteer-Petris Act and the 1975 San Francisco Waterfront Special Area Plan, which ruled out conversion to non-water oriented uses on public lands. Reviews of policies for the piers in the 1990s produced a physical and policy plan for the area between Pier 35 and China Basin that responds to the port's commercial realities.

Public benefits of this plan include: removal of deteriorating piers that pose a threat to navigation and public safety and health, restoration of areas of open water for ecological health and recreation, an integrated public access network, and design policies that will preserve historic resources along the waterfront, enhance bay views, and provide opportunities to enjoy water areas adjacent to the Embarcadero.

The Port of San Francisco has been working to transform the piers into public attractions. With this goal in mind, Robin Chiang, an architect practicing in San Francisco, created this drawing to celebrate the piers' future with images of the festivities that could enliven them. The city in the background is depicted as a fantasy island.

The drawing is described by its maker as executed "from memory and wishful thinking." A base drawing on bond paper was executed in ball point and flow pen; scanned and printed at 100 percent size on bond paper for final application of coloring pencils and flow pen.

Title: Perspectival Rendering of a Section of San Francisco
Date: Created in March 2006
Cartographer: Skidmore, Owings & Merrill, San Francisco
Unpublished Colored Projection of seismic hazard information,
variable dimensions
Collection of Skidmore, Owings & Merrill, San Francisco

In the mid-nineteenth century, San Francisco's skyline was dominated by high hills—Telegraph, Russian, and Nob—near the center of the expanding city, and higher ones such as Lone Mountain and Twin Peaks, far from the developed areas. But by the beginning of the twenty-first century, manmade peaks have come to rival the city's natural features, as these last views reveal.

The technology used to create these two city views surpasses aerial and satellite photography in its capacity to astonish. One of the important services the new digital technology can offer San Franciscans is the ability to assess where the greatest damage and destruction from earthquakes might occur. The pictorial rendering of the areas with the greatest potential for liquifaction—shown here by the red tentacles of liquifaction snaking their way through the city—is appropriately terrifying. All the more so because the data for the image was created by the Division of Mines and Geology in the California Department of Conservation; the City of San Francisco made it publicly available in May 2000.

This information has been published in other formats that also show streets and topographic features. But the combination of identifiable buildings with the seismic hazard data makes it dramatically clear that much of the densely built parts of the city are in hazard zones.

Title: Perspectival Rendering of the Downtown Area of San Francisco
Date: Created in March 2006
Cartographer: Skidmore, Owings & Merrill, San Francisco
Unpublished Colored Projection showing buildings, variable dimensions
Collection of Skidmore, Owings & Merrill, San Francisco

Like the previous city view, this map was created by a team of architects headed by Mark Schwettmann in the San Francisco office of Skidmore Owings & Merrill. The motivation for the map project was the desire for a tool that would show the physical context of building projects and thereby enable architects to make better design decisions and communicate them to clients, colleagues, consultants, and the larger community.

Working with a combination of two-dimensional CAD (Computer Aided Design), GIS (Geographic Information Systems), and three-dimensional computer modeling, the SOM team has spent two years developing a three-dimensional computer model of San Francisco.

Although products that represented parts of San Francisco three dimensionally were available in the marketplace, none of them met SOM's specific goals of accuracy, flexibility in visualization and modification, and geographic consistency with data from other fields such as urban planning, civil engineering, and real estate.

The model's concept and the mapping and modeling techniques for its development began in 2004. The creation of a system that would organize the information so that many designers could contribute to it and future users could comprehend it was the first step. Between June and August of 2005 the city's ground plane was replicated by "draping" its streets and blocks over a three-dimensional model created from contour files made available to the public by the city's GIS Department.

Two-dimensional outlines of building masses were projected onto the sloping ground plane and then extruded vertically to create three-dimensional buildings. The task of modeling the form of individual buildings was substantially complete for the downtown core by January of 2006.

As of this writing, the topography and streets of the entire city have been mapped three-dimensionally with some precision. Beyond San Francisco, the bay area's neighboring counties are represented by USGS digital elevation model maps, which do not show manmade features. Buildings rendered with a relatively high degree of detail now exist for the center-city area east of Van Ness Avenue and north of Howard Street. Less detailed buildings are shown for the Mission district north of 16th Street and the area east of Arguello Boulevard.

SOM's map project has enabled its participants to examine the city's physical form from any vantage point at any scale while, at the same time, overlaying it with geospatial data related to specific projects. The model has already been used for projects in San Francisco ranging from downtown high-rise buildings to plans for entire neighborhoods outside of the center-city area.

The team's effort to bring greater depth and more interactivity to projects by integrating three-dimensional data with outside sources of information continues. Future use of two- and three-dimensional mapping with the new possibilities offered by digital information technology will undoubtedly inform the process of designing urban forms here and elsewhere in the country.

If seeing is believing, it is hard to imagine a better conclusion than this image to the survey of San Francisco's evolving form over its more than 200 years of history.

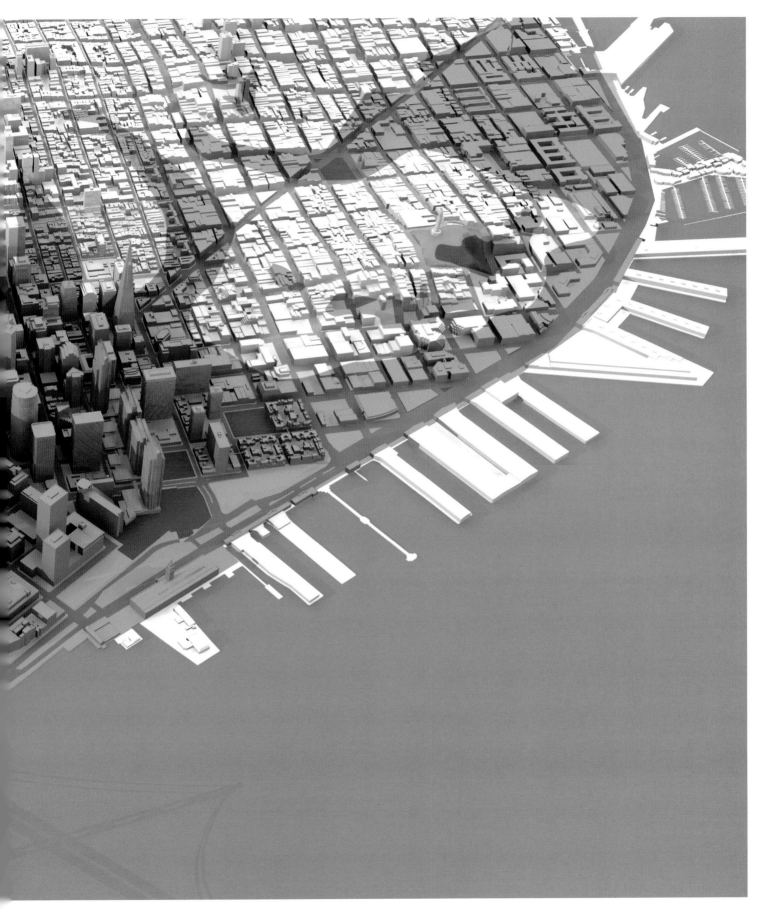

CODA

Curiosity about the west coast of the North American continent grew steadily in the sixteenth and seventeenth centuries, particularly after the discovery of the San Francisco Bay in 1769 by Juan Rodrigues Cabrillo and its exploration in 1774–75 by Juan Bautista de Anza and subsequently by others. But the focus of this curiosity was not the look of the land, but rather that of the waters that surrounded the land that had to be navigated by explorers from Spain, England, and France, and traders and privateers who had practical reasons for wanting to tour the coast and the bay. It is then no wonder that charts tracing the shorelines and recording the depths of the water, as well as obstacles such as reefs, were most wanted.

After the discovery of gold and the rush to San Francisco, the gateway to the mining country, the demand for maps of the city and the surrounding country accelerated until the bay was of less interest than the land around it. While real estate maps were of prime importance for practical purposes, panoramic maps and bird's-eye views fed the public's desire for visual information. The latter were published as early as the 1830s and peaked in popularity in the 1880s. The firms of Britton & Rey and A. L. Bancroft were the most active in printing panoramic maps and views.

The federal government also played a strong cartographic role with the establishment of the U. S. Coastal Survey during Thomas Jefferson's administration as an agency of the Treasury Department. Between 1867 and 1879 the federal government sponsored four geographical and geological surveys of the West later known as "The Great Surveys." To coordinate further governmental expeditions and surveys, the U. S. Geological Survey was established in the Department of the Interior where it continues to function today.

Most of the early maps and views of San Francisco from the 1830s to the 1880s were lithographs produced by a few firms, some of them quite small, and individuals. Eastern printing firms relied on images that were sent to them rather than on artists sent to California to create them firsthand. Many pictorial views were made from daguerreotypes and other photographic processes. Thus the volume of prints was relatively small, and of these many were destroyed in the various catastrophes—fires and earthquakes—that beset the Bay Area particularly in the early decades. For example, Britton & Rey, the firm that produced most of the lithographed views and maps, lost its records and inventory in the fire after the 1906 earthquake.

The early views were mainly black and white, though often printed on tinted paper. The paper was both low quality and thin so that it could be folded and sent as a letter. These so-called letter-sheets were the forerunners of the post card. Scenes of the Gold Rush—of both miners and sites—were the most popular and sellable.

Experimentation with color was ongoing during the period from 1849 to 1915. Although chromolithography produced multi-toned printing in imitation of oil painting with tints of increasing chromatic intensity, intense colors were not popular with San Francisco lithographers who were apparently attached to their custom of printing a few carefully planned tones to gain an overall effect of light and atmosphere. They adopted the practice of printing from many stones, but restricted the range of color. Views of the city from the 1850s and 1860s show black with beige with light brown or brown-gray sometimes warmed to a grayed orange. The blue for sky and water verged on blue-green; green was achieved by printing blue over yellow. It was a color scheme well suited to the area's natural landscape.

San Francisco cannot boast of great age in comparison with other cities, but it still counts as the earliest American settlement on the Pacific coast worthy of being called a city. Even in the late nineteenth century, a person seeking transportation to San Francisco from, say, Seattle could simply ask for a ticket to "the city" and expect to get one to San Francisco.

Maps of San Francisco have evolved from a focus on navigation of the bay with little notice taken of the land around it, to guide maps that not only inform people about all there is to see, but also tell them the various ways they may use to see it all. More people seeing more will not exhaust the city's resources if they are cared for and described well. Indeed, we may never finish seeing San Francisco.

APPENDIX

SELECTED MAKERS OF MAPS AND
VIEWS OF SAN FRANCISCO

Nineteenth Century

Before coming to San Francisco on November 28, 1849, **Alexander Zakrzewski** was a captain in the Polish army who fought in the 1830–31 insurrection. Born in Poland on January 1, 1799, Zakrzewski was educated as a military engineer. He had published several maps of Warsaw, and in Paris, where he went after an unsuccessful uprising, he made some engravings but apparently did not remain there to pursue a career. He then traveled around the world, living in Tahiti and Madagascar, and eventually arrived in San Francisco. He made some early maps of the city including the one reproduced on (p. 34) which he prepared following the field notes of City Surveyor William M. Eddy.

Zakrzewski was listed as a lithographer in San Francisco's first city directory of 1850. At that time he lived on Clay Street between Dupont (now Grant Avenue) and Kearny streets; in 1854 he listed his topographical office at Washington and Montgomery Streets. Zakrzewski's work was not limited to San Francisco. In 1852, he lithographed a plan of Marysville, a city northeast of San Francisco; in 1857, he published a map of Arizona. Around 1859, he was a draughtsman in the U. S. Surveyor-General's office in San Francisco where his salary was $2,000 a year. Zakrzewski was also a photographer in this early period of San Francisco's history and apparently continued this work when he returned to Poland in 1863. He died in Cracow on April 22, 1866.

Edward Bosqui, the publisher of Captain W. F. Swasey's famous 1846–47 *View of San Francisco before the Discovery of Gold*, was a French Canadian born in Montreal who arrived in San Francisco for the Gold Rush in 1850, served as cashier of the city's first bank, and was fortunate in getting the job of private secretary to General John Fremont. It is not clear where he got his training, but he opened a printing plant in 1859 at Clay and Leidesdorff Streets where he remained until 1898. He did bookbinding, printing, and lithography, and printed the *Evening Bulletin* along with numerous commercial labels. Although lithographed views were not his main stock-in-trade, he was a member of the city's artistic community, having been a founder of the Bohemian Club, the School of Design, and the Art Association of San Francisco.

Britton & Rey, the city's largest printing firm, began in 1852 at Montgomery and California Streets. **Joseph Britton**, an Englishman born in Yorkshire in 1825, came to the United States in 1835, and lived in New York City until the age of 24. He is credited with having produced a lithographed music sheet in 1847 from an office at 559 Hudson Street, but left for California in 1849. Unsuccessful in the gold fields, he came to San Francisco where, in 1852, he formed a partnership with **Jacques Joseph Rey** in the lithography business.

Rey was born in Bouxviller, Alsace in 1820 and studied art and lithography in his youth. In about 1850 he came to California but did not go to the gold fields; what he did prior to joining Britton is not known. Apparently Rey was the firm's artist, and Britton handled the business, although he did sketches as well. The pair was the western counterpart of Currier & Ives in the East. Over the years, the firm's name changed several times, sometimes incorporating different partners, and had three locations. From 1868 to 1880, their offices were at Commercial and Leidesdorff Streets, near Edward Bosqui. Britton & Rey executed numerous plates depicting the life and work of miners. (One of their city maps is shown on pp. 52-53).

Britton participated in the city's public sphere and, according to his obituary, engaged in several enterprises including joining with A. S. Hallidie, Henry L. Davis, and James Moffitt in constructing the first-ever cable railroad, the Clay Street cable car line. He was a member of the Board of Supervisors in the early 1860s and in 1870. Both Britton and Rey had extensive real estate holdings and interests in various mining firms, some of which they received in lieu of payment for lithographic services. Rey died in 1892 and Britton in 1901.

William H. Dougal was born in New Haven, Connecticut about 1808. In 1853 he worked for the U. S. Treasury Department and traveled around the Bay Area and Sacramento where he made a number of sketches of views of landscapes and cities. His View of San Francisco from Yerba Buena Island was appended to the 1852 chart on (pp. 44-45). Dougal then left California and later wrote a book titled, *Off for California: The Letters, Log and Sketches of William H. Dougal, Gold Rush Artist.*

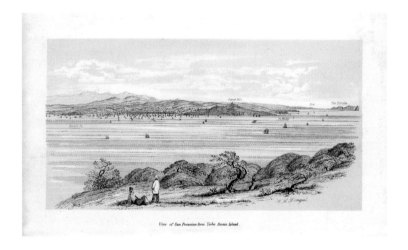

View of San Francisco from Yerba Buena Island.

The Englishman **George Henry Goddard** (1817–1906)—artist, architect, surveyor, civil engineer, mapmaker, and architect—lived for much of his long life in San Francisco. He arrived in the city on October 2, 1850, after 180 days aboard the ship *Diana*, which had sailed from Bristol, England, on April 15. Although Goddard had come to California to make his fortune, he was not without means. He was one of only three first class passengers on board the *Diana*, which carried 35 passengers in steerage and a cargo that included 21 packaged iron houses. (The iron buildings were in demand in San Francisco because they were supposedly fireproof. However, when exposed to intense fire, they became ovens, and some even melted.)

Before leaving England, Goddard had attended Oxford and earned some success as an artist, having exhibited at the Royal Academy in 1837 and 1850. The 1848–49 London post office directories listed him as an architect, and in 1850 he was listed as a civil engineer. Although Goddard intended to be a miner in California, he had little success and turned instead to various business ventures. He sketched the mining country in the Columbia-Sonora region and later published his lithographic views, including some of San Francisco, in the 1850s. Lithography, though popular, turned out to be a risky business because, as Goddard complained in letters to his brother in England, the stones had to be left in the lithographers' offices where letter-sheet prints were made and sold without any benefit to the artist.

Goddard then turned to surveying and joined an expedition to explore the Sonora Pass in search of a possible railroad route across the Sierra. While the expedition was not successful, Goddard's future as a surveyor and civil engineer was helped along by this experience. His next career opportunity came in 1854 when George Gorden hired him to be the architect for South Park, Gordon's fashionable development in the shadow of the city's first upper class residential area on Rincon Hill. Gordon's fortunes failed before most of the houses on the South Park crescent were built, but it was well publicized and, until the decline of Rincon Hill, successful. Still, Goddard wrote his brother in England that large architectural commissions for public works that paid well were only obtained through politics and intrigue.

Surveying appeared to be the career path most suited to Goddard's skills and opportunities. Not only was California's eastern boundary not settled but a practical route for the Emigrant Road west had not yet been determined. In 1855, Goddard undertook a survey for the Surveyor General of California to establish whether Carson Valley was in California or Utah. As a result of his work he prepared a topographical map of California and one of the Great Basin of Utah with a portion of New Mexico and of the Gadsden Purchase. Even here he had trouble getting paid on time because the work was completed under a new Surveyor General. However, the new official praised his work, commended the "valuable" information about the immigrant wagon roads and mountain passes, and hired him to conduct other surveys.

In 1857, Goddard was finally able to write his brother that surveying business was increasing and he often had more work than he could do. His California map was published in that year and recognized as the most accurate and complete map to date of California and its gold regions, rendering the other maps obsolete. Thereafter Goddard's production of maps increased, and by 1860 he had completed a set of maps recording the Pacific railroad exploration for the U. S. War Department as well as maps for California cities and counties.

During his years of struggle, Goddard continued to paint, winning compliments for his work at the 1859 State Fair from the well-known California author Bayard Taylor. He was a member of the San Francisco Art Association, founded in 1871, and had a studio in the Mercantile Library on the northeast corner of Van Ness and Golden Gate Avenue. In 1861 he became a United States citizen and in 1864 won the great honor of having a peak in the Sierra over 13,000 feet high named for him.

Goddard continued his many-sided career with survey work on the Western and the Central Pacific Railroads as well as civil engineering and architectural projects. He had joined the Academy of Sciences in 1854 and had collected, catalogued, and labeled over 3,000 specimens of rocks collected during his years of surveying. In 1903 at the age of 86, he prepared a seven-page type-written description of his collection that listed, among other things, the 500 colored views of California and Nevada, some 600 maps, and notes and journals of his surveys and explorations beginning in 1850. He recommended that it be kept intact and given to an institution of learning. Stanford University was interested in the whole collection, but Mrs. Stanford offered only $16,000 of the $40,000 that Goddard asked for it. Negotiations continued, but ended unfortunately when the fire following the 1906 earthquake destroyed Goddard's Van Ness Avenue home and with it his collection. His death on December 27, 1906, was attributed by members of his family to his grief over his losses.

Goddard is one of the few California mapmakers whose life was well known, largely because of his extraordinary breadth of interests and achievements. He is represented in this book by his 1868 panoramic view of San Francisco on (pp. 76-77).

Although no works by **George Holbrook Baker** are reproduced in this book, he was one of the most famous artists of the Gold Rush era; his life reflects the varied opportunities and accomplishments that those who produced the visual accounts of early San Francisco and California experienced. Born in Massachusetts in 1827, his forebears had fought in the American Revolution. He apparently sketched and painted as a young man and spent three years in New York City as an apprentice to a commercial artist where he drew maps until boredom caused him to leave. After some time as a student at the National Academy of Design, Baker caught the Gold Rush fever and joined a group of 12 men led by Captain A. Paul that left Boston on January 8, 1849. After various adventures he arrived in San Francisco in May 1849. Like many other 49ers, Baker did not prosper in the gold fields and returned to San Francisco where he open a business with merchandise of an unknown kind sent to him by his family. For the next few years he pursued whatever business ventures came his way with whichever partners he found, achieving neither great success nor failure. At one point, he even operated a mail service, Baker's Express, from San Francisco to the Feather River mines, a 290-mile trip. In 1852, he moved to Sacramento and for the next 10 years was in the general merchandising business.

Circa 1854, having kept up his sketching while traveling, Baker entered into a partnership with a man named Barber and printed views of California from woodcuts. Later he became an independent lithographer and in 1862 returned to San Francisco where he established another lithography business. He died in January 1906. During his years in Sacramento he and George Goddard were close friends but apparently never collaborated. Several of Baker's subjects were also depicted by other artists. One such was a view of the port of San Francisco in 1849 from Rincon Hill with the bay and Angel Island in the distance. The *New York Tribune* published it on August 28, 1849. The focus of this view was the "About 200 vessels then detained here their crews leaving for the mines on arrival in port," a most dramatic situation. The same subject was depicted in the map titled *The Port of San Francisco, 1849, from Rincon Hill*, drawn on the spot by Henry Firks, shown on (pp. 38-39).

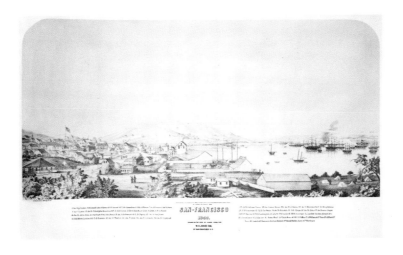

A. L. Bancroft & Company operated a printing business located at 721 Market Street in 1872. The firm produced a number of lithographed views of California cities and places of interest from Healdsburg, San Jose, Los Angeles, San Diego, and other places. Judging by its output, the company was an important one, but this writer has found no biographic information on it. The large *Official Guide Map of the city and county of San Francisco, compiled from official maps in the surveyor's office*, is reproduced on (p. 80).

The firm **Currier & Ives** dates from 1857 when James Merrit Ives became a partner in the firm Nathaniel Currier had with his brother Charles in New York City. The firm's more than 7,000 lithographs of American scenes included some of topical interest of California, which may have been executed to broaden their selection. The large view of San Francisco dated 1878 on (pp. 88-89) was drawn by **C. R. Parsons**, a New Yorker who spent some of his youth in San Francisco where he was a close friend of Joseph Britton of Britton & Rey. Parsons also lithographed *The City of San Francisco from Rincon Point* shown on (p. 57) for Endicott & Company. According to Henry T. Peters, author of *California on Stone*, William and Charles Endicott produced a huge volume of work in lithographs that were the first machine-made lithographic prints in mass circulation. They employed the artist C. R. Parsons for many years and worked for and with Currier & Ives in New York City.

Another prominent artist who has left little biographical information is **Charles B. Gifford**, represented here by three panoramic views: *North Beach, San Francisco from Russian Hill* (pp. 68-69), *A Bird's-eye View of San Francisco* (pp. 72-73), and *San Francisco Looking South from North Point* (pp. 86-87), published by G. T. Brown & Company. Gifford also executed a view of Hayes Valley, *North Beach, San Francisco from Russian Hill* of 1864 and a few other city views.

Gifford was associated with W. Vallance Gray for a *Bird's-Eye View of the City of San Jose*, printed by L. Nagel and published by George H. Hare in San Jose in 1869. In 1868, these two produced a *Bird's-Eye View of the Bay of San Francisco* that was published by A. L. Bancroft & Company.

Today **Rand McNally & Company** is known worldwide for its maps. Although it rose to prominence in the nineteenth century, its greatest growth was in the twentieth century. The company's founder, **William H. Rand**, had studied printing in Boston, but the Gold Rush lured him to California in 1849. When the gold fields proved unrewarding, he moved to Los Angeles where he worked for several years as a printer and newspaper reporter. In 1855, he moved to Chicago and began preparing and printing directories and guidebooks. In 1858, he hired **Andrew McNally**, a young Irish printer, who became his partner 10 years later. The partners first gained access to the burgeoning railroad industry by printing railroad tickets. They soon expanded their business, printing annual reports, timetables, and coupons. In 1871, they began publishing railway guides. The 1897 map of San Francisco shown on (pp104-105) appeared in Rand McNally's *Indexed Atlas of the World*.

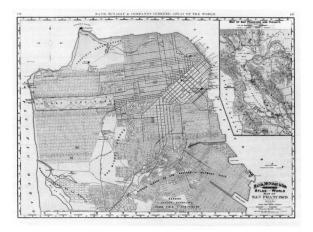

By 1900, Rand McNally & Company was no longer dependent on the railroads for business. While many maps of the country and individual states showed railroad lines, they also had automobile routes, bicycle paths, and even airline routes.

Twentieth / Twenty-First Century

Late-twentieth- and early-twenty-first-century graphic designers have increasingly used computer programs to create views and maps. Yet this practice has not meant the end of hand-drawn images. The *Axonometric View of the City by the Bay* issued in 1998 by the **mapPoster** division of the **Ludington Ltd.** company in Hastings-on-Hudson, New York, was based on a combination of aerial photographs by Alex McLean, ground photography, and records of building footprints. A team of designers then divided up the tasks of rendering the colors and building types and drew the map street by street, a process that took from six months to a year. The software program Adobe Illustrator was used to produce the map. The poster map is reproduced on (p. 137). MapPoster.com grew out of a graphic services company, Graphic Chart and Map Company, Inc, which creates custom maps for customers around the world.

Jack and **Gay Reineck** established the small design studio of **Reineck & Reineck** in 1972. Although the Reinecks employ some cartographic methods, they consider themselves designers of information graphics rather than cartographers.

While studying existing maps in preparation for a project in the late 1970s, Jack and Gay realized that the cartographic language used by most mapmakers for street and other types of maps had not incorporated graphic design methods to improve their maps. Since then the firm has developed a visual language for maps based on a hierarchy of information related to that of color and typography. Map projects often include bird's-eye views for three-dimensional effects. Reineck & Reineck serve a wide variety of clients from parks, zoos, universities, real estate firms, and public agencies. They have designed the maps for the Bay Area Rapid Transit system, BART; the most recent one is reproduced on ((p. 145). Four San Francisco maps designed by Reineck & Reineck are shown on (pp. 138, 140-141, 142-143, 146-147).

Gay Reineck holds a Design Diploma from Kingston University and a graduate degree from the London College of Printing. She worked in England as a graphic designer until the Walker Art Institute in Minneapolis recruited her to be the museum's graphic designer. After working with Interdesign, an interdisciplinary design group in Minnesota, Gay moved to Los Angeles where she worked in the offices of Saul Bass and Charles Eames.

Jack Reineck has a B. Arch and has worked in the fields of architecture, planning, industrial and graphic design.

Rick Waterman created the map on (p. 151) titled, *Site Suitability Analysis: Home Purchase in San Francisco*, using ArcMap by ESRI, of GIS (Geographic Information System) software. He chose the map's subject while working toward a graduate degree in cartography at San Francisco State University in 2004. Several color schemes were considered to express the physical criteria of elevation, slope, and proximity to specific roadways, open space, schools, and bicycle routes. The colors were personal choices and not based on traditional map colors.

BIBLIOGRAPHY

Baird, Joseph A., Jr., and Edwin C. Evans. *Historic Lithographs of San Francisco*. San Francisco: Burger and Evans, 1972.

Barry, Theodore Augustus, and Benjamin Adam Patten. *Men and Memories of San Francisco*. San Francisco: Burger and Evans, 1972.

Benedict, Burton. *The Anthropology of World's Fairs: San Francisco's Panama-Pacific International Exposition of 1915*. San Francisco: Scholar Press, 1983.

Bloomfield, Anne B. "A History of the California Historical Society's New Mission Street Neighborhood," *California History: The Magazine of the California Historical Society*. Vol LXXIV No.4, Winter 1995/96.

Clarke, Dwight L. *William Tecumseh Sherman: Gold Rush Banker*. San Francisco: California Historical Society, 1969.

Dana, Richard Henry. *Two Years Before the Mast*. New York: Harper and Bros., 1840.

Dwinelle, John W. *The Colonial History, City of San Francisco*. San Francisco: Ross Valley Book Co., 1978.

Ethington, Philip J. *The Public City, The Political Construction of Urban Life in San Francisco, 1850-1900*. Berkeley and Los Angeles: University of California Press, 2001.

Harlow, Neil. *California Conquered, War and Peace on the Pacific, 1846-1850*. Berkeley and Los Angeles: University of California Press, 1982.

———. *The Maps of San Francisco Bay, from the Spanish Discovery in 1769 to the American Occupation*. San Francisco Book Club of California, 1950.

Harris, David, and Sandweiss, Eric. *Eadweard Muybridge and the photographic panorama of San Francisco, 1850-1880*. Montreal: Canadian Centre for Architecture, 1993.

Hart, James D. *A Companion to California*. Berkeley and Los Angeles: University of California Press, 1987.

Hartman, Chester with Sarah Carnochan. *City for Sale, The Transformation of San Francisco*. Berkeley and Los Angeles: University of California Press, 2002.

Issel, William, and Robert W. Cherny. *San Francisco, 1865-1932: Politics, Power, and Urban Development*. Berkeley and Los Angeles: University of California Press, 1986.

Kirker, Harold. *California's Architectural Frontier: Style and Tradition in the Nineteenth Century*. San Marino, California: Huntington Library, 1960.

Knowles, Anne Kelly, ed. *Past Time, Past Place, GIS for History*. Redlands, California: ESRI Press, 2002.

Lotchin, Roger. *San Francisco, 1846-1856: from Hamlet to City*. Lincoln: University of Nebraska Press, 1979.

Polledri, Paolo, ed. *Visionary San Francisco*. Munich: Prestel-Verlag in association with the San Francisco Museum of Art, 1990.

Reps, John W. *Cities on Stone: Nineteenth Century Lithograph images of the Urban West*. Fort Worth: Amon Carter Museum of Western Art, 1976. An exhibition catalog.

Ristow, Walter. *American Maps and their Mapmakers: Commercial Cartography in the Nineteenth Century*. Detroit: Wayne State University Press, 1985.

Rumsey, David, and Edith M. Punt. *Cartographica Extraordinaire, The Historical Map Transformed*. Redlands, California: ESRI Press, 2004.

Scott, Mel. *The San Francisco Bay Area: A Metropolis in Perspective*. Berkeley and Los Angeles: University of California Press, 1959.

Vance, James E., Jr. *Geography and Urban Evolution in the San Francisco Bay Area*. Berkeley: Institute of Governmental Studies, University of California, Berkeley, 1964.

Wahrhaftig, Clyde. *Streetcar to Subduction and other Plate Techtonic Trips by Public Transportation in San Francisco*. American Geophysical Union, revised edition, 1984.

Woodbridge, Sally B. *John Galen Howard and the University of California*. Berkeley and Los Angeles: University of California Press, 2002.

INDEX

702   700   GEARY ST.   KEARNY ST.   CHRONICLE BUILDING, ELEVATOR 652   640 638   634   632   630   628   624

MARKET ST.—NORTH SIDE—CORNER GEARY AND KEARNY STS.

706. **PACIFIC TELEPHONE & TELEGRAPH CO.**
SUNSET TELEPHONE & TELEGRAPH CO.,
Connecting all towns in California with
Long Distance Telephones and Metallic
Copper Loop Lines.

702. **THOS. NORFFEW, D.D.S.,** 2d Floor, Dentist

702. **DRS. CARVER & LEANER,** 3d Floor,
Chiropodists—Pedicure & Manicure Parlors

702. **L. MONACO,** 4th Floor, Photographer

5M Kearny St. B. J. BURR & CO., 2d Floor,
Successors to Burr & Fink, Merchant Tailors

9 Geary St. S. W. WOLF, Rooms 4, 8, 9,
Merchant Tailor, Cleaning, Dying Repairing

11 Geary St. LUCAS DETECTIVE AGENCY,
A. E. Lucas & Co., Props. Agents in all parts
of U. S., Canada and Mexico.

13 Geary St. JOHN NORGROVE, Mfr. Trunks
and Valises. Travelers' Outfittings.
Offices Chronicle Building, 652

OREIAN B. BURNS, Rooms 8 and 9, Dentist

**MERCHANTS' RETAIL COMMERCIAL
AGENCY,** of Chicago, Ill., Rooms 31 and 32

MORAGA LAND ASS'N, J. A. Burton, Sec.
The Moraga Rancho. Choice Fruit Lands

FRED. S. WILLIAMS, Steam Power Plants,
Constructing and Mechanical Engineer

J. P. McELROY, Room 51
Attorney and Counsellor at Law

M. M. HEINEMAN, Rooms 81 to 84
Importer of Diamonds, Watches, Jewelry,
Jewelry Sold on Installments.

634. **THE BOUQUET,** Thos. W. Shaw

638. **EASTON, ELDRIDGE & CO.,** Corporation
Real Estate Agents and Auctioneers
House and Insurance Brokers

638. **NORTHERN PACIFIC R. R.,**
T. K. Stateler, General Agent
The Only All-Rail Line to Yellowstone Park

540. **T. ELLSWORTH,** General Agent of the
Preferred Accident Insurance Co., and
Manager of Hartford Life and Annuity Ins. Co'

628. **CHICAGO & ALTON R. R.**
Union Overland Ticket Office
Frank G. High, General Passenger Agent

626. **J. W. WRIGHT,** Loans
Real Estate and Financial Agent

630. **MORRIS & MERSION,** Real Estate and Ins.
Agts. Palo Alto Property at Stanford University

632. **MERCHANT'S PUBLISHING CO.,**
Pacific Coast Business Directory

633. **T. P. RIORDAN,**
Real Estate Agent and Insurance Broker

5